Ainsley's
FRIENDS & FAMILY COOKBOOK

Ainsley's
FRIENDS & FAMILY
COOKBOOK

TED SMART

CONTENTS

6 Introduction

How to use this book

Notes on the recipes

Essential equipment

Unusual ingredients

Handy hints for shopping,
   cooking and eating

Freezing

Healthy cooking and eating

18 Breakfasts and brunches

*Quick and nutritious ways to
start the day.*

38 Lunch on the go

*Deliciously different ideas for a
satisfying midday meal.*

54 Home alone

*Quick and easy dinners for
one or two.*

74 After-work suppers

*Tasty mid-week suppers ready in
less than half an hour.*

96 Friends for dinner

*Prepare-ahead dishes that leave you
time for entertaining.*

120 Spice it up

Spicy dishes from around the world.

140 Family favourites

*Family favourites from fish pie to
bread-and-butter pudding.*

166 After-eight dinners

*Extra-special dishes for an indulgent
evening in.*

188 Al fresco eating

Fresh ideas for outdoor entertaining.

216 Back to basics

*Vegetable dishes, sauces and much
more besides.*

237 Index

240 Acknowledgements

Introduction

It's great to know that so many of you have enjoyed my range of cookery books, which includes *Meals in Minutes*, *Barbecue Bible* and *Gourmet Express* to name but a few. Your feedback has been really positive. You generally seem to want the same things when it comes to recipes: good, delicious, nutritious meals that are easy to prepare and guaranteed to have everyone coming back for seconds.

I've certainly kept this in mind when coming up with the ideas for my new *Friends and Family Cookbook* – after all, these people are the most important in our lives, so when it comes to mealtimes we want to give them the best we can. For me there is nothing better than cooking and eating really good home-cooked food with people I really care about.

I've also tried to make this book much more than just another recipe collection by including tips on shopping for the week ahead, menu ideas and lots of basic recipes. It should be the type of cookbook that will become an essential handbook and make life in the kitchen an altogether easier and more enjoyable experience for you.

The book is divided up into sections that reflect the whole range of occasions you might want to cater for such as: *Breakfasts and Brunches*, with lots of yummy dishes to kick off the day; *Lunch on the Go*, full of new and exciting ways with packed lunches; *Friends for Dinner*, plenty of quick, tasty and satisfying dishes for that casual dinner party; *Spice It Up*, with spicy ideas for that Friday-night curry fix; *Home Alone*, for that effortless treat for one or two; and *Al Fresco Eating*, for those summer days when you want to get together with your mates for a bit of outdoor entertaining.

You can of course mix and match the dishes, but I hope that whatever the occasion, you'll be able to pick up this book and find a chapter that fits the bill. Another of my favourite sections is *After-work Suppers*, as I often have to dash home after a hectic day and whip-up some family treats such as *Smoked Bacon, Creamed Tomato and Pea Penne*, *Crispy Salmon Fingers with Sun-blushed Dipping Sauce*, *Chicken Pasta Salad with Pine Nuts* or *American Hot Pizza*, all of which are great because they're easy to prepare and can be multiplied up if the kids bring some of their friends home for tea. Just as well that the fabulous desserts are also quick to make, and you can easily conjure up treats such as *Butterscotch Whip in a Whirl*, *Chocolate Mousse in Minutes* and *Baked Bananas with Greek Yoghurt* – yum!

Sometimes, though, it's not just finding that key recipe that's the problem, it's planning an entire menu. If you want to cook that special Valentine's Day dinner, where do you start? What do you prepare for a Girls' Night In ...? Throughout the book I've included some menu spreads to help you out, and all of the menus have been thought through so that you've got time to entertain and enjoy the meal yourself. There are also tips for preparing ahead and advice on what wines to swig as well.

The Back to Basics section is packed with great salads and dressing ideas, fresh exciting ways to serve vegetables and instructions on how to make pastry and sauces from scratch. I'm not against taking short-cuts and using ready-made ingredients to save time, but it's also good to know how to make some of the basics. After all, you can't spend your whole life being terrified of making pastry – go on have a go you'll be amazed at how easy it is.

So now it just remains for me to say that I hope you thoroughly enjoy using my *Friends and Family Cookbook*. Please feel free to experiment with your own variations on the recipes because cooking should be lots of fun. I hope that in this book I've given you a wide and varied range of recipes and lots of helpful advice that will make your kitchen a happy and stress-free place to be. Enjoy!

Nutritional Information

As you flick through the book you'll see that each recipe includes some nutritional information to help ensure that you and your family are eating a balanced diet.

For most of the dishes the information given is per portion, so provided you stick to the exact recipe you can calculate precisely how much fat etc. you are eating. Any side dishes or sauces that you choose to add will obviously involve extra calories, fat, and so on. Occasionally, the information will apply to an entire recipe so, for example, the information for the pastry recipe in the Back to Basics section, is for the entire amount. Where this is the case I've mentioned it in the recipe introduction so that you're not overly alarmed if the calories or fat content look unusually high.

⭐ Where recipes contain less than 12 g of fat you'll see the star symbol (left) beside the recipe title. For those of you watching what you eat, these are the dishes to choose as they're officially classed as low-fat. Of course that doesn't mean they're not delicious. I pride myself on creating great tasting low-fat food, as the wife insists we do our best to be healthy. But don't take my word for it, look through the book and you'll see exactly what I mean.

How to use this book

The recipes in this book are divided into chapters, which I think reflect the way we live today.

Breakfasts and Brunches includes quick, nutritious ways in which to start the day, plus a few slightly more elaborate ideas for lazy weekend brunches.

Lunch on the Go gives you ideas for a satisfying midday meal, whether you are at home, on the move or at work.

Home Alone includes lots of ideas for just one or two people. So whether you live alone, the rest of the household have skipped out for the evening, or you just want to have some quiet time catching up with a friend, these dishes will provide suppers that are quick and easy to shop for, prepare and cook.

After-work Suppers provides you with inspiration for tasty mid-week meals that you can put together in less than half an hour, whether you've had a hard day, are short on time or someone has to rush out for the evening.

Friends for Dinner is full of dishes that you can prepare in advance or that require very little attention once the cooking is under way, leaving you plenty of time to chat and catch up.

Spice It Up offers a selection of spicy dishes from around the world that will provide you with an alternative to take-away curry on a Friday night. They are mostly quick to cook and informal in style, both of which are important after a busy week. Only a couple take a little longer to cook, and these can be made in advance and reheated quite quickly – in the time that it takes to cook the accompanying rice.

Family Favourites gives you a selection of classic comfort foods for family mealtimes, suitable for both weekdays and weekends, that everyone will enjoy. They take a little more time to prepare, but most can be made in advance and then take a relatively short time to cook.

After-eight Dinners provides a selection of adult-style dishes that are perfect for just two people, but can also be multiplied up if you want to throw a dinner party. They use slightly unusual or extra special ingredients, too.

Al Fresco Eating offers you lots of ideas for summertime food, particularly barbecues.

Back to Basics provides everything you'll need in the way of simple and slightly more elaborate accompaniments to your meal, such as vegetables, salads, rice and sauces, as well as some of the basic elements that need to be made ahead, such as stocks and pastry.

All the main recipes are interchangeable, so feel free to mix and match between the chapters, and to serve them at any time you like. And once you are familiar with the cooking method for a recipe, do alter the flavours and ingredients to suit your own taste.

Notes on the recipes

- All these recipes supply both metric and imperial measures, but when cooking them, stick to one system or the other, not a mixture.

- All teaspoon and tablespoon measurements are level unless stated otherwise, and are based on measuring spoons, where 1 teaspoon = 5 ml and 1 tablespoon = 15 ml. Don't be tempted to use a coffee spoon or an old-fashioned serving-sized tablespoon instead.

- All preparation times and cooking times are approximate.

- All recipes have been tested in a conventional oven. If you have a fan oven, you will probably need to adjust the dial slightly, by about 20°C. So for 200°C, set the dial at about 180°C. I always keep an oven thermometer hanging on one of the racks so that I can check the temperature before I start cooking.

- All herbs are fresh unless stated otherwise. And instead of giving amounts of chopped herbs in tablespoons, I have tried to write the recipes around those plastic packets of supermarket herbs. As a rule of thumb, one 20-g (¾-oz) packet (or 1 small bunch) minus the stalks yields about 3 tablespoons of chopped herbs. There is no need to remove the stalks from basil and coriander.

- Free-range eggs are recommended in all recipes and should be medium sized unless the recipe says otherwise.

- Recipes made with raw or lightly cooked eggs should be avoided by anyone who is pregnant or in a vulnerable health group.

- Where salt is used in the cooking process, fine cooking salt is quite acceptable, but for flavour in salads, or when serving and garnishing, use fine sea salt flakes instead, as these have a lovely flavour and texture. All pepper, whether black or white, is best freshly ground.

Essential equipment

Be kind to yourself when buying equipment. Good-quality stuff will last for years and actually improve your cooking.

Air-tight plastic containers – have a selection for storing cakes, biscuits and ice-cream, and for freezing leftovers.

Baking beans – you don't need to bother with those ceramic baking beans; I think they are a bit too heavy anyway. I use dried red kidney beans.

Baking tray & sheet – you will need a large tray with sides and a large flat sheet. Sturdy metal ones are a good investment, as they will last for years. Cheap ones will buckle and twist in the heat of the oven.

Chopping board – a thick, chunky wooden one is easy to scrub clean, is kind to your knives and will last you a lifetime.

Colander – plastic or metal are both fine, but make sure you choose a large one.

Digital kitchen timers – have a couple of these; they're more precise than the wind-up types.

Electric hand mixer – great for making light work of cakes, whisking batters and egg whites, and making mayonnaise.

Electric scales – choose a model that works in both imperial and metric; those on which you can rest a bowl and add and weigh are fantastic.

Flameproof casserole – this means one which you can use on top of the stove as well as in the oven. Choose a large, deep one with a lid, which holds about 3½–4 litres (6–7 pints).

Food processor – this is probably one of the most expensive pieces of equipment you are likely to buy for the kitchen, but if you hunt around for one with a powerful motor, it will last for many years, and enable you to do even the most laborious tasks effortlessly. It is great for puréeing soups, chopping onions, slicing potatoes, shredding cabbage, grating carrots and other vegetables, rubbing fat into flour for pastry and crumbles, making ice-cream, and a variety of other tasks.

General cooking utensils – balloon whisk, box grater, fish slice, horseshoe potato peeler, kitchen scissors, large metal spoons, pastry brush, potato masher, rolling pin, rubber spatulas, slotted spoon, soup ladle, wooden spoons.

Glass mixing bowls – have a selection of stackable bowls in various sizes.

Knives – you can have a large array of knives if you like, but most people find that two sizes are all that's really needed: a cook's knife with a wide 20-cm (8-inch) blade that juts below the handle (the wide bit is known as the 'heel'), is ideal for chopping, slicing, carving, etc., and a small kitchen knife with a 10-cm (4-inch) blade is good for slightly more fiddly work. In addition, a bread knife with a serrated blade is great for cutting bread, cakes and tomatoes.

Knife sharpener – a metal steel is one of the best things on which to sharpen a knife, once you've mastered the action. However, manual knife sharpeners, which have two sharpening wheels or crossed steel bars that you hold flat on the work surface and then drag the blade across, work beautifully, too.

Measuring jug – a see-through 1.2-litre (2-pint) jug with 25-ml (1-fl oz) divisions up the sides is indispensable.

Non-stick frying pans – you'll need three of these: a shallow 18-cm (7-inch) one, a 20–23-cm (8–9-inch) ovenproof one, and a deep 30-cm (12-inch) one.

Non-stick saucepan – a medium-sized pan 18–20 cm (7–8 inches) is great for scrambled eggs, porridge, custards, etc.

Ovenproof dishes – have a selection of shallow dishes in the following sizes: 1 x 1.5 litre (2½ pint), 1 x 1.75 litre (3 pint), 1 x 2.25 litre (4 pint) and 2 x 600 ml (1 pint).

Roasting tin – choose a sturdy metal one measuring about 25 x 35 cm (10 x 14 inches). But make sure it's not too heavy – just remember that you have to put ingredients in it, too!

Saucepans – choose thick pans, as deep as possible, with thick, heavy bases; you'll need one in each of the following sizes: 15 cm (6 inches), 20 cm (8 inches), 25–30 cm (10–12 inches).

Sieve – choose a metal one about 20 cm (8 inches) in diameter.

Skewers – have both long metal ones and bamboo ones for barbecuing, plus a couple of shorter ones for testing cakes and roast chicken.

Tongs – essential for chargrilling, barbecuing and frying.

Wrapping/lining materials – aluminium foil, cling film, greaseproof paper and non-stick baking parchment.

Useful extra equipment

The following items are not essential, but will make life a lot easier and also enable you to make all the recipes in this book.

Coffee grinder (for spices) – a cheap electric one is perfect for grinding spices to a fine powder. Don't be tempted to use the same machine for grinding coffee beans: the spices will taint the coffee and vice versa.

Deep-fat fryer – this is much safer than using a saucepan of hot oil, for which you would also need a sugar thermometer to check the temperature. The fryer is thermostatically controlled so that it maintains a constant temperature during cooking, and cannot overheat and catch fire. You can leave it filled with oil until it is ready to be changed, and store it in a cupboard when not in use. Most fryers dismantle for ease of cleaning.

Flan tins – choose loose-bottomed ones which are 4 cm (1½ inches) deep, in a selection of sizes: 1 x 20 cm (8 inches), 1 x 23 cm (9 inches) and 1 x 25 cm (10 inches).

Griddle pan – a ridged, cast-iron pan is great for cooking chicken, steaks and chops on top of the stove. Griddling also uses a minimum amount of oil, so this is a great investment if you're trying to cut down your fat intake.

Ice-cream maker – if you like ice-cream and make it a lot, this little machine makes life so much easier. You don't need to buy an expensive model with its own refrigeration unit, either; one with a gel-filled bowl that you keep in the freezer works just as well. All you are trying to do is break down the ice crystals in the mixture as it freezes so that the end result is nice and smooth.

Liquidizer – great for making smoothies, soups and sauces. Many also have an ice-crushing facility – a handy luxury if you want to make those smoothies really cold.

Mandolin – this is useful for thinly slicing and grating potatoes, carrots and similar hard vegetables. But do be very careful, and always use the guard, as the blade is extremely sharp.

Mortar and pestle – a large, deep mortar and heavy pestle will make grinding spices very much easier. However, you could use a coffee mug and the end of a rolling pin if the mixture doesn't have to be very fine.

Muffin tray – choose one with 12 compartments, and buy paper cases to fit. You can now buy flexible non-stick muffin trays that make turning out the cakes very easy.

Potato ricer – these might sound a bit cheffy but, believe me, they make the very best mashed potato. If you overwork the starch in the potatoes it becomes 'gluey', whereas what you are looking for is 'fluffy'. Pressing the potatoes through the ricer keeps the starch granules separate, and then all you have to do is quickly stir in some softened butter, a little milk to get the consistency you like, and some salt and pepper to taste, and you get really yummy mash. One of the best ones on the market is by Metaltex and is made of white plastic, has interchangeable metal plates with different sized holes, depending on what you want to mash, and is dishwasher proof. They are relatively inexpensive, too.

Salad spinner – there is no better way of drying salad leaves and spinach.

Unusual ingredients

Most of the recipes in this book use readily available ingredients with which everyone will be familiar. However, there are some more unusual ones, so here is a little more information about them to help you on your way.

Ackee – the fruit of a tree from West Africa and the West Indies. When ripe, it splits open to reveal the edible segments, which are pale yellow and very soft. It has a delicate and unique flavour. In the UK it is available in cans, preserved in brine, and is found in West Indian and Asian grocery shops and some delicatessens. It just needs to be drained before using.

Amaretti – small, hard, macaroon-like biscuits from Italy, flavoured quite strongly with almond. They are sometimes wrapped in patterned tissue paper.

Bulgar wheat – bulgar wheat is a nutty-tasting cracked wheat, which just needs to be rehydrated in hot water, then drained before using. One of my favourite salads is made by cooking and cooling the wheat, then mixing it with olive oil, spring onions, herbs and tomatoes (see page 68).

Buttermilk – traditionally the liquid that was left after cream had been turned into butter, but it is now commercially manufactured from skimmed milk. It has a mild, slightly tangy taste. It is usually found in the chill cabinet near the dairy produce, but if you can't find it, just mix some low-fat natural yoghurt with a little milk.

West Indian hot pepper sauce – a chilli sauce made from chillies, vinegar and salt. It can vary immensely in flavour, from warm to mind-blowingly hot, so start with a mild one. A brand to look out for, and which is ideal for serving with the Jamaican ackee and salt fish on page 34, is Encona.

Chillies – in the UK, unfortunately, fresh chillies are not labelled, so the buyer has no way of knowing what type they are or the amount of heat they generate. The general rule is that the smaller their size, the hotter they are. The most versatile ones are also those most easily available. They are long and slim, about 10–12 cm (4–5 inches), and bright red or vibrant green in colour and will give you a medium amount of heat. Red chillies are ripe green chillies and sweeter in flavour. Other widely available chillies, also red and green, are much smaller and more triangular in shape and give a similar amount of heat. Very small red, green and yellow chillies, packed full of little seeds and often sold in packets with a few other ingredients specifically for making

curries, are called bird's-eye chillies and these are very, very hot.

Scotch bonnet chillies, also called rocotillo or West Indian chillies, got their name because they resemble little squashed bonnets. They come in yellow, red or green, depending on ripeness. They are extremely hot and must be handled with care – I oil my hands before using them, which seems to work.

Look for those that have a firm skin and a fresh-looking stalk. Once they become wrinkled, they go bad very quickly.

Chorizo – an air-dried Spanish pork sausage flavoured with garlic and paprika. It comes in two forms: the fatter version can be thinly sliced and eaten like salami, while the smaller version needs cooking. Use the smaller type for the recipes in this book, such as the Jambalaya on page 131.

Ciabatta – a slightly waxy, open-textured bread from Italy, usually dusted lightly with semolina. You can now buy it as a part-baked loaf, which can be handily stored in the freezer until you are ready to bake it.

Cornmeal– also known as polenta, becomes a bland porridge when mixed with water, so it needs lots of flavouring. Salt, pepper and cheese are popular additions for a savoury mixture. Traditional cornmeal takes 20 minutes to cook, but you can now buy quick-cook polenta too.

Halloumi – a hard salty cheese, mildly flavoured with mint, which has been preserved in whey. It is sold in blocks and can be found in the chill cabinet. It is useful in cooking because it can be fried or barbecued and does not melt when it's heated.

Harissa paste – A North African chilli and spice paste that comes either in tubes or small jars. Once opened it will keep in your fridge for a few weeks.

Lychee – tropical fruit covered in a knobbly pink skin, which, when peeled away, reveals a very soft, pearly white, jelly-like fruit underneath with a hard black stone in the centre.

Pancetta – An Italian type of streaky bacon that comes either thinly sliced in packets, or in cartons, cut into short fat strips called lardons. Great for flavouring dishes such as spaghetti alla carbonara (see page 63), it is also fantastic added to stews with vegetables and herbs.

Plantain – a member of the banana family, and looks very similar, but is green when unripe, becoming yellow, then black as it ripens. It can be eaten at any stage but must be cooked first. Like bananas, plantain should not be refrigerated once you get them home. They are available from West Indian grocers and some supermarkets.

Ricotta – a very mild-tasting, moist, grainy cheese from Italy, which comes in plastic tubs and is found next to the mascarpone and mozzarella in the supermarket. It is used a lot in Italian cooking.

Salt cod – also called bacalão or salt fish, is a speciality of Portugal and the Caribbean. The cod is heavily salted, then dried, and is now conveniently sold in boneless fillet form. Available only from ethnic grocers, it can be hard to find, but undyed smoked haddock makes a pretty good substitute, although the flavour is a lot more subtle.

Sambal oelek – an Indonesian paste made from fresh chillies and salt, this is a useful standby to use in place of fresh chillies. If you can't find the authentic stuff, you can also buy little jars of minced red chilli in most supermarkets now, which does exactly the same job.

Semi-sun-dried tomatoes – otherwise known as sun-blushed or mi-cuit tomatoes, these need no soaking. You'll find them in supermarkets on the deli counter, or packed in cartons in the chilled section.

Sweet chilli sauce – basically a chilli sauce made from red chillies, sugar, vinegar and salt.

Sweet soy sauce – also known as 'ketchup manis', this is an Indonesian soy sauce to which sugar and an individual blend of spices have been added. It is available in most large supermarkets, but if you can't find it, just mix dark soy sauce with an equal amount of clear honey.

Thai fish sauce – nam pla, as it is known in Thailand, is an amber-coloured liquid made from fermented salted anchovies. It has a very distinctive smell, but it adds a very authentic, savoury taste to all Thai food. It is available in most supermarkets, but keep an eye on the sell-by date, as it darkens with age and gets a bit overpowering in smell and flavour.

Wasabi – this is the name of a hot, bright green Japanese paste that is traditionally used in the making of sushi. It is similar in taste to horseradish and although it can be bought in powdered form, it is now available ready-mixed in tubes and is available from larger supermarkets and Asian grocers.

Handy hints for shopping, cooking and eating

Most of us lead very busy lives these days and there just never seem to be enough hours in the day to achieve everything we want. But with a little thought and forward planning it is still possible to shop for, prepare, cook and eat interesting, tasty and healthy food.

Planning ahead

- Take a look at the lists overleaf and keep your store-cupboard, fridge and freezer well stocked with the basic, non-perishable things.

- Set aside some time each week to plan your food and shopping for the forthcoming week. Just one hour of constructive thinking will save you time later on in the week.

- Get into the habit of eating breakfast, and make sure you always have the basics to hand so that you don't run out and end up grabbing a packet of crisps at coffee time.

- If you take lunch with you to work, which is far cheaper and usually a far healthier way to eat, think about what you fancy in advance, then make sure you shop for everything at the weekend. Eat the perishable things early on in the week, and leave the eggs, cheese and canned tuna, for example, to the end.

- If you plan on entertaining mid-week, cook something very simple for which you have to buy only one or two fresh ingredients at the most on the day itself. If possible, cook something in advance and freeze or refrigerate it for re-heating on the night.

Shopping

- Check through your store cupboard, fridge, freezer, vegetable rack and fruit basket from time to time. Turf out anything past its sell-by date; although it is probably still edible, it has often lost the best of its flavour, which in turn will make your food taste inferior.

- Keep an on-going shopping list in the kitchen. I know this might sound obvious, but I can never remember what it was I needed when I come to make my list. As things run out, jot them down, then expand on the list just before you go shopping.

- Try not to buy too much at any one time. Overbuying creates storage problems, and you run the risk of foods going off or out of date before you have the chance to eat them. Buy little and often, or as often as you can; most of us can squeeze in one trip to the supermarket each week.

- Have a think about your food for the week ahead. With careful shopping, you should be able to make it through to the following weekend, with maybe a quick shop once or twice for some fresh salads, vegetables or fruit.

Adapting ready-made ingredients

There are hundreds of ready-made products available to us today, and although many are high in fat and salt, some of them are pretty good. So why not use them to your advantage when you are in a hurry? Here are some of my favourites.

- Take a thin-crust Margherita pizza and add a few extra toppings. I like pepperoni sausage, chopped chilli and more cheese. You could also add ham, sliced tomatoes and cheese; cooked spinach and blue cheese; or tinned tuna, sweetcorn and grated Cheddar.

- A cheat's vegetarian lasagne can be made with fresh lasagne sheets layered with a fresh tomato sauce and a mixture of thawed and chopped leaf spinach, ricotta cheese and grated Parmesan. Top with a tub or two of four-cheese sauce, sprinkle with grated cheese and bake for 30–40 minutes at 180°C/350°F/Gas Mark 4.

- You can now buy sachets of cooked basmati rice. Heat 1 tablespoon curry paste and a little oil in a frying pan or wok, add the rice, some shredded cooked chicken or cooked peeled prawns, frozen peas and cashew nuts and stir-fry for a few minutes until hot. Stir in lots of coriander and serve drizzled with some sweet chilli sauce.

- For pretty instant nachos, spread some tortilla chips over a plate and spoon over some ready-made chilli tomato salsa, chopped spring onions and grated Cheddar cheese. Place under a medium heat and grill for 2–3 minutes until the cheese has melted, spoon over teaspoonfuls of guacamole and soured cream and serve.

- Mix some natural yoghurt, or a vanilla-flavoured one, with a little cream, then layer with some ready-made fruit compote, such as rhubarb or apricot, some crunchy de luxe muesli and clear honey.

Shopping checklist

I always keep a supply of basic foodstuffs in the cupboard, fridge and freezer so that I can rustle up something at short notice, as well as lessen the amount of stuff I need to buy when I fancy cooking something new.

Store-cupboard basics

Cans: Chick peas
Chopped tomatoes (large and small)
Coconut milk
Evaporated milk (small)
Red kidney beans
Sweetcorn kernels (no added sugar)
Tuna (in olive oil, sunflower oil or spring water)
White beans, such as cannellini or butter beans

Dry goods: Baking powder
Cornflour
Cornmeal or polenta
Couscous
Dried pasta (macaroni, spaghetti, tagliatelle, etc.)
Flour (plain, self-raising and wholemeal)
Lentils (dried red and Puy)
Porridge oats, rolled
Rice (basmati, long-grain, risotto, e.g. Arborio, and pudding)

Spices and flavourings:
Cardamom pods
Cayenne pepper
Chillies (dried, crushed)
Chilli powder
Cinnamon sticks
Cloves
Cooking salt
Coriander (ground and seed)
Cumin (ground and seed)
Oregano (dried)
Garam masala
Mustard seeds (black)

Nutmegs (whole)
Peppercorns (black)
Paprika
Sea salt flakes
Turmeric (ground)
Vanilla extract

Buy these regularly in small amounts, and keep an eye on the sell-by date as they soon start to taste a bit like dust. Grinding whole spices, where possible, just before you use them is always the best option, but ready-ground spices are fine as long as they are fresh.

Sugar: Caster
Demerara
Icing
Light soft brown or light muscovado

Vegetable stock powder (good quality, such as Marigold)

Jars/bottles: Brown sauce
Coconut cream (small cartons)
Curry paste (mild or medium)
Dark soy sauce
Honey (clear)
Jam
Mango chutney
Maple syrup
Marmalade
Mustard (Dijon and wholegrain)
Passata
Tomato ketchup
Worcestershire sauce

Oils: Olive oil (ordinary and a good extra virgin oil)
Sunflower oil
Toasted sesame oil

Vinegars: Red wine
White wine
Balsamic

Vegetable rack

Garlic
Lemons
Onions
Potatoes
Root ginger, fresh

Fridge

Butter
Cheese (Cheddar and Parmesan wedges)
Crème fraîche
Eggs , half dozen
Fruit juice (orange or apple)
Garlic and ginger, prepared jars (although not as fresh-tasting as the real thing, these products cut down enormously on preparation time and are a great standby)
Greek yoghurt
Lard
Mayonnaise
Milk
Stock cubes (chicken, vegetable and beef)
Tomato purée, tube
Yoghurt, natural

Freezer

Bread (including pitta, naan and chapatis)
Ice-cream, vanilla
Ice cubes
Milk
Peas
Puff pastry
Spinach (leaf)
Stock, home-made

Freezing

I don't tend to use my freezer for storing lots of uncooked ingredients, such as meat and fish, but rather as a source of emergency foods and for storing leftovers and basics. I have listed, left, a few things that I always have in the freezer, but I also keep a pizza in there, to which I add a few extra toppings, and I always have tubs of home-made soup for lunches, which I make in large batches and freeze in single-person portions. I also make a batch of bolognese sauce for pasta or lasagne, and I make stock when I can and freeze it in 300-ml (10-fl oz) pots.

- When freezing any foods, whether home-made or bought, always label them with the date and the year. It's scary how time can slip by. It is a fallacy that you can store food in a freezer forever: this is definitely not the case, as you will know if you have ever thawed and tried to eat something that has been in there far too long. Freezing merely slows down the deterioration of food; it does not preserve it forever. In the end the continual presence of ice in the food breaks down its structure and makes it unpalatable.

- Make sure you pack things adequately to protect them. If they are exposed to the ice and air, they will dry out and go white, which is known as 'freezer burn'. The food is then ruined. The package needs to be airtight. Plastic freezer bags are strong and designed specifically for this purpose. When using them, try to remove as much air as possible and then seal the bag well. Small, stackable plastic boxes are ideal for portions of soup, pasta sauces, casseroles and curries.

- Allow home-cooked foods for the freezer to cool down to room temperature before freezing them.

- Be aware of the star system on ready-made products. Domestic freezers and frozen food compartments in fridges have different star ratings according to what temperature they operate at. This, together with the best-before date on the packet, determines how long certain products can be stored.

  - * frozen food compartment with a temperature of -6°C. Store up to 1 week.

  - ** frozen food compartment with a temperature of -12°C. Store up to 1 month.

  - *** frozen food compartment with a temperature of -18°C. Store until best-before date.

- **** a food freezer with a temperature of -18°C or colder. Store until best-before date.

- Here is a rough guide to the maximum storage time for certain foods stored at -18°C:

  4 months – fish, sausages, ready meals, cakes and pastries

  6 months – meat and poultry

  8 months – vegetables and fruit

- Try to transfer frozen food from the shop to your home freezer as soon as possible. If necessary, and especially in warm weather, take lots of newspapers or even a cooler box with you so that it can't thaw out on the way home. And, if necessary, stick your freezer on fast freeze for a few hours once you place the food in it. This is especially true for non-frozen foods that you want to freeze.

- Do not overcrowd the freezer. Your freezer manual will tell you its maximum capacity.

- Thawed frozen foods become as perishable as fresh, so use them straight away.

- Never refreeze thawed frozen foods – you run the risk of food poisoning.

- Thaw and clean out your freezer at least three times a year. As it ices up, it begins to work less efficiently, shortening the safe storage time of your food. Thick ice also takes up lots of useful space.

Healthy cooking and eating

Today we are constantly being reminded of how important it is to eat healthily. But most of us lead busy lives and time is precious, so good food is often pushed aside in favour of convenience. If we all took more time to eat properly, there wouldn't be the tendency to snack throughout the day on the vast array of not-such-healthy products available to us. We should all try to make the time to sit down at a table for at least one meal during the day, and also consciously make an effort to eat three meals a day at regular intervals.

Breakfast is the most important meal of the day. If you can make time for something substantial, such as porridge, muesli or eggs, you will have a lot more energy and be able to make it through until lunchtime without snacking. And at lunchtime, even if you are constantly on the go, it's far better to eat something that's filling, healthy and interesting to see you through until the evening rather than opting for fast food fixes. And if that option is not easily available to you, the best solution is to take lunch with you so that you can avoid the temptation to stray from the healthy path. A soup or salad, interchanged with a sandwich or two throughout the week, will give you a far better balanced diet and, I hope, something to look forward to.

Healthy eating is not a fad or a diet: it is a way of life that we can all adjust to with a little time, thought and effort. We are surrounded today by countless fashionable diets, but as research has shown, most don't work, at least not long term, and the information given by one seems to contradict that of the others – and it's all very confusing. Food should be fun, sociable, interesting and enjoyable. So here are a few suggestions that can help you achieve this.

Healthy cooking

- Try to cook using methods that don't require too much fat. Instead of deep- or shallow-frying, try griddling your meat and vegetables on a ridged cast-iron griddle. It is quick, requires very little oil and tastes fantastic.

- Grilling is also an excellent way of cooking because the food sits on a rack and any excess fat drips into the tray below. Roasting is great too. Just remember to skim off the excess fat from the juices before making the gravy.

- Stir-frying is ideal as the food is cut into small pieces and is cooked very quickly in relatively little oil, retaining maximum nutrients and flavour.

- Steaming is one of the healthiest methods of cooking, and works well with fish, chicken and vegetables, but is not particularly favoured because the food can taste quite bland. The trick is to serve it with a zappy, well-flavoured sauce.

- Another healthy cooking technique is poaching where the food is cooked very gently just below the boiling point in water or stock. You can poach many types of food including fish, eggs, poultry and meat. Poaching does give the food a very delicate flavour, however, so bear this in mind if you decide to try it.

- Plunge green vegetables into well-salted boiling water and cook for as short a time as possible, until just tender. Alternatively, steam them and season them afterwards.

- Try to use olive oil instead of butter when cooking.

- In a recipe that requires ingredients to be fried in a few tablespoons of oil or butter, such as in a stir-fry or at the start of making a soup, try cutting the fat back by half. Quickly fry the ingredients until they start to take on a little colour, then add a couple of tablespoons of water, cover with a lid and continue cooking until tender.

Healthy eating

• Try to eat five portions of fruit and vegetables every day, excluding potatoes. Fruit and vegetable juices and smoothies are a great way of meeting your daily target. A single portion = roughly 85 g (3¼ oz).

• Try to drink 2 litres (3½ pints) of water a day – the equivalent of eight large glasses. It seems like a lot, but with practice it gets easier, honestly. I have even been known, on a very busy day, to set my watch to bleep at one-hour intervals as a reminder. If you work in an office, keep a glass of water beside you at all times and you'll son find that you've drunk your daily quota. Coffee and tea don't count. If you like the odd glass or two of wine or beer, then match each one with an extra glass of water.

• Try to eat more fish, especially oily fish, which is an excellent source of omega-3 fatty acid – essential for a healthy heart.

• Try to eat less protein. Our bodies only really need 75 g (3 oz) per day, but if this seems a little bit stingy, why not double up this amount on those days when you do want meat, fish or eggs, and eat vegetable-based meals on the other days? There are loads of great Italian and Indian veggie dishes.

• Try to cut down on fat and avoid too many buttery sauces, mayonnaise, creams and ice-cream.

• Try to eat plenty of fibre to maintain a healthy digestive system. You'll find it in brown bread, wholegrain cereals and rice, vegetables, nuts and pulses, such as peas, beans and lentils.

• Try to eat less refined sugar (found in chocolate bars and sweets, soft drinks, ice-cream, biscuits, cakes and sweetened breakfast cereals). Eat some fresh fruit, dried fruit, or nuts and seeds if you are feeling a bit peckish, or drink fresh fruit juice diluted with water.

BREAKFASTS AND BRUNCHES

fruit smoothies

The perfect start to the day – breakfast in a cup. So break out the blender and get whizzing.

Just make sure you use really ripe fruit, and sweeten to taste with a little sugar or honey if you wish.

serves 1 • preparation 2 mins, if that • cooking none

mango, passion fruit and coconut

Energy 293 kcals • Protein 4.0 g • Carbohydrate 34.3 g • Fat 16.6 g
Saturated fat 13.9 g • Fibre 4.4 g • Salt 0.31 g • Added sugars none

½ medium-sized mango, peeled and flesh cut
    away from the stone
100 ml (3½ fl oz) canned coconut milk
2 passion-fruit, halved and the juice rubbed
    through a sieve
2 teaspoons fresh lime juice
150 ml (5 fl oz) orange juice
a handful of ice cubes

1 Simply put all the ingredients for the smoothie into a liquidizer and blend until smooth. Alternatively, you can put everything into a large measuring jug and blend with a hand-held blender, moving it up and down, until smooth. Pour into a chilled glass and serve.

✪ frozen berry and lemon yoghurt

Energy 231 kcals • Protein 6.0 g • Carbohydrate 52.9 g • Fat 1.0 g
Saturated fat 0.6 g • Fibre 2.6 g • Salt 0.21 g • Added sugars 23.1 g

100 g (4 oz) frozen fruits of the forest mix
100 g (4 oz) lemon-flavoured yoghurt
200 ml (7 fl oz) orange juice
1 tablespoon clear honey

1 Put all the ingredients for the smoothie into a liquidizer and blend until smooth. Alternatively, put everything into a large measuring jug and blend with a hand-held blender until smooth and serve in a chilled glass if you wish.

✪ pear, banana, oat and honey

Energy 426 kcals • Protein 11.2 g • Carbohydrate 93.8 g • Fat 3.4 g
Saturated fat 1.1 g • Fibre 6.5 g • Salt 0.22 g • Added sugars 11.5 g

1 ripe, juicy pear, peeled and cored
1 ripe banana, peeled and sliced
25 g (1 oz) porridge oats
1 tablespoon clear honey
100 g (4 oz) natural yoghurt
250 ml (8 fl oz) cloudy apple juice
A handful of ice cubes

1 Place all the ingredients for the smoothie into a liquidizer and blend until smooth. Alternatively, you can put everything into a measuring jug and blend with a hand-held blender, moving it up and down, until smooth. Pour into a chilled glass and serve.

✪ pineapple, lime and ginger

Energy 155 kcals • Protein 1.8 g • Carbohydrate 39.0 g • Fat 0.3 g
Saturated fat none • Fibre 0.2 g • Salt 0.06 g • Added sugars none

250 g/9 oz prepared fresh pineapple
Juice 1 lime
Juice 1 orange (about 150 ml/5 fl oz)
½ teaspoon finely grated fresh ginger
1 teaspoon caster sugar (optional)

1 Simply put all the ingredients for the smoothie into a liquidizer and blend until smooth. Alternatively, you can put everything into a large measuring jug and blend with a hand-held blender, moving it up and down, until smooth. Serve in a chilled glass if you wish.

CLOCKWISE FROM TOP: *mango, passion fruit and coconut; pear, banana, oat and honey; pineapple lime and ginger; and frozen berry and lemon yoghurt.*

✪creamy apple, lemon and honey muesli with fruit and nuts

Jumbo oats, available from health-food shops, give this muesli an even nuttier texture. Even children will enjoy this delightful, healthy cereal.

serves 4 • preparation 3–4 mins + soaking • cooking none

Energy 310 kcals • Protein 12.6 g • Carbohydrate 58.3 g • Fat 4.5 g
Saturated fat 1.1 g • Fibre 7.0 g • Salt 0.13 g • Added sugars 8.6 g

- 225 g (8 oz) rolled porridge oats
- 300 ml (10 fl oz) cold water
- 100 ml (3½ fl oz) apple juice or orange juice
- 225 ml (8 fl oz) whole-milk natural yoghurt
- 3 tablespoons clear honey
- finely grated zest of 1 small lemon
- 2 dessert apples, quartered, cored and coarsely grated

CHOICE OF TOPPINGS

- 225 g (8 oz) raspberries and 50 g (2 oz) coarsely chopped toasted almonds
- 225 g (8 oz) blackberries and 50 g (2 oz) coarsely chopped toasted hazelnuts
- 225 g (8 oz) cored and chopped apple and 50 g (2 oz) crumbled pecan nuts
- 225 g (8 oz) blueberries and 25 g (1 oz) freshly grated coconut

1 Mix the oats, water and fruit juice together in a bowl. Cover with cling film and leave in the fridge overnight.

2 The next morning, stir in the yoghurt, honey, lemon zest and grated apples. Spoon into individual bowls and top with the fruit and nuts.

✪cornmeal porridge with nutmeg

This porridge is more like a semolina, made extra delicious by the addition of evaporated milk and nutmeg. A Caribbean classic, it's a winter warmer that will set you up for the day.

serves 4 • preparation none • cooking 10–12 mins

Energy 317 kcals • Protein 10.8 g • Carbohydrate 46.2 g • Fat 11.1 g
Saturated fat 6.5 g • Fibre 0.6 g • Salt 0.64 g • Added sugars 15.8 g

900 ml (1½ pints) full-cream milk
300 ml (10 fl oz) water
100 g (4 oz) cornmeal or polenta
a pinch of salt
¼ teaspoon freshly grated nutmeg
4 tablespoons caster sugar
4 tablespoons evaporated milk

TO SERVE
muscovado or demerara sugar
single or double cream (optional)

1 Put the milk and water into a pan and bring to the boil. Slowly pour in the cornmeal, stirring all the time with a wooden spoon to prevent it from going lumpy. Add the salt, nutmeg, sugar and evaporated milk and leave to simmer gently, stirring every now and then, for 10–12 minutes.

2 Serve sprinkled with some brown sugar and a little chilled cream, if you wish.

VARIATIONS

TRADITIONAL SCOTTISH PORRIDGE

Replace the cornmeal or polenta with rolled porridge oats and leave out the nutmeg, sugar and evaporated milk. Simmer for just 5 minutes, stirring occasionally and serve topped with extra cold milk, or a little cream and a sprinkling of demerara sugar.

go to work on an egg

During the week, most of us are in a rush to leave the house, and an egg is the perfect way to start off the day. Each recipe serves 4.

SOFT-BOILED EGGS

Bring a pan of water to the boil. Meanwhile, prick the wider end of 4–8 eggs with a pin (this will release the air trapped in a little pocket here and stop the eggs from cracking while they cook). Gently lower the eggs into the water and boil medium-sized ones for 4 minutes, large ones for 4½ minutes, turning them over once or twice during cooking.

To serve, crack off the top of the eggs, add a small knob of butter, if you wish, and a little salt and freshly ground black pepper. Serve with toast soldiers, spread with butter, and a little Marmite if you wish. Toasted flavoured breads also make a nice change: try herby foccaccia, black olive or sun-dried tomato ciabatta, or cheese and onion loaf.

SCRAMBLED EGGS

Break 8 large eggs into a bowl and season with salt and pepper. Beat together lightly with a fork. Melt 25 g (1 oz) butter in a large non-stick pan. Swirl it around the pan so that it coats the sides, add the eggs and cook over a medium heat, stirring all the time, for about 2 minutes, or until the eggs are half set. Take the pan off the heat, add 25 g (1 oz) butter, and (if you wish) 4 tablespoons double cream, and keep stirring, returning to the heat briefly if necessary, until the eggs are soft and creamy. Serve inside split, warmed croissants or toasted muffins, sprinkled with a few chopped chives if you wish.

FRIED EGGS

Heat a thin layer of oil in a non-stick frying pan over a medium-high heat. Reduce the heat a little, break in 4 large eggs and leave them to fry, spooning a little of the hot oil over the yolks, until they are just set. Serve with bread toasted on a hot, ridged cast-iron griddle pan and drizzled with a little olive oil. Sit the eggs on top, sprinkle with some sea salt flakes and freshly ground black pepper and serve with a spicy tomato ketchup or tomato sauce.

POACHED EGGS

Heat 4 cm (1½ inches) water in a large, deep frying pan until little bubbles begin to appear on the surface. Add 1 tablespoon white wine vinegar and ½ teaspoon salt. Break a very fresh egg into a teacup, then slide it gently into the water. Repeat with 3 more eggs. Cook for 3½ minutes, making sure that the water stays at a very gentle simmer. Lift them out of the water with a slotted spoon and drain them briefly on kitchen paper before serving.

If you want to do more than 4 eggs, cook them for just 3 minutes, then lift them out into a bowl filled with tepid water. When you have cooked all your eggs, slip them back into the barely simmering water for 30 seconds just to finish off the cooking and heat them through.

Top half a toasted and lightly buttered English muffin with grilled small bacon steaks or back bacon rashers and a poached egg. Spoon over a little hollandaise sauce (see page 234) and serve.

WHAT'S THE DIFFERENCE?

There are several categories of eggs available today, but what do all the words mean?

Organic eggs All organic eggs are free-range, i.e small flocks of birds are allowed to range freely outside, with easy access to shelter and have been fed a primarily organic diet with no genetically modified ingredients or colourings to enhance the colour of the yolk.

Free-range eggs The birds are reared in barns and have daytime access to open-air runs that are mainly covered in vegetation. However, the more dominant birds can still prevent some birds from getting to the outside.

Barn eggs Very large flocks of birds are housed in barns that have the addition of nesting boxes and perches, but they are still reared entirely indoors.

Battery eggs The majority of eggs sold in the UK are battery eggs. Tens of thousands of birds are housed in large, artificially lit barns, three to five birds to a cage, which have sloping floors so that eggs can roll away to await collection.

HOW TO USE EGGS SAFELY:

- Stored properly, a fresh egg will keep for up to a month.
- Keep them at a cool and constant temperature, or in the least cold part of the fridge, which is often nearest the top (but check with the fridge manufacturer's instructions).
- Keep them on a shelf away from raw meat and other raw products.
- Use eggs before the 'best before' date printed on the box and the egg.
- Allow eggs to come to room temperature before using.

- Avoid buying eggs in reusable egg boxes, which could be contaminated, or in boxes containing the remains of broken eggs.
- Very slightly cracked eggs should be used immediately, and only where they are going to be fully cooked e.g. in cakes. Crack them into a tea cup first to check they are still fresh.
- Any recipes featuring raw or lightly cooked eggs should be avoided by anyone who is pregnant or in a vulnerable health group.

✪ buttermilk pancakes

These are fantastic for breakfast and very easy to make. Buttermilk is available in most supermarkets and gives a lovely texture and flavour. The pancakes are nice spread with butter and jam, too. The nutritional information below is for each pancake, so if you're calorie counting you'll need to multiply up depending on how many you have.

makes 20 • preparation 5 mins • cooking 3 mins per batch

Energy 83 kcals • Protein 2.2 g • Carbohydrate 12.3 g • Fat 3.1 g
Saturated fat 1.7 g • Fibre 0.3 g • Salt 0.34 g • Added sugars 2.7 g

50 g (2 oz) butter
225 g (8 oz) self-raising flour
2 teaspoons baking powder
50 g (2 oz) caster sugar
175 ml (6 fl oz) buttermilk
2 eggs
175 ml (6 fl oz) full-cream milk
1 teaspoon vanilla extract
maple syrup and lemon wedges, to serve

1 Melt the butter in a small pan over a low heat. Pour off the clear liquid into a bowl and discard the milky-white residue that will have settled to the bottom of the pan. The end product is called 'clarified butter'.

2 Sift the flour, baking powder and sugar into a bowl. Make a well in the centre, add the buttermilk, eggs and milk and whisk together to make a smooth, thickish batter. Stir in the vanilla extract.

3 Heat a large, non-stick frying pan over a medium heat. Brush the base with a little of the clarified butter, add 3 large spoonfuls of the batter, spaced well apart, and cook for 2 minutes until bubbles start to appear on the surface of the pancakes and they are golden brown underneath. Turn over and cook for another minute. Lift onto a plate and keep warm while you cook the remainder.

4 To serve, pile the pancakes onto warmed plates, drizzle with the remaining clarified butter and the maple syrup, garnish with the lemon wedges and eat straight away.

VARIATIONS

APPLE PANCAKES

Stir 300 g (11 oz) peeled, cored and coarsely grated cooking apples into the batter before cooking, and serve with toffee sauce (see page 94) and yoghurt.

SAVOURY PANCAKES

Leave out the sugar and vanilla and stir in 100 g (4 oz) coarsely grated Cheddar cheese and ¼ teaspoon salt and eat the pancakes with grilled bacon and lashings of tomato ketchup.

✪ american sweetcorn pancakes

Serve these with whatever you fancy. I like tomatoes and thickly sliced cooked ham, but scrambled eggs with a bit of grated cheese stirred in and crispy bacon are also a wicked treat. The nutritional information given below is for each pancake, so if you're calorie counting you'll need to multiply up depending on how many you have.

serves 4 • preparation 5 mins • cooking 4 mins per batch

Energy 180 kcals • Protein 3.9 g • Carbohydrate 23.9 g • Fat 8.3 g
Saturated fat 2.9 g • Fibre 1.0 g • Salt 1.03 g • Added sugars 2.0 g

1 x 330-g (11½-oz) can sweetcorn kernels
25 g (1 oz) cornflour
½ teaspoon baking powder
1 large egg, beaten
2 spring onions, trimmed and thinly sliced (optional)
1 tablespoon sunflower oil
15 g (½ oz) butter
salt and freshly ground black pepper

1 Drain the sweetcorn well, then tip it into a food processor and blend to a coarse purée. Transfer to a mixing bowl and stir in the cornflour, baking powder, egg, spring onions, ¼ teaspoon salt and some black pepper.

2 Heat the oil and butter in a non-stick frying pan over a medium-high heat. Add 4 spoonfuls of the batter, spaced well apart, and cook for 2 minutes on each side until richly golden. Remove from the pan and keep warm while you make the remaining 4 pancakes. Serve straight away.

full english breakfast

The quantities below are enough for one person. If cooking for more than one, multiply the quantities up accordingly.

serves 1 • preparation 5 mins • cooking 25 mins

Energy 656 kcals • Protein 33.7 g • Carbohydrate 27.6 g • Fat 46.5 g
Saturated fat 11.2 g • Fibre 3.5 g • Salt 4.71 g • Added sugars none

1–2 meaty pork sausages
sunflower oil, for frying
1 medium-sized tomato, halved
butter, for grilling and frying
2 rindless back bacon rashers
1 slice white bread, cut into 2 triangles
50 g (2 oz) button mushrooms, wiped clean
1–2 eggs
salt and freshly ground black pepper

1 Pre-heat the oven to 150°C/300°F/Gas Mark 2 and pre-heat the grill to high.

2 Fry the sausages in a little sunflower oil over a medium heat, turning them every now and then, for 8–10 minutes until cooked through. Put onto a baking tray and slide into the oven to keep hot.

3 Put the tomatoes cut-side up onto the rack of the grill pan, dot each one with a little butter and season. Grill for 4 minutes, then keep warm with the sausages.

4 Meanwhile, wipe out the frying pan, add a teaspoon or two of oil and fry the bacon for 1–2 minutes until crisp and golden on both sides. Keep warm with the sausages and tomatoes.

5 Heat another tablespoon of oil with the bacon fat left in the frying pan, add the bread and fry for 1–2 minutes on each side until crisp and golden. Put onto a second baking tray and slide into the oven.

6 Melt a small knob of butter in a medium-sized frying pan, add the mushrooms and some seasoning and cook over a high heat for 2–3 minutes. Set to one side.

7 Wipe the frying pan clean again, then heat a thin layer of oil in it over a medium-high heat and fry the egg(s) (see page 24). Alternatively, for larger numbers, scramble the eggs instead (see page 24). Serve with tomato ketchup or brown sauce.

tortilla weekend brunch

Here is a full-English-breakfast version of the classic Spanish omelette conveniently cooked in one pan.

serves 4 • preparation 15 mins • cooking 15 mins

Energy 471 kcals • Protein 23.8 g • Carbohydrate 11.8 g • Fat 36.9 g
Saturated fat 12.1 g • Fibre 1.3 g • Salt 2.63 g • Added sugars none

225 g (8 oz) potatoes, peeled and cut into small chunks
4 meaty pork sausages
3 tablespoons sunflower oil
4–6 rindless back bacon rashers, halved
25 g (1 oz) butter
100 g (4 oz) button mushrooms, wiped clean
6–8 eggs
2 tomatoes, cut into wedges
salt and freshly ground black pepper

1 Boil the potatoes in salted water for 7–8 minutes until just tender. Drain and set aside.

2 Cut the sausages in half lengthways and then cut each piece across into two. Heat 2 tablespoons of the oil in a 23-cm (9-inch) non-stick frying pan, add the sausages and fry for 2 minutes, turning until golden. Transfer to a plate, then fry the bacon pieces for 1 minute on each side. Set aside with the sausages.

3 Add the remaining oil and half the butter to the pan, add the potatoes and fry for 5–6 minutes until crisp and golden. Season and set aside.

4 Place the rest of the butter in the pan with the mushrooms and some seasoning and fry briskly for 1 minute. Return the sausages, bacon and potatoes to the pan and arrange them over the base so that eventually each slice will get a little bit of everything. Beat the eggs with some salt and pepper, pour into the pan and cook over a low heat for 15 minutes until almost set.

5 Pre-heat the grill to medium-high. Season the tomato wedges with a little salt and pepper and arrange them over the top of the tortilla. Slide the pan under the grill for 2–3 minutes until the omelette has lightly browned and the tomatoes are hot. Serve cut into wedges.

how to make muffins

These bun-like muffins originated in the USA and are very easy to make. You can even prepare the bowls of dry ingredients and wet ingredients in advance and simply mix them together just before you cook. The trick to fluffy muffins is to fold the wet and dry ingredients together as briefly as possible until just combined; don't worry if the mixture still looks a little lumpy. The nutritional information below is per muffin, so if you're calorie counting, you'll need to multiply up, depending on how many you have.

✪ marmalade muffins

makes 10 • preparation 5 mins • cooking 20–25 mins

Energy 240 kcals • Protein 3.8 g • Carbohydrate 37.5 g • Fat 9.3 g
Saturated fat 5.6 g • Fibre 1.0 g • Salt 0.80 g • Added sugars 17.2 g

200 g (7 oz) plain flour
1 tablespoon baking powder
a small pinch of salt
40 g (1½ oz) stoneground wholemeal flour
75 g (3 oz) caster sugar
175 ml (6 fl oz) milk
1 medium egg, beaten
100 g (4 oz) butter, melted
finely grated zest of 1 orange
100 g (4 oz) thick-cut marmalade
2 tablespoons demerara sugar, for sprinkling

1 Pre-heat the oven to 200°C/400°F/Gas Mark 6. Line a muffin tray with 12 deep paper cases.

2 Sift the plain flour, baking powder and salt into a bowl. Stir in the wholemeal flour and caster sugar. Beat the milk, egg, warm melted butter and orange zest together, add to the bowl of dry ingredients with the marmalade and stir until only just mixed.

3 Spoon the mixture equally into the paper cases and sprinkle the tops with a little demerara sugar. Bake for 20–25 minutes until well risen and golden brown. Leave to cool for 5 minutes, then serve warm. The muffins are best served on the day they are made.

VARIATIONS

BLUEBERRY, COCONUT AND LEMON MUFFINS

Sift 240 g (8½ oz) plain flour with the baking powder and salt. Stir in 150 g (5 oz) caster sugar and 40 g (1½ oz) desiccated coconut. Beat together the milk, egg, melted butter and the finely grated zest of ½ lemon. Stir in with 100 g (4 oz) blueberries. Bake as before.

CHEESY CORNMEAL AND BACON MUFFINS

Fry 175 g (6 oz) chopped rindless back bacon rashers in 1 teaspoon oil until crisp and golden. Spoon onto kitchen paper and leave to drain. Sift 120 g (4½ oz) plain flour with 100 g (4 oz) cornmeal (polenta), the baking powder and ¼ teaspoon of salt. Stir in 50 g (2 oz) grated Cheddar cheese and the bacon. Beat the milk, egg and melted butter together and stir in. Bake as before.

crunch brunch mushrooms

For vegetarians, leave out the bacon and add one skinned, seeded and diced tomato with the breadcrumbs and herbs.

serves 4 • preparation 10 mins • cooking 12–15 mins

Energy 337 kcals • Protein 10.3 g • Carbohydrate 21.8 g • Fat 23.9 g
Saturated fat 9.4 g • Fibre 2.6 g • Salt 1.97 g • Added sugars none

- 8 large open-cup field mushrooms, wiped clean
- 3–4 tablespoons olive oil
- 4 rindless smoked back bacon rashers, chopped
- 50 g (2 oz) butter
- 1 small onion, finely chopped
- 2 garlic cloves, crushed
- 100 g (4 oz) fresh white breadcrumbs
- the leaves from ½ x 20-g (¾-oz) packet parsley, chopped
- the leaves from 3 sprigs of thyme
- 1 tablespoon lemon juice
- salt and freshly ground black pepper

1 Pre-heat the oven to 230°C/450°F/Gas Mark 8, or as high as it will go. Remove the stalks from the mushrooms and roughly chop. Heat 1 tablespoon of the oil in a frying pan, add the bacon and fry for a minute or two until golden. Add the butter, mushroom stalks, onion and garlic and fry gently for 5 minutes until the onion is soft.

2 Season to taste with salt and pepper and stir in the breadcrumbs, parsley and thyme. Put the mushrooms rounded-side down onto a lightly oiled baking sheet and drizzle with the rest of the olive oil and the lemon juice. Season with a little salt and pepper, then divide the breadcrumb topping between each one, spreading the mixture out to the edges of each cap.

3 Bake the mushrooms for 12–15 minutes until the mushrooms are tender and the topping is crisp and golden.

sweet soy mushrooms on ciabatta toast

Sweet soy sauce, also called 'ketchup manis', is available in most supermarkets now, but if you can't find it, just use dark soy sauce mixed with a little clear, runny honey instead.

serves 2 • preparation 2–3 mins • cooking 3–4 mins

Energy 488 kcals • Protein 13.1 g • Carbohydrate 62.4 g • Fat 20.8 g
Saturated fat 11.3 g • Fibre 4.6 g • Salt 5.58 g • Added sugars 1.4 g

40 g (1½ oz) butter, plus a little extra for spreading
1 small garlic clove, finely chopped
350 g (12 oz) small chestnut or button mushrooms, wiped clean and halved
½ ciabatta loaf, sliced
2 tablespoons sweet soy sauce
a small bunch of chives, garlic ones if possible, snipped into long lengths
salt and freshly ground black pepper

1 Melt the butter in a large frying pan. Add the garlic and mushrooms and stir-fry them over a high heat for 2–3 minutes. Meanwhile, toast about 6 slices of the ciabatta bread.

2 Add the sweet soy sauce to the mushrooms and toss over a high heat for a few seconds more – it will caramelize instantly. Season to taste with salt and pepper.

3 Put the toast onto warmed plates, and spread with a little butter if you wish. Spoon on the mushrooms and sprinkle with the chopped chives. Serve straight away.

hot-smoked salmon and egg kedgeree

The beauty of this dish is that it can be cooked in advance, covered with cling film and reheated in the microwave on full power for 4–5 minutes, forking through the rice halfway through. It is equally good made with cooked flaked smoked haddock, smoked cod, kippers or even cooked peeled prawns.

serves 4 • preparation 7–8 mins • cooking 15 mins

Energy 618 kcals • Protein 34.1 g • Carbohydrate 74.2 g • Fat 22.6 g
Saturated fat 9.7 g • Fibre 0.6 g • Salt 3.39 g • Added sugars none

50 g (2 oz) butter
1 medium onion, finely chopped
seeds from 4 green cardamom pods
¼ teaspoon turmeric powder
a small piece of cinnamon stick
350 g (12 oz) basmati rice
600 ml (1 pint) chicken stock, ideally fresh (see page 231)
2 bay leaves
4 eggs
350 g (12 oz) hot-smoked salmon, broken into flakes
1 tablespoon lemon juice
the leaves from 1 x 20-g (¾-oz) packet curly parsley, chopped
salt and freshly ground black pepper

1 Melt half the butter in a 20-cm (8-inch) heavy-based pan, add the onion and cook gently for 5 minutes until soft but not browned. Add the cardamom seeds, turmeric and cinnamon stick and cook for 1 minute.

2 Add the rice to the buttery onions and stir well. Add the stock, bay leaves and ¼ teaspoon of salt. Bring to the boil, stir once, then cover with a well-fitting lid and leave to cook very gently over a low heat for 12 minutes.

3 Meanwhile, hard-boil the eggs for 8 minutes, then drain, peel and cut into small chunky pieces.

4 Uncover the rice and remove the bay leaves and cinnamon stick. Gently fork in the hot-smoked salmon and eggs, re-cover and cook for a further 3–4 minutes until they have heated through. Melt the remaining butter. Uncover the rice once more and fork through the lemon juice, parsley, melted butter and some salt and pepper to taste.

Jamaican ackee and salt fish in de pan

You can now buy packets of salt cod fillet with the skin and bones already removed, which makes it a lot quicker to prepare, and cooked salt fish, called bacalão, is available in cans. Ackee is the fruit of a Jamaican tree and has a texture very much like scrambled eggs. It is handily available in cans.

serves 4 • preparation 10 mins • cooking 30 mins

Energy 496 kcals • Protein 49.7 g • Carbohydrate 7.4 g • Fat 30.1 g
Saturated fat 5.1 g • Fibre 2.3 g • Salt 1.89 g • Added sugars 0.7 g

450 g (1 lb) salt cod fillet, soaked overnight in plenty of cold water
2 large eggs
2 tablespoons sunflower oil
1 red pepper, seeded and chopped
1 green pepper, seeded and chopped
4 fat spring onions, trimmed and sliced
the leaves from 3 sprigs of thyme
½ medium-hot red chilli, seeded and chopped
4 tomatoes, skinned, cut into thin wedges and the seeds removed
1 x 450-g (1-lb) can prepared ackee, drained
the leaves from ½ x 20-g (¾-oz) packet flat-leaf parsley, chopped
freshly ground black pepper
West Indian hot pepper sauce, to serve

1 Bring a pan of water to the boil. Add the drained, soaked salt cod, bring back to the boil and simmer for 15 minutes. Drain, flake and set aside.

2 Lower the eggs into another pan of boiling water and boil for 8 minutes. Meanwhile, heat the oil in a large frying pan. Add the red and green peppers and fry over a medium-high heat for 5 minutes until tender. Add the spring onions, thyme leaves, chilli and tomatoes and fry for 3–4 minutes more.

3 Add the salt cod and ackee to the chilli mixture and cook for 2 minutes or so, carefully turning over now and then until heated through. (Try to avoid breaking up the ackees.) Meanwhile, drain and peel the eggs and cut into quarters.

4 Arrange the egg quarters on top. Sprinkle with the chopped parsley and some freshly ground black pepper. Serve with hot pepper sauce for that extra kick!

caribbean brunch

There's nothing nicer at the weekend than a leisurely brunch. It allows everyone the luxury of a lie-in and then time to catch up with each other on the events of the week. You can then usually forget about lunch, having consumed enough food to keep you going until supper.

menu

Mango, passion fruit and coconut smoothies
(see page 20)

Jamaican ackee and salt fish in de pan
(see page 34)

Fried plantains or bananas
(see page 226)

Cheesy cornmeal and bacon muffins
(see page 30)

Coffee (Blue Mountain for the connoisseurs)

CARIBBEAN COOL

If you have room, put some tall glasses into the freezer to get cold overnight. This helps to keep the smoothies cold for longer, and gives the glasses a nice frosted look.

time plan

The day before
Soak the salt cod in plenty of cold water.
Make some ice for the smoothies.

In advance on the day
Prepare bowls of wet and dry ingredients for the muffins, but don't mix together.
Pre-heat the oven and line the muffin tray with paper cases.
Prepare the ingredients for the smoothies.
Prepare the ingredients for the ackee and salt fish.
Cook and flake the salt cod and set aside.

time plan for an 11 a.m. brunch

10.30 a.m.	Make the muffins and put them in to bake.
10.40 a.m.	Put the eggs on to boil. Start the salt fish and ackee.
10.50 a.m.	Fry the plantains or bananas and keep warm.
10.55 a.m.	Make the smoothies.

LUNCH ON THE GO

✿ spicy chick pea, cumin and coriander soup

This is a rich, intensely spicy soup, which reminds me of Moroccan holidays. It can be made almost entirely from the store-cupboard.

serves 4 • preparation 5 mins • cooking 20 mins

Energy 226 kcals • Protein 11.1 g • Carbohydrate 25.2 g • Fat 9.7 g
Saturated fat 0.8 g • Fibre 5.8 g • Salt 1.71 g • Added sugars none

2 tablespoons extra virgin olive oil,
   plus extra to garnish
1 large onion, finely chopped
2 large garlic cloves, finely chopped
2 teaspoons ground cumin
2 × 400-g (14-oz) cans chick peas, drained and rinsed
900 ml (1½ pints) vegetable or chicken stock
   (see page 231)
½ x 20-g (¾-oz) packet coriander, chopped
a few drops of Tabasco
juice of ½ lemon
salt and freshly ground black pepper

1 Heat the oil in a large pan and add the onion and garlic. Sauté for about 5 minutes until well softened but not browned. Stir in the cumin and cook for a minute or so, stirring. Add the chick peas, then pour in the stock. Season generously and bring to the boil, then reduce the heat and simmer for 10 minutes until the flavours are well combined.

2 Add the coriander to the chick pea mixture, then blitz with a hand-held blender or process until smooth. Add the Tabasco and lemon juice and season to taste. Serve garnished with swirls of olive oil.

✿ easy home made chicken and sweetcorn soup

This is a variation on an old favourite that appears on every Chinese take-away menu in the country. I really like the fresh flavours of this version. It makes a truly satisfying meal in a cup.

serves 4 • preparation 5 mins • cooking 20 mins

Energy 265 kcals • Protein 24.6 g • Carbohydrate 21.9 g • Fat 9.3 g
Saturated fat 1.8 g • Fibre 1.05 g • Salt 2.29 g • Added sugars 2.25 g

1 tablespoon sunflower oil
2 garlic cloves, finely chopped
2.5 cm (1 inch) fresh root ginger, peeled and finely chopped
2 green bird's-eye chillies, seeded and finely chopped
2 skinless chicken breast fillets, halved lengthways
   and finely sliced or diced
1 tablespoon mild curry paste
1 teaspoon cornflour
1.2 litres (2 pints) chicken stock (see page 231)
1 × 350-g (12-oz) can sweetcorn kernels, drained,
   or 225 g (8 oz) frozen kernels
2 eggs
1 teaspoon sesame oil
about 2 teaspoons dark soy sauce

1 Heat the sunflower oil in a large pan, add the garlic, ginger and chillies and stir-fry for 30 seconds or so. Add the chicken and stir-fry for 2–3 minutes until sealed, then stir in the curry paste and stir-fry for a further minute. Mix the cornflour with a little of the stock and add to the pan with the remaining stock and the sweetcorn. Bring to the boil, stirring continuously, and simmer gently for about 5 minutes.

2 Beat together the eggs and sesame oil and slowly trickle into the chicken and sweetcorn mixture, stirring with a chopstick or fork to make egg strands. Season to taste with the soy sauce and serve.

sandwiches

There are many types of bread available now and my favourites for sandwiches include malted rye and sourdough breads. You can also serve any of these ideas as open sandwiches – just garnish with a sprig of parsley or watercress. All the recipes take just minutes to make and should serve 4 (or 2 greedy adults).

ALL-AMERICAN CLUB SANDWICH (BELOW)
This is a triple-decker sandwich. Pre-heat the grill and cook 12 **rindless, smoked streaky bacon rashers** until crisp and lightly golden. Mix 1 tablespoon **wholegrain mustard** with 6 tablespoons **mayonnaise** and some seasoning. Toast 12 slices **white bread** and spread with the mustard mayonnaise. Finely shred 25 g (1 oz) **crisp lettuce** and divide half between 4 slices of the toast. Arrange 2 sliced **tomatoes** on top. Cut 1 small **white onion** into wafer-thin slices and place half over the tomato. Season to taste. Cover the tomato and onion layer with 100 g (4 oz) **wafer-thin chicken slices** and place a slice of toast on top, mayonnaise-side up. Add the remaining lettuce followed by 4 **thin slices Swiss cheese**, such as Emmenthal, the crispy bacon and the

rest of the onion. Cover with the remaining slices of toast and press down lightly. To serve, cut each sandwich into four triangles and secure each piece with a cocktail stick or small plastic skewer.

CRAB WITH ROCKET AND LEMON AÏOLI
Place 4 tablespoons **mayonnaise** in a bowl and beat in ½ small, crushed **garlic clove**, ½ teaspoon **Dijon mustard**, 2 teaspoons **fresh lemon juice** and a pinch of **minced red chilli**. Season to taste. Spread 8 slices **crusty white bread** with the lemon aïoli. Arrange 40 g (1½ oz) **wild rocket** on 4 slices and pile 350 g (12 oz) **fresh white crabmeat** on top. Season to taste, then sandwich with the remaining slices of bread. Press down lightly, cut on the diagonal and serve.

PASTRAMI, DILL PICKLE AND MUSTARD MAYONNAISE
I like to serve this sandwich with crinkle-cut chips on the side. Mix 2 tablespoons **American mustard** (from a squeezy bottle) with 2 tablespoons **mayonnaise** and season to taste. Spread over the 8 slices **crusty Granary bread**, then divide 12 **thin slices pastrami** between 4 slices. Arrange 4 thinly sliced **dill pickles** (large gherkins), on top and cover with the remaining slices of bread. Cut the sandwiches in half and serve.

HOT-SMOKED SALMON AND WATERCRESS
Split 4 **crusty Granary rolls** and smear them with 3 tablespoons **mayonnaise**. Arrange 50 g (2 oz) trimmed **watercress** on the bottom halves followed by 350 g (12 oz) **hot-smoked salmon**. Add a squeeze of **lemon juice** and season to taste. Press the tops down lightly, cut each one in half and serve.

ROQUEFORT, GRAPE, RADICCHIO AND WALNUT
It is a good idea to allow the cheese to come up to room temperature before using – this normally takes about an hour. Cut 1 small **brown farmhouse loaf** into 8 slices, discarding the ends, and butter lightly. Take 275 g (10 oz) **Roquefort**, cut off any rind, then cut the cheese into thin slices and divide between 4 slices of the bread. Shred 1 small head **radicchio**, place in a bowl and add about 2 tablespoons **extra virgin olive oil** and 1 teaspoon **red wine vinegar** – just enough to barely coat the leaves. Season to taste and pile on top of the cheese. Scatter with 50 g (2 oz) halved **seedless red grapes** and 25 g (1 oz) chopped **walnut halves**, then cover with the remaining slices of bread. Cut each sandwich on the diagonal and serve.

ROAST PORK, BEETROOT AND HORSERADISH

Spread 8 slices of **light rye** or **country-style bread** with butter and smear with **creamed horseradish**. Pile slices of **cooked roast pork** on half of them and top with a layer of thinly sliced **cooked beetroot**. Add a few **crisp lettuce leaves**, if liked, then cover with the remaining slices of bread. Cut in half on the diagonal and serve.

BEEF AND ROCKET WITH MUSTARD DRESSING *(ABOVE)*

To make the dressing, place 2 tablespoons of **sunflower oil** and 1 tablespoon of **walnut oil** in a screw-topped jar with 2 teaspoons of **Dijon mustard** and 1 tablespoon of **white wine vinegar**. Season to taste and shake well to combine. Spread 8 slices of **crusty brown or white bread** with butter and arrange slices of **cooked roast beef** on half of them. Use just enough of the dressing to barely coat 50 g (2 oz) of wild rocket, then pile on top. Cover with the remaining slices of bread, cut in half on the diagonal and serve.

SPICED CHICKEN WITH APRICOT

Gently fry an **onion** in a knob of **butter**. Add 1 tablespoon **mild curry paste**, 1 tablespoon **clear honey**, a glass of **white wine** and a handful of finely chopped **ready-to-eat apricots**. Simmer, uncovered, for about 15 minutes until nearly all the liquid is gone. Leave to cool, then stir in 4 tablespoons of **mayonnaise** and 2 tablespoons of **crème fraîche**. Cut 350 g (12 oz) of **cooked roast chicken** into bite-sized pieces, then fold into the apricot mixture. Spread 8 slices of **Granary** or **brown bread** with butter and divide the chicken mixture between half of them. Pile **crisp shredded lettuce** on top with some thinly sliced **cucumber** and **spring onions**, if liked. Cover with the remaining slices of bread, cut on the diagonal and serve.

chunky greek salad with feta cheese

This summer salad conjures up images of sunny tavernas, where the salad is always dressed just with olive oil, never with vinaigrette. It is a very transportable feast and needs nothing more than a hunk of crusty bread and a glass of gutsy red wine to make a lovely light lunch.

serves 4 • preparation 5 mins • cooking none

Energy 201 kcals • Protein 7.1 g • Carbohydrate 5.6 g • Fat 16.9 g
Saturated fat 6.0 g • Fibre 1.5 g • Salt 2.0 g • Added sugars none

  1 red onion, roughly chopped
  225 g (8 oz) cherry tomatoes, halved
  $\frac{1}{2}$ cucumber, peeled and cut into chunks
  150 g (5 oz) feta cheese, cut into thin slices
  a handful of good-quality black olives
  a pinch of dried oregano
  3–4 tablespoons extra virgin olive oil
  salt and freshly ground black pepper

1 Soak the onion in a bowl of salted water for 5–10 minutes to remove the sharpness. Drain well on kitchen paper. Place in a serving bowl with the tomatoes and cucumber, then mix gently to combine. Scatter with the feta and olives, then sprinkle over the oregano. Season to taste and drizzle with the olive oil. Serve at once.

italian bean salad with griddled red onion and tuna

This salad, which needs to be served at room temperature, should be made with the best-quality ingredients. It makes excellent picnic food, or use as an addition to an antipasti platter or as an instant lunch.

serves 4 • preparation 5 mins • cooking 10 mins

Energy 475 kcals • Protein 32.7 g • Carbohydrate 28.0 g • Fat 26.7 g
Saturated fat 3.9 g • Fibre 7.7 g • Salt 2.15 g • Added sugars 0.5 g

  2 red onions, cut into wedges but root left intact
  120 ml (4 fl oz) extra virgin olive oil
  juice of $\frac{1}{2}$ lemon
  a pinch of sugar
  2 × 400-g (14-oz) cans cannellini beans, drained
    and rinsed
  the leaves from 1 x 20-g ($\frac{3}{4}$-oz) packet flat-leaf parsley,
    roughly chopped
  1 × 400-g (14-oz) can tuna in oil, drained and flaked
  salt and freshly ground black pepper

1 Pre-heat a griddle pan. Toss the onion wedges in a bowl with 2 tablespoons of the oil and season generously. Add to the griddle pan and cook for 6–8 minutes until cooked through and lightly charred, turning occasionally.

2 Meanwhile, place the remaining olive oil in a screw-topped jar with the lemon juice and sugar, and season to taste. Shake until well combined and pour into a serving dish large enough to hold the beans. When the onions are cooked through, add them to the dressing, turning gently to combine, then fold in the beans, parsley and tuna. Season to taste and serve at once.

bagels

The great New York bagel lends itself to any number of fillings, so here are just a few ideas. All serve 4 people and take 10 minutes to make.

SALMON ROYAL BAGEL *(BELOW)*
Pre-heat the grill. Split 4 **plain bagels**, then lightly toast, cut-side up. Spread thickly with 120 g (4½ oz) **full-fat soft cheese** and arrange 225 g (8 oz) **smoked salmon** on the bottom halves. Slice 2 **ripe tomatoes**, layer them over the salmon and season to taste. Slice ½ small **red onion** and separate into rings. Arrange over the tomato and scatter with 1 tablespoon **capers** (optional). Sandwich together, then cut each bagel in half and serve.

GRIDDLED CHICKEN WITH TOMATO AND CHILLI MAYONNAISE AND ROCKET
Heat a heavy-based griddle pan until smoking hot. Place 225 g (8 oz) **mini chicken fillets** or chicken fillet strips in a bowl and add 2 tablespoons **olive oil**. Season, toss the chicken until evenly coated, then add to the pan. Reduce the heat and cook for 2–3 minutes, turning once until cooked through and lightly charred. Transfer to a plate and leave to cool.

To make the tomato and chilli mayonnaise, place 4 tablespoons **mayonnaise** in a bowl and beat in 1 small, crushed **garlic clove**, ½ teaspoon **tomato purée** and 2 teaspoons **sweet chilli sauce**. Set aside.

Split 4 **caramelized onion bagels** and toast them, cut-side down, on the griddle pan until lightly charred. Spread with the flavoured mayonnaise and divide 25 g (1 oz) **wild rocket** between the bottom halves. Top with the chicken fillets and sandwich together. Cut each bagel in half and serve.

ULTIMATE TUNA MAYONNAISE
Pre-heat the grill. Split 4 **poppy-seed bagels** and toast them, cut-side up. Place 6 tablespoons **mayonnaise** in a bowl and beat in 4 chopped **spring onions**, 2 tablespoons rinsed **capers**, 1 teaspoon **Dijon mustard**, 1 teaspoon **grated horseradish** and a squeeze of **lemon juice**. Season to taste and fold in 400 g (14 oz) **canned tuna**. Divide the tuna mayonnaise between the bottom halves of the bagels, sandwich together, cut each one in half and serve.

baguettes

The French answer to a sandwich, baguettes are best served the day they are bought. If you do have any left-overs they can be used to make French-bread pizza. Filled baguettes also have the advantage of transporting well if wrapped up in cling film, making them perfect for picnics. I've also included a couple of ideas for hot baguettes, which are ideal for weekend lunches. None of these recipes take long to prepare and each one serves 4.

PAN BAGNAT (RIGHT)

Often served in Provence as a mid-morning snack, *pan bagnat* is basically *salade niçoise* between bread. I think it is best made a few hours in advance so that all the flavours have a chance to combine.

Place 2 **eggs** in a small pan, just cover with boiling water and cook for 10 minutes. Drain and rinse under cold running water, then remove the shells and cut into slices. Place 4 tablespoons **extra virgin olive oil** in a small bowl, mix in 1 crushed **garlic clove** and season to taste. Split 4 small baguettes, then brush the oil mixture all over the inside of each one. Separate the leaves of 1 **gem lettuce**, slice 2 **ripe tomatoes** and thinly slice 1 small **red onion**. Layer on the bottom halves of the baguettes. Drain and flake 1 × 400-g (14-oz) **can tuna** and place on the onion. Add the hard-boiled eggs and 100 g (4 oz) **pitted black olives**, seasoning as you go. Finish with 50 g (2 oz) **drained anchovies**. Add a **squeeze of lemon** to the remaining **garlic oil** and drizzle on top. Cover with the remaining baguette halves, wrap tightly with cling film and chill for up to 2 hours, or until ready to serve.

FRENCH BREAD PIZZA TOASTS

Pre-heat the oven to 200°C/400°F/Gas Mark 6. Cut 1 large **baguette** in half lengthways, then cut into eight equal-sized pieces. Spread a layer of **passata** over each piece, season to taste and sprinkle lightly with **dried oregano**. Drizzle with **olive oil** and scatter 100 g (4 oz) **grated mozzarella** and 50 g (2 oz) **grated mature Cheddar** on top. Arrange on baking sheets and bake for 15–20 minutes until the cheese has melted and the pizzas are lightly toasted.

SAUSAGE TORPEDOES WITH CARAMELIZED ONIONS

Pre-heat the grill. Mix 6 tablespoons **tomato ketchup** with 1 tablespoon **dark soy sauce**, 1 teaspoon **Dijon mustard** and 1 teaspoon **clear honey**. Place 4 good-quality **jumbo pork sausages** in a non-metallic dish. Pour in half the honey mixture and spread it on the sausages. Grill for 10–15 minutes, turning and basting occasionally. Meanwhile, cut 1 large **onion** into thick slices, separate into rings and dust in 2 tablespoons **seasoned flour**. Heat 2 tablespoons **sunflower oil** in a frying pan and sauté the onion rings for 8–10 minutes or until crisp and lightly golden. Drain on kitchen paper. Split 4 small **baguettes** and place the sausages on the bottom halves. Scatter the onion rings on top, then drizzle with the rest of sauce and serve.

how to make tortillas

A Spanish omelette, otherwise known as a tortilla, is thick, cooked until firm and golden brown on the outside, and is traditionally filled with potatoes. It makes an inexpensive lunch or, served cold, it makes fantastic picnic food. I find it keeps covered in the fridge for up to two days. I like to use a non-stick frying pan but a well-seasoned heavy-based frying pan also works well, it's just more difficult to turn over.

spanish tortilla with parma ham and caramelized red onions

serves 4 • preparation 5 mins • cooking 55 mins

Energy 310 kcals • Protein 12.6 g • Carbohydrate 58.3 g • Fat 4.5 g
Saturated fat 1.1 g • Fibre 7.0 g • Salt 0.13 g • Added sugars 8.6 g

3 tablespoons olive oil
1 large onion, thinly sliced
350 g (12 oz) small potatoes, peeled
6 eggs
175 g (6 oz) sliced Parma ham
salt and freshly ground black pepper

TO SERVE
caramelized red onions (from a jar)
green salad with vinaigrette (see page 228)

1 Heat 2 tablespoons of the oil in a non-stick frying pan with a base that is 20 cm (8 inches) in diameter. Add the onion and sauté for about 5 minutes until softened but not coloured. Thinly slice the potatoes using a food processor or even a potato peeler. Dry well in a clean tea towel and add to the pan, tossing to combine. Season generously, reduce the heat and cover with a lid or flat plate, then cook gently for 20–25 minutes until tender. Turn them over once or twice and shake the pan occasionally to ensure they cook evenly.

2 Break the eggs into a large bowl, add a good pinch of seasoning, then whisk lightly with a fork. When the onion and potato mixture is cooked, drain off any excess oil and quickly stir into the beaten eggs. Wipe out the pan and use to heat the remaining tablespoon of oil. Tip in the potato and egg mixture, pressing it down gently, and reduce the heat to its lowest setting. Cook for 15–20 minutes, and when there is virtually no raw egg mixture left on top of the omelette, invert it onto a flat plate. Slide the omelette back into the pan and cook for another 5 minutes. Turn off the heat and set aside for 5 minutes to finish cooking. It should be cooked through, but still moist in the centre.

3 To serve warm or cold, turn the tortilla onto a chopping board and cut into four wedges. Place a wedge on each serving plate. Arrange a tumble of Parma ham beside or on top of each tortilla wedge and add a dollop of the caramelized red onions. Serve at once with a bowl of green salad.

VARIATIONS

ROASTED RED PEPPER AND GOATS' CHEESE
Replace the potatoes with two large red peppers that have been halved, seeded and thinly sliced, and cook as for the potatoes. Crumble 100 g (4 oz) of mild, creamy goats' cheese on top and finish under a hot grill for about 5 minutes instead of inverting onto a plate.

PEA AND HAM WITH NEW POTATOES
Use 225 g (8 oz) scrubbed new potatoes cut into 1-cm (½-inch) discs. Stir 50 g (2 oz) frozen peas into the beaten egg with 100 g (4 oz) diced ham. Cook as described above.

ciabatta

Ciabatta is an Italian loaf – its shape is supposed to resemble a slipper. It should have large holes and a soft but chewy, floury crust. All the ideas below serve 4 and can be made in 30 minutes.

PEPERONATA WITH BUBBLING GOATS' CHEESE *(ABOVE)*
Heat 4 tablespoons **chilli-infused oil** in a large, heavy-based frying pan. Deseed and thinly slice 2 **red peppers** and 2 **yellow peppers** and place in the pan with 2 teaspoons **cumin seeds**. Fry over a high heat for 2–3 minutes, then season generously, reduce the heat and stir in 1 large, crushed **garlic clove**. Cook for another 10 minutes, stirring occasionally until the peppers have caramelized around the edges. Remove from the heat and leave to cool a little. Pre-heat the grill. Cut a 150-g (5-oz) **round goats' cheese** into 4 equal slices. Cut 1 **ciabatta loaf** in half lengthways, then in half widthways to give 4 pieces. Spoon on the pepper mixture and place a slice of goats' cheese on top. Place under the grill for a couple of minutes until bubbling, then serve sprinkled with some **chopped fresh parsley**.

BLT
Pre-heat the oven to 180°C/350°F/Gas Mark 4. Place 4 part-baked, small **ciabatta loaves** on a large baking sheet and bake for 8–10 minutes, or according to the instructions on the packet. Transfer to a wire rack and leave to cool a little. Pre-heat the grill and cook 8 **rindless bacon rashers** (dry-cured, if possible) until crisp and golden. Drain well on kitchen paper. Meanwhile, split the loaves and smear with 4 tablespoons **mayonnaise**, then spread 1 tablespoon **Dijon mustard** on the bottom halves and 2 tablespoons **tomato ketchup** on the top halves. Shred 1 **cos lettuce** and slice 4 **ripe plum tomatoes**. Pile the lettuce and tomatoes on the bottom halves and season generously. Add the bacon and cover with the top halves. Press down lightly, cut each sandwich into 3 pieces and serve.

MARINATED STEAK WITH CRISPY ONION RINGS
This recipe produces a medium-rare steak, so grill for 2 minutes on each side if you prefer it rare, and 6–7 minutes on each side for well done.

Trim the fat off 4 × 100-g (4-oz) **sirloin steaks**, about 2 cm (¾ inch) thick. Season well and place in a non-metallic dish. Mix together 3 tablespoons **olive oil**, 1 tablespoon **red wine vinegar**, 1 large, crushed **garlic clove** and 1 teaspoon **fresh thyme leaves** and spoon over the steaks, turning to coat. Cover and leave to marinate for at least 15 minutes and up to 24 hours in the fridge.

Cut 1 **Spanish onion** into 1-cm (½-inch) slices and separate into rings. Place in 150 ml (5 fl oz) milk and leave to soak for at least 15 minutes. Shake the steaks to remove any excess marinade, place on a grill rack and grill for 3–4 minutes on each side. Meanwhile, heat 5 cm (2 inches) sunflower oil in a frying pan. Transfer the steaks to a warm place and leave to rest for a couple of minutes. Drain the onion rings and toss in 6 tablespoons **seasoned flour**, then deep-fry in batches for 2–3 minutes until crisp and golden. Drain on kitchen paper.

Cut 1 **ciabatta loaf** in half lengthways, then widthways to give 4 equal pieces. Spread with 2 tablespoons **Dijon mustard** and pile 40 g (1½ oz) torn **frisée lettuce** on top. Place each piece on a warmed serving plate and put a rested steak on top. Scatter with the onion rings and serve at once.

pittas and wraps

Pitta bread and soft flour tortillas offer a healthy, but tasty alternative to traditional breads. All of the following recipes take less than 15 minutes to prepare and each one will serve 4.

AVOCADO, ROCKET AND PRAWN (*BELOW*)

Heat a heavy-based frying pan. Cut 1 large **ripe avocado** in half and remove the stone, then scoop the flesh into a bowl and add a good dash of **balsamic vinegar** and 2 tablespoons **mayonnaise**. Season to taste and mash with a fork to a smooth purée. Heat 4 **soft flour tortillas** for 30 seconds in the frying pan, turning once. Spoon the avocado mash down the middle of each heated tortilla and divide 50 g (2 oz) **wild rocket** and 350 g (12 oz) large, **cooked peeled prawns** between them. Season to taste, roll up to enclose the filling, then cut each one on the diagonal and serve.

CAJUN CHICKEN

Pre-heat a griddle pan. Place 2 teaspoons **Cajun seasoning** on a plate and season generously, then use to coat 2 **boneless chicken breasts**. Lightly brush the griddle pan with a little oil and add the chicken, skin-side down. Cook for 5 minutes until the skin is crisp and golden, then turn over and cook for another 3–4 minutes until cooked through but still juicy. Transfer to a plate and set aside for a couple of minutes to rest. Meanwhile, quickly warm 4 **soft flour tortillas** on the griddle pan. Spoon dollops of **soured cream** down the middle of each tortilla and divide 50 g (2 oz) **mixed salad leaves** and 75 g (3 oz) **semi-sun-dried tomatoes** between them. Carve the chicken into slices and arrange on top, then roll up to enclose the filling. Cut in half on the diagonal and serve.

HUMMUS, ROASTED RED PEPPER AND SPINACH

Place 2 roughly chopped **garlic cloves**, 1 seeded and roughly chopped **mild red chilli**, and a handful of **fresh flat-leaf parsley leaves** in a food processor and whizz until finely chopped. Add half a 400-g (14-oz) can drained **chick peas** with 2 tablespoons **extra virgin olive oil** and 1 tablespoon **sesame oil** (optional), and whizz again until smooth. Add the remaining chick peas and pulse for another 10 seconds, until just combined. Season to taste. Pre-heat the grill or a griddle pan and quickly warm 4 **white pitta breads** on both sides. Drain and slice 400 g (14 oz) **roasted red peppers** (from a can or jar). Split open the pittas and stuff with the hummus, 50 g (2 oz) **tender, young spinach leaves** and the peppers.

✪iced lemon pumpkin bars

These bars are a real treat for adults and children alike. Pumpkin purée is now readily available in cans and jars, but you could follow the recipe below and make your own. The nutritional informaton given below is per bar, so you'll need to multiply up accordingly if you have more than one.

makes about 24 • preparation 15 mins • cooking 1 hr 30 mins

Energy 184 kcals • Protein 2.4 g • Carbohydrate 28.7 g • Fat 7.5 g
Saturated fat 2.6 g • Fibre 0.7 g • Salt 0.07 g • Added sugars 16.0 g

- 400-g (14-oz) slice fresh pumpkin,
  - or 150 g (5 oz) canned pumpkin purée
- 150 g (5 oz) unsalted butter, softened
  - plus extra for greasing
- 225 g (8 oz) light muscovado sugar
- 2 eggs
- 275 g (10 oz) plain flour
- 1/2 teaspoon baking powder
- 1 teaspoon ground cinnamon
- 1/2 teaspoon ground ginger
- 1/2 teaspoon ground allspice
- 100 g (4 oz) sultanas
- 100 g (4 oz) pecan nuts, chopped
- 3–4 tablespoons milk
- 150 g (5 oz) icing sugar, sifted
- finely grated rind and juice of 1 lemon

1 Pre-heat the oven to 180°C/350°F/Gas Mark 4. Using a large spoon, scoop out the pumpkin seeds, then cut the piece in half widthways. Smear all over the flesh with 25 g (1 oz) of the butter, then place on a baking sheet. Roast for 50–55 minutes, or until completely tender. Leave to cool, then scoop out the flesh, discarding the skin, and whizz to a purée in a food processor. This will give you 150 g (5 oz).

2 Grease a 30 × 23-cm (12 × 9-inch) baking tin and line the bottom with baking parchment. Cream the remaining 100 g (4 oz) of the butter with the muscovado sugar until light and fluffy, then add the pumpkin purée and the eggs; don't worry if it curdles slightly. Sift the flour, baking powder and spices into a bowl, then gradually add to the creamed mixture. Stir in the sultanas and nuts, then add enough milk to give the mixture a dropping consistency. Pour into the prepared baking tin and spread evenly. Bake for 30–35 minutes until golden brown and just firm to the touch. Leave to cool for 5 minutes in the tin.

3 Meanwhile, mix the icing sugar in a bowl with the lemon rind and juice. Turn the cake out onto a wire rack, then carefully turn right side up. While still warm, spread with the icing. When cold, cut into bars and start munching.

chocolate krispie fridge cake

As there's no cooking involved in this cake, it can be safely made by children. The mixture can be formed into individual truffles, if you like. The nutritional information given below is per slice, so you'll need to multiply up if you eat more than one piece.

makes a 1.5-litre (2½-pint) cake (approx. 12 slices) • preparation 2 hrs 45 mins • cooking none

Energy 411 kcals • Protein 5.0 g • Carbohydrate 46.8 g • Fat 24.0 g
Saturated fat 14.3 g • Fibre 0.5 g • Salt 0.42 g • Added sugars 31.8 g

- 400 g (14 oz) milk or plain chocolate, broken into pieces
- 100 g (4 oz) unsalted butter
- 225 g (8 oz) Madeira cake, crumbled
- 1 × 30-g (1¼-oz) packet Rice Krispies
- 50 g (2 oz) raisins
- 75 g (3 oz) Maltesers, chopped (2 × 37-g packets)
- 2 Twix bars, finely chopped
- 2 tablespoons golden syrup

1 Line a 1.5-litre (2½-pint) loaf tin with baking parchment. Melt 275 g (10 oz) of the chocolate in a large bowl set over a pan of simmering water or in the microwave. Melt the butter in a small pan or in the microwave and add to the melted chocolate with the Madeira crumbs. Add the Rice Krispies, raisins, Maltesers, Twixes and golden syrup, and mix until well combined. Spoon into the prepared loaf tin, then place in the fridge and allow to set for at least 2 hours, or overnight, until completely firm.

2 To serve, remove the cake from the tin and carefully peel away the parchment. Place on a flat serving plate. Melt the remaining 100 g (4 oz) of chocolate as before and pour over the cake, swirling with the back of a spoon to spread evenly, then set aside for at least 30 minutes and up to 1 hour to set. Cut into slices with a knife dipped in hot water. Wrap any remaining cake in parchment and foil, and store in the fridge until needed.

HOME ALONE

2 While the chicken is simmering, make the noodles according to the directions on the packet, then drain. Sprinkle half the onions and peanuts into the bottom of 2 large warmed bowls, and add the cooked noodles and lettuce.

3 Ladle the flavoured stock into the bowls, season with the soy sauce, then scatter over the remaining onions and peanuts. Garnish with the coriander and offer the chilli sauce separately.

mushroom and cheese omelette

Omelettes make a fabulous super-quick meal. Take care not to overbeat the eggs as it will spoil the texture.

serves 1 • preparation 5 mins • cooking 15 mins

Energy 604 kcals • Protein 37.2 g • Carbohydrate 0.3 g • Fat 50.5 g
Saturated fat 19.9 g • Fibre 0.6 g • Salt 1.75 g • Added sugars none

    2 teaspoons sunflower oil
    15 g (½ oz) unsalted butter
    50 g (2 oz) chestnut mushrooms, wiped clean and sliced
    3 eggs
    a small bundle of chives, snipped
    50 g (2 oz) Gruyère or Roquefort cheese, thinly sliced
    salt and freshly ground black pepper
    rocket and crusty bread, to serve

1 Pre-heat the grill and heat a 20-cm (8-inch) non-stick frying pan. Add half the oil and butter and, once the butter is foaming, tip in the mushrooms. Season to taste, then sauté for 2–3 minutes until tender. Tip into a bowl and keep warm.

2 Wipe out the frying pan and return to the hob. Break the eggs into a bowl, add the chives and some seasoning, then beat lightly. When the pan is hot, add the remaining oil and butter, swirling it so that the base and sides get coated. While the butter is still foaming, pour in the egg mixture, tilting the pan from side to side. Use a fork or wooden spatula to draw the mixture from the sides to the centre as it sets. When the eggs have almost set, scatter over two-thirds of the cheese and place under the pre-heated grill for 1–2 minutes until melted.

3 Tilt the pan away from you and use a knife to fold over a third of the omelette to the centre, then fold over the opposite third. Slide onto a plate, flipping it over so that the folded side is underneath. Lightly press the omelette into a cigar shape and cut a slit. Spoon the mushrooms inside the slit and scatter over the remaining cheese. Serve with rocket and crusty bread.

chicken noodle soup with lettuce

Noodle soups are the ultimate comfort food. They take very little time to prepare and are also low in fat.

serves 2 • preparation 10 mins • cooking 10 mins

Energy 387 kcals • Protein 31.7 g • Carbohydrate 18.9 g • Fat 21.0 g
Saturated fat 3.5 g • Fibre 2.3 g • Salt 3.18 g • Added sugars 2.8 g

    1 tablespoon sunflower oil
    175 g (6 oz) boneless, skinless chicken, cut into small pieces
    900 ml (1½ pints) chicken stock (see page 231)
    1 teaspoon sugar
    1 × 85-g (3¼-oz) packet chicken-flavoured instant noodles
    2 spring onions, finely sliced
    50 g (2 oz) salted peanuts, roughly chopped
    50 g (2 oz) crisp lettuce leaves, shredded
    dark soy sauce, to taste
    ½ x 20-g (¾-oz) packet coriander, chopped
    chilli sauce or oil, to serve

1 Heat the oil in a large pan. Add the chicken and stir-fry for 2–3 minutes until lightly browned and just tender. Pour in the stock, add the sugar, then bring to a gentle simmer and cook for 5 minutes.

how to make stir-fries

Stir-frying is a traditional Chinese cooking technique that is very easy to master. To check if the vegetables are cooked, pierce them with the tip of a knife: the vegetables should feel as soft as butter.

fragrant pork and vegetable stir-fry

serves 2 • preparation 20 mins • cooking 20 mins

Energy 334 kcals • Protein 23.8 g • Carbohydrate 22.3 g • Fat 16.9 g
Saturated fat 2.9 g • Fibre 4.4 g • Salt 2.72 g • Added sugars 1.0 g

- 2 teaspoons dark soy sauce
- 1 teaspoon sesame oil
- 1 teaspoon dry sherry
- 1 teaspoon cornflour
- 175 g (6 oz) pork tenderloin (fillet) or boneless loin chops, well trimmed
- 2 tablespoons sunflower oil
- 2 garlic cloves, crushed
- 2 spring onions, finely chopped
- 2 teaspoons freshly grated root ginger
- 1 onion, thinly sliced
- 1 carrot, peeled and sliced on the diagonal
- 50 g (2 oz) baby sweetcorn, split in half lengthways
- 1 red pepper, halved, seeded and sliced
- 50 g (2 oz) sugarsnap peas
- 2 tablespoons oyster sauce (from a jar or sachet)
- egg-fried rice, to serve (see page 232)

1 Place the soy sauce, sesame oil and sherry in a bowl, then stir in the cornflour until smooth. Cut the pork against the grain into small, thin strips and add to the soy mixture, stirring to combine. Cover with cling film and set aside for 10 minutes, or up to 24 hours in the fridge.

2 Heat a wok until it is very hot, then add the sunflower oil and heat until it is almost smoking. Remove the pork from the marinade with a slotted spoon and stir-fry in the wok for a few minutes. Transfer to a sieve or colander to drain off all the excess oil, leaving only one tablespoon behind in the wok.

3 Add the garlic, spring onions and ginger and stir-fry for 20 seconds, then tip in the onion and stir-fry for another minute. Add the carrot and stir-fry for 2 minutes until softened, sprinkling over a tablespoon of water if the mixture is getting too dry. Add the sweetcorn and pepper and stir-fry for 1–2 minutes, again adding a little water if necessary, then add the sugarsnap peas and stir-fry for another minute.

4 Stir in the oyster sauce and toss the vegetables until coated. Return the pork to the pan and stir-fry for 1–2 minutes until the pork is tender and heated through. Serve at once with the rice.

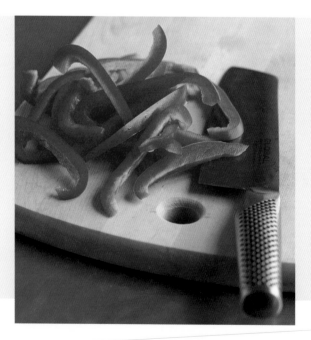

VARIATIONS

BEEF AND VEGETABLES WITH BLACK BEAN SAUCE

Replace the pork with fillet or sirloin steak that has had all the fat removed, and use black bean sauce instead of oyster sauce.

NUTTY VEGETABLE STIR-FRY

Omit the pork and oyster sauce. Mix together 2 teaspoons each of mild curry paste, soy sauce and honey. Add an extra carrot and yellow pepper to help bulk out the vegetables. Tip in 50 g (2 oz) salted cashew nuts with the sugarsnap peas, then pour over the curry paste mixture and stir-fry for another minute or two until well combined.

american-style seared chicken salad

This is a variation on the famous Caesar salad but is much easier to prepare. If time allows, rub the paprika mixture into the chicken, cover with cling film and chill overnight to allow the flavours to penetrate the flesh.

serves 2 • preparation 10 mins • cooking 15 mins

Energy 759 kcals • Protein 48.1 g • Carbohydrate 24.7 g • Fat 52.6 g
Saturated fat 12.5 g • Fibre 1.9 g • Salt 2.43 g • Added sugars 0.1 g

3 tablespoons mayonnaise
  (see page 230, or use ready-made)
1 tablespoon crème fraîche
2 garlic cloves, crushed
1 teaspoon Dijon mustard
1 teaspoon Worcestershire sauce
¼ teaspoon Tabasco
2 anchovy fillets, crushed to a paste
4 tablespoons olive oil
1 teaspoon sweet paprika
the leaves from ½ x 20-g (¾-oz) packet flat-leaf parsley,
  chopped
2 chicken breast fillets
2 slices country-style bread, crusts removed and
  cut into cubes
1 large cos lettuce
40 g (1½ oz) freshly grated Parmesan cheese
salt and freshly ground black pepper

1 Place the mayonnaise in a small bowl with the crème fraîche. Add half the garlic, the mustard, Worcestershire sauce, Tabasco and anchovies, then beat until well combined. Season to taste. Cover with cling film and chill until ready to use.

2 Heat a griddle pan until searing hot. Place half the olive oil in a shallow, non-metallic dish with the remaining garlic plus the paprika, parsley and a teaspoon each of salt and pepper. Slash the chicken fillets and rub the oil mixture into the flesh, then place in the griddle pan and cook for 10–12 minutes, turning once, until cooked through and completely tender. Transfer to a plate and leave to rest for a minute or two.

3 Meanwhile, make some croûtons. Heat a frying pan. Toss the bread cubes in a bowl with the remaining oil and season generously. Add to the heated pan and sauté for 6–8 minutes until evenly golden.

4 Break the large outer lettuce leaves roughly, keeping the smaller leaves whole. Toss with the mayonnaise mixture and two-thirds of the grated Parmesan. Arrange the leaves in the centre of 2 plates, scatter with the croûtons, then garnish with the remaining Parmesan. Carve each chicken breast on the diagonal and arrange on the salads to serve.

cheesy nachos with avocado and sweetcorn salsa

This is wicked comfort food at its best – perfect for a night in with a good movie. Make sure you follow it with one of my ice-cream suggestions at the end of this chapter (see page 72).

serves 2 • preparation 5 mins • cooking 15 mins

Energy 330 kcals • Protein 6.7 g • Carbohydrate 33.9 g • Fat 19.5 g
Saturated fat 5.2 g • Fibre 4.3 g • Salt 1.48 g • Added sugars 0.6 g

100 g (4 oz) canned or frozen sweetcorn kernels
1 ripe tomato, seeded and diced
1 small, ripe avocado, peeled, stoned and diced
4 spring onions, thinly sliced
25 g (1 oz) sliced jalapeño chillies (from a jar or can),
  drained and chopped
1 × 175-g (6-oz) packet tortilla chips
3–4 tablespoons soured cream
25 g (1 oz) Cheddar cheese, grated
salt and freshly ground black pepper

1 Pre-heat the oven to 200°C/400°F/Gas Mark 6. If using frozen sweetcorn, place it in a pan of boiling, salted water and cook for a few minutes until just tender, then drain and refresh under cold running water. Place in a large bowl with the tomato, avocado, onions and chillies. Stir to combine and season to taste.

2 Tip the tortilla chips into a shallow ovenproof dish and scatter the avocado and sweetcorn salsa on top. Spoon over the soured cream and top with the Cheddar. Bake for about 10 minutes until the Cheddar is bubbling. Serve at once straight from the dish.

roasted vegetable couscous with lemon hummus

This dish is delicious hot or cold. Try using any combination of Mediterranean vegetables you fancy. However, it's important that the vegetables are not too crowded in the roasting tin, otherwise they'll stew rather than roast. Try to ensure that they are spread across the tin in a single layer, and if you don't have a large enough pan to enable you to do this, roast the vegetables in a couple of smaller roasting tins.

serves 2 • preparation 10 mins • cooking 45 mins

Energy 577 kcals • Protein 15.2 g • Carbohydrate 55.6 g • Fat 34.1 g
Saturated fat 5.5 g • Fibre 9.2 g • Salt 1.39 g • Added sugars none

1 red pepper, halved, seeded and cut into 2.5-cm (1-inch) squares
1 yellow pepper, halved, seeded and cut into 2.5-cm (1-inch) squares
1 large courgette, cut into 2.5-cm (1-inch) pieces
1 small aubergine, cut into 2.5-cm (1-inch) pieces
1 large red onion, cut into 2.5-cm (1-inch) pieces
4 tablespoons extra virgin olive oil
a handful of fresh basil leaves
1 × 120-g (4½-oz) carton hummus
3 tablespoons Greek yoghurt
juice of 1 lemon
100 g (4 oz) couscous
salt and freshly ground black pepper

1 Pre-heat the oven to 230°C/450°F/Gas Mark 8. Heat a large roasting tin. Place the red and yellow peppers, courgette, aubergine and onion in a large bowl and drizzle over half the oil, tossing to coat evenly, then tip into the heated roasting tin. Season generously and roast for about 40 minutes, or until the vegetables are completely tender and lightly caramelized, tossing from time to time to ensure they cook evenly. About 5 minutes before the vegetables are ready, quickly chop up the basil. Scatter over the vegetables, tossing to combine, then return to the oven to finish cooking.

2 Place the hummus in a bowl and whisk in the yoghurt and half the lemon juice, then season to taste. Cover with cling film and chill until needed.

3 Place the couscous in a large bowl and drizzle over the remaining olive oil with the rest of the lemon juice, stirring to combine. Pour over 120 ml (4 fl oz) boiling water, then stir well, cover and leave to stand for 5 minutes before gently separating the grains with a fork. Season to taste and place in a pan to re-heat, stirring continuously with a fork. Serve with the roasted vegetables piled on top and the hummus mixture drizzled around the edge.

creamy spaghetti carbonara

For a change, you could replace the bacon in this recipe with strips of smoked salmon, which obviously don't need any cooking, and use dill instead of parsley.

serves 2 • preparation 5 mins • cooking 15 mins

Energy 771 kcals • Protein 35.3 g • Carbohydrate 66.3 g • Fat 42.3 g
Saturated fat 19.1 g • Fibre 2.8 g • Salt 2.89 g • Added sugars none

175–225 g (6–8 oz) spaghetti
1 tablespoon olive oil
1 shallot, finely chopped
1 small garlic clove, finely chopped
100 g (4 oz) pancetta or streaky bacon lardons
1 egg
3 tablespoons double cream
50 g (2 oz) freshly grated Parmesan cheese
the leaves from 1/2 x 20-g (3/4-oz) packet flat-leaf parsley,
   chopped
salt and freshly ground black pepper

1 Plunge the spaghetti in a large pan of boiling, salted water, stir once and cook at a rolling boil for 10–12 minutes until *al dente*.

2 Meanwhile, heat the oil in a frying pan. Add the shallot and garlic and sauté for 2–3 minutes until softened but not coloured. Stir in the pancetta and cook for another 2–3 minutes until sizzling and lightly golden.

3 Break the egg into a bowl and add the cream, two-thirds of the Parmesan and all the parsley. Add some seasoning, then whisk lightly.

4 Drain the spaghetti and return to the hot pan. Quickly pour in the egg mixture and the pancetta mixture and toss well to combine; the heat from the spaghetti will cook the egg. Serve with the remaining Parmesan scattered on top.

PERFECT BAKED POTATOES

The baked potato is undoubtedly one of the greatest standby meals. Choose a floury variety, such as Maris Piper, King Edward or Golden Wonder; a 200-g (7-oz) potato is the perfect size for a single serving. Scrub the potato clean and prick it a few times with a fork to allow steam to escape while it's baking. Place directly on the shelf in an oven pre-heated to 200°C/400°F/Gas Mark 6, and cook for 1½ hours or until it feels soft when gently squeezed. My wife, Clare, often gives baking potatoes a head start in the microwave, heating them on high for 5 minutes if she's short of time. This halves the overall cooking time.

To serve, cut a deep cross in the baked potato and, using a clean tea towel, gently press in the sides so that the flesh rises slightly above the skin. I love mine with just a pinch of Maldon sea salt and a generous knob of butter, plus a crisp green salad on the side. If you're feeling more adventurous, try some of the topping suggestions below.

TOPPING SUGGESTIONS

SOURED CREAM AND CHIVES
Add a generous dollop of soured cream and a few snipped fresh chives and mix into the potato flesh with the butter.

BAKED BEANS AND CHEDDAR
Enrich a 100-g (4-oz) can of baked beans with a knob of butter and a tablespoon of cream. Spoon over the split potato, cover with grated Cheddar cheese and flash under the grill until bubbling.

SALMON AND CREAM CHEESE
Mix a 50-g (2-oz) can of drained salmon with 2 tablespoons of Boursin (full-fat garlic and herb soft cheese) until well combined, and season to taste.

ANCHOVY BUTTER
Mash together 1 anchovy, 1 small, crushed garlic clove, a little chopped flat-leaf parsley, a knob of butter and plenty of freshly ground black pepper. Mix into the potato flesh.

BACON AND AVOCADO
Grill 2 rindless streaky bacon rashers until crisp, then gently crumble into a bowl. Add a small avocado that has been peeled, stoned and diced and mix together with 2 tablespoons mayonnaise and 1 finely chopped salad onion. Season to taste and pile into the baked potato.

TUNA SALAD
Mix a 200-g (7-oz) can of drained tuna in brine with 4 finely chopped spring onions, the grated rind of 1 lime, ½ x 20-g (¾-oz) packet of chopped fresh flat-leaf parsley or coriander and 4 tablespoons of soured cream (or mayonnaise, or Greek yoghurt). Season to taste and pile into the baked potato.

CARAMELIZED CHERRY TOMATO AND FETA

Saute 1 thinly sliced onion in a knob of butter and a dash of oil until golden. Tip in 100 g (4 oz) of cherry tomatoes and continue to sauté until the skins are lightly charred and just beginning to split. Remove from the heat and fold in 100 g (4 oz) feta cheese cubes. Season with pepper and pile into the baked potato.

HOT CHILLI BEAN

Fry 2 spring onions until softened and then stir in a 200-g (7-oz) can drained kidney beans and a 200-g (7-oz) can chopped tomatoes. Add a tablespoon of chilli sauce, season to taste and simmer for about 10 minutes, stirring occasionally, until reduced and thickened. Pile into the baked potato.

PESTO AND MOZZARELLA

Mix 50 g (2 oz) of cubed mozzarella cheese with a tablespoon of home-made or shop-bought pesto. Season to taste and pile into the baked potato.

corned beef hash with poached egg

Originally from the southern states of the USA, this terrific comfort food can also be served with a fried egg (see page 24) and a good dollop of tomato ketchup on the side.

serves 2 • preparation 5 mins • cooking 20 mins

Energy 578 kcals • Protein 34.0 g • Carbohydrate 55.3 g • Fat 25.9 g
Saturated fat 8.6 g • Fibre 5.2 g • Salt 2.77 g • Added sugars none

550 g (1¼ lb) potatoes, cut into 1-cm (½-inch) cubes
2 tablespoons olive oil
1 large onion, chopped
a knob of butter
1 × 200-g (7-oz) can corned beef, cut into 1-cm (½-inch) cubes
the leaves from ½ × 20-g (¾-oz) packet flat-leaf parsley, chopped
salt and freshly ground black pepper
poached eggs, to serve (see page 24)

1 Place the potatoes in a pan and cover with boiling water. Add a pinch of salt and bring to the boil, then cover and simmer for 5 minutes.

2 Meanwhile, heat the oil in a large, heavy-based, non-stick frying pan. Add the onion and sauté for 3–4 minutes until softened.

3 Drain the potatoes, then add the butter to the onion mixture. Once it is foaming, tip in the potatoes, season and sauté for 8–10 minutes until the potatoes are crisp and golden.

4 Prepare the poached eggs as described on page 24. Add the corned beef to the potato and onion mixture and continue to sauté for another 3–4 minutes until the corned beef has broken down and crisped up in places. Stir in the parsley and season to taste. Serve with a poached egg on top.

pan-fried plaice with crispy bacon

The combination of fish and bacon may not be an obvious one, but it really is a winner. Use dry-cured streaky bacon, if possible, or pancetta, the Italian equivalent.

serves 2 • preparation 5 mins • cooking 10 mins

Energy 485 kcals • Protein 45.8 g • Carbohydrate 10.6 g • Fat 29.2 g
Saturated fat 15.7 g • Fibre 0.4 g • Salt 2.98 g • Added sugars none

6 thin, rindless streaky bacon rashers

25 g (1 oz) seasoned flour

4 × 100-g (4-oz) plaice fillets, skinned

50 g (2 oz) unsalted butter

1 tablespoon chopped mixed herbs
   (parsley, chives and tarragon)

½ lemon, pips removed

salt and freshly ground black pepper

crushed new potatoes, to serve (see page 220)

1 Heat a large, heavy-based frying pan and pre-heat the grill. Arrange the bacon on a grill rack and cook for a minute or so on each side until crisp. Drain on kitchen paper and allow to crisp up completely.

2 Meanwhile, place the seasoned flour on a plate and lightly dust 2 of the fish fillets with it, shaking off any surplus. Add a knob of the butter to the pan and, when it foams, add the floured plaice flesh-side down. Cook for 2 minutes until lightly golden, then turn over and cook for another 1–2 minutes, depending on the thickness of the fillets. Transfer to a serving plate and keep warm.

3 Add another knob of butter to the pan. Lightly dust and cook the remaining 2 plaice fillets as before, then keep warm. Using scissors, snip the bacon rashers over the fish. Wipe out the pan and add the remaining butter, allowing it to melt over a moderate heat. When it turns to light brown foam, quickly add the herbs and a squeeze of lemon juice, swirling to combine. Spoon this mixture over the plaice and bacon, then serve with crushed new potatoes.

tabbouleh with roasted spiced salmon

A Lebanese speciality, tabbouleh is a mixture of bulgar (cracked wheat), fragrant herbs and lemon juice, which is simplicity itself to make. It can be used immediately or will keep happily in the fridge for up to two days if covered with cling film.

serves 2 • preparation 30 mins • cooking 15 mins

Energy 644 kcals • Protein 39.9 g • Carbohydrate 26.3 g • Fat 42.5 g
Saturated fat 7.1 g • Fibre 1.7 g • Salt 0.49 g • Added sugars 1.1 g

50 g (2 oz) bulgar wheat

4 tablespoons extra virgin olive oil

2 garlic cloves, crushed

juice of 1 lemon

½ teaspoon ground cumin

2 × 175-g (6-oz) thick salmon fillets, skinned and boned

a good pinch of ground cinnamon

a good pinch of ground allspice

a pinch of caster sugar

2 vine-ripened tomatoes, halved, seeded and diced

the leaves from 1 x 20-g (¾-oz) packet flat-leaf parsley, chopped

a small handful of fresh mint leaves, chopped

4 spring onions, finely chopped

salt and freshly ground black pepper

1 Place the bulgar in a bowl and pour over enough hot water to cover. Set aside for 30 minutes, or according to the packet instructions, then tip into a sieve and rinse well under cold running water. Drain thoroughly and tip into a bowl.

2 Pre-heat the oven to 200°C/400°F/Gas Mark 6 from cold. Place 1 tablespoon of the oil in a small roasting tin with half the garlic, half the lemon juice and all the cumin. Add the salmon fillets, turning to coat, then arrange skinned-side down and roast for 10–12 minutes until cooked through but still moist inside.

3 Meanwhile, make a dressing by placing the remaining lemon juice in a screw-topped jar with the rest of the garlic and all the cinnamon, allspice and sugar. Season to taste and shake until the salt has dissolved. Add the remaining 3 tablespoons olive oil and shake again until well combined.

4 Add the tomatoes, parsley, mint and onions to the drained bulgar, then pour over the dressing and stir gently until well combined. Season to taste and set aside at room temperature, while the salmon cooks, to allow the flavours to develop. Serve the salmon with a little of their juices and offer the tabbouleh separately.

caramelized leek and bacon pilaff

This spiced rice dish originated in the East. I like to serve it with a dollop of creamy garlic yoghurt; and it would also be wonderful simply served with a roasted chicken breast.

serves 2 • preparation 5 mins • cooking 25 mins

Energy 565 kcals • Protein 17.0 g • Carbohydrate 45.4 g • Fat 36.2 g
Saturated fat 19.4 g • Fibre 3.1 g • Salt 2.66 g • Added sugars none

- 50 g (2 oz) unsalted butter
- 2 leeks, trimmed, cleaned and finely sliced
- a good pinch of ground allspice
- 100 g (4 oz) rindless, unsmoked streaky bacon rashers, finely chopped
- 100 g (4 oz) basmati rice
- 450 ml (12 fl oz) vegetable or chicken stock (see page 231)
- the leaves from $\frac{1}{2}$ x 20-g ($\frac{3}{4}$-oz) packet flat-leaf parsley, chopped
- 4 tablespoons Greek yoghurt
- 1 small garlic clove, crushed
- salt and freshly ground black pepper

1 Melt the butter in a heavy-based pan with a lid. Add the leeks and a pinch of allspice and sauté for about 3–4 minutes until softened and just beginning to brown around the edges. Add the bacon and cook for another 2–3 minutes until sizzling and lightly golden.

2 Stir the basmati rice into the pan and pour in enough stock to cover by 5 mm ($\frac{1}{4}$ inch). Season and cover with a circle of non-stick baking parchment. Bring to the boil, then cover with a lid and simmer for 10–12 minutes, or until all the liquid is absorbed. Fold in the parsley and season to taste.

3 Meanwhile, place the yoghurt in a bowl and mix in the garlic, a pinch of allspice and some seasoning. Offer separately with the finished pilaff.

cheesy baked ham with cabbage

This would also be delicious served with brown wheaten bread or with a jacket potato smothered with butter (see page 64).

serves 2 • preparation 10 mins • cooking 25 mins

Energy 493 kcals • Protein 34.7 g • Carbohydrate 6.4 g • Fat 36.7 g
Saturated fat 21.3 g • Fibre 3.7 g • Salt 3.92 g • Added sugars 0.5 g

- a knob of butter, plus extra for greasing
- 225 g (8 oz) Savoy cabbage, trimmed and cut across the grain into 1-cm ($\frac{1}{2}$-inch) slices
- 4 spring onions, finely sliced
- 175 g (6 oz) chunky pieces hand-carved ham
- 100 g (4 oz) mature Cheddar cheese, grated
- 3 tablespoons double cream
- 2 teaspoons Dijon mustard
- salt and freshly ground black pepper
- boiled new potatoes, to serve

1 Pre-heat the oven to 200°C/400°F/Gas Mark 6. Place the butter and a teaspoon of water in a sauté pan with a lid over a high heat. When the butter mixture is bubbling, add the cabbage and onions with a pinch of salt. Cover, shake vigorously and cook over maximum heat for $1\frac{1}{2}$ minutes. Stir well, then cover again, giving the pan a good shake. Cook for another minute, then remove from the heat and season with pepper.

2 Butter a 20-cm (8-inch) ovenproof dish. Place one third of the cabbage in the dish in an even layer. Sprinkle half the ham on top, then add another third of the cabbage. Repeat until all the ingredients are used up, finishing with a layer of cabbage.

3 Place the Cheddar in a bowl, fold in the cream and mustard, then season with pepper. Spread over the cabbage in an even layer and bake for 15–20 minutes until bubbling and golden brown. Serve immediately with boiled potatoes.

✪ espresso and crumbled biscotti

A sophisticated dessert that would make a wonderful finale to any meal.

serves 2 • preparation 5 mins • cooking none

Energy 150 kcals • Protein 2.7 g • Carbohydrate 21.5 g • Fat 6.5 g
Saturated fat 4.1 g • Fibre 0.1 g • Salt 0.19 g • Added sugars 11.5 g

2 scoops vanilla ice-cream
50 ml (2 fl oz) strong, black coffee, such as espresso
2 biscotti biscuits, roughly smashed

1 Divide the ice-cream between tall glasses and pour a shot of espresso over each one. Sprinkle with roughly smashed biscotti biscuits to serve.

strawberry pancakes

This recipe would also work well with split croissants that have three to four squares of white chocolate put inside each one before being warmed in an oven preheated to 180°C/350°F/Gas 4, for about 5 minutes.

serves 2 • preparation 5 mins • cooking 5 mins

Energy 780 kcals • Protein 12.5 g • Carbohydrate 83.2 g • Fat 46.4 g
Saturated fat 18.2 g • Fibre 1.0 g • Salt 0.45 g • Added sugars 51.2 g

100 g (4 oz) bar of white chocolate
2 tablespoons double cream
knob of unsalted butter
4 ready-made griddle-style or Scotch pancakes
4 scoops strawberry or vanilla ice-cream
100 g (4 oz) strawberries, hulled and halved

1 To make a white chocolate sauce, melt the white chocolate in a heatproof bowl with the cream and butter over a pan of simmering water; or in a microwave on high for 2 minutes, stirring halfway through.

2 Meanwhile, heat the pancakes for about 30 seconds on each side in a frying pan or on high in the microwave for 20 seconds. Overlap 2 pancakes on each plate and top with the scoops of strawberry or vanilla ice-cream. Scatter over the strawberries and drizzle with the sauce to serve.

caramelized pineapple with rum and raisin

If you haven't got a baby pineapple a can of pineapple slices in natural juice makes a good alternative.

serves 2 • preparation 5 mins • cooking 10 mins

Energy 286 kcals • Protein 2.7 g • Carbohydrate 32.4 g • Fat 15.2 g
Saturated fat 9.7 g • Fibre 1.0 g • Salt 0.12 g • Added sugars 12.4 g

1 ripe baby pineapple
icing sugar, to dust
25 g (1 oz) unsalted butter
good dash of dark rum
25 g (1 oz) raisins
2 scoops chocolate ice-cream

1 Heat a large non-stick frying pan. Peel the pineapple and cut into four even-sized slices then, using a sharp knife or apple corer, cut out the cores. Sprinkle thickly with icing sugar.

2 Melt the butter in the frying pan and once it stops foaming add the coated pineapple rings. Fry for a minute or two on each side until caramelized. Add the rum and raisins, swirling the pan to make a smooth sauce. Top each serving with a scoop of the chocolate ice-cream.

lemonade float

This thirst quencher appeals to adults and children alike, especially on a warm summer's day.

serves 2 • preparation 5 mins • cooking none

Energy 387 kcals • Protein 5.4 g • Carbohydrate 63.8 g • Fat 14.0 g
Saturated fat 7.8 g • Fibre none • Salt 0.27 g • Added sugars 27.8 g

300 ml (½ pint) exotic fruit juice, well chilled
4 scoops vanilla ice-cream
300 ml (½ pint) old-fashioned sparkling lemonade, well chilled
25 g (1 oz) Smarties, lightly crushed

1 Half fill tall glasses with the exotic fruit juice and add the scoops of vanilla ice-cream and fill up with traditional sparkling lemonade. Decorate with lightly crushed Smarties to serve.

AFTER-WORK SUPPERS

italian fusilli sausage 'ragu'

This pasta dish is quick and easy to make and perfect for a cold winter's night. The 'ragu' or sauce seems to taste even better the next day, and makes a nice change from your average tomato-flavoured sauce.

serves 4 • preparation 5 mins • cooking 25 mins

Energy 765 kcals • Protein 26.8 g • Carbohydrate 87.9 g • Fat 34.3 g
Saturated fat 10.4 g • Fibre 6.8 g • Salt 3.05 g • Added sugars none

2 tablespoons olive oil

450 g (1 lb) cocktail sausages

1 red pepper, halved, seeded and thinly sliced

1 yellow pepper, halved, seeded and thinly sliced

1 large red onion, thinly sliced

2 garlic cloves, crushed

1 teaspoon dried crushed chillies

450 g (1 lb) fusilli pasta (twists)

120 ml (4 fl oz) red wine

1 × 400-g (14-oz) can chopped tomatoes

1 tablespoon sun-dried tomato purée

salt and freshly ground black pepper

1 Heat half the oil in a frying pan and sauté the sausages for about 5 minutes until lightly golden. Drain well on kitchen paper. Wipe out the pan and use to heat the remaining tablespoon of oil, then add the peppers and onion and sauté for 5 minutes until softened. Add the garlic and chillies and cook for another minute until well combined.

2 Meanwhile, plunge the fusilli into a large pan of boiling, salted water; stir once, then cook for 10–12 minutes until *al dente* or according to the packet instructions.

3 Return the sausages to the pan, pour in the wine and allow to bubble down. Add the tomatoes and tomato purée, then season to taste. Cover with a lid and simmer for 8–10 minutes until slightly reduced and thickened, stirring occasionally.

4 When the pasta is cooked, drain, rinse briefly if neccesary (see page 84), then fold the sausage mixture into the pasta. Season to taste and serve at once.

smoked bacon, creamed tomato and pea penne

This is the kind of pasta dish I tend to make when there's nothing much left in the fridge. It takes virtually no time to prepare, and is great served with a light rocket salad and a glass of decent wine.

serves 4 • preparation 5 mins • cooking 20 mins

Energy 708 kcals • Protein 20.4 g • Carbohydrate 76.9 g • Fat 35.4 g
Saturated fat 16.3 g • Fibre 4.6 g • Salt 2.04 g • Added sugars 1.1g

2 tablespoons olive oil

8 rindless, smoked streaky bacon rashers, cut into strips

1 red onion, finely chopped

450 g (1 lb) penne pasta (quills)

120 ml (4 fl oz) dry white wine

300 ml (½ pint) passata

a large pinch of chopped fresh oregano

150 ml (5 fl oz) double cream or crème fraîche

100 g (4 oz) frozen peas

salt and freshly ground black pepper

freshly grated Pecorino cheese, to serve

1 Heat the oil in a frying pan and fry the bacon for 2–3 minutes until lightly browned. Add the onion and cook for another minute or two until softened.

2 Meanwhile, plunge the penne into a large pan of boiling, salted water; stir once, then cook for 10–12 minutes until *al dente*, or according to the instructions on the packet.

3 Pour the wine into the bacon mixture and allow to bubble down, then stir in the passata and oregano. Bring to a simmer, then stir in the cream. Season to taste, cover and simmer for 5 minutes until slightly reduced and thickened. Stir in the peas and cook for another 3–4 minutes until tender.

4 When the pasta is cooked, drain, rinse briefly if necessary (see page 84), shaking the pasta well to get the water out of the pasta tubes. Fold in the bacon and pea mixture. Season to taste and serve scattered with the Pecorino.

fettuccine with melting courgettes and parmesan

This recipe is really stunning. Use the smallest courgettes you can find; they have a nuttier flavour and seem to ooze much less water.

serves 4 • preparation 5 mins • cooking 25 mins

Energy 397 kcals • Protein 13.7 g • Carbohydrate 40.0 g • Fat 21.2 g
Saturated fat 6.8 g • Fibre 2.7 g • Salt 2.74 g • Added sugars none

4 tablespoons olive oil
2 shallots, finely chopped
450 g (1 lb) courgettes, trimmed and diced
2 garlic cloves, finely chopped
the leaves from 3 sprigs of thyme
$\frac{1}{2}$ teaspoon dried crushed chillies
275 g (10 oz) dried egg fettuccine
25 g (1 oz) butter
the leaves from $\frac{1}{2}$ x 20-g ($\frac{3}{4}$-oz) packet flat-leaf parsley, chopped
4 tablespoons freshly grated Parmesan cheese
salt and freshly ground black pepper

1 Heat the oil in a heavy-based frying pan. Add the shallots and sauté for about 5 minutes until softened but not coloured. Add the courgettes, garlic, thyme, chillies and seasoning and cook for another 15 minutes until completely softened, stirring occasionally.

2 Meanwhile, plunge the fettuccine into a large pan of boiling, salted water, stir once and cook for 5 minutes until just tender, or according to the instructions on the packet. Drain, then toss in the butter and parsley. Stir in the courgette mixture and serve with a good grinding of black pepper and a scattering of Parmesan.

gratin of penne with spinach and tomatoes

This recipe is easy enough for everyday eating, but good enough to serve to friends. If you haven't got time to make a cheese sauce, simply replace with a tub of mascarpone cheese and a couple of handfuls of freshly grated Parmesan.

serves 4 • preparation 5 mins • cooking 30 mins

Energy 541 kcals • Protein 20.5 g • Carbohydrate 57.3 g • Fat 26.7 g
Saturated fat 13.5 g • Fibre 4.0 g • Salt 1.71 g • Added sugars none

275 g (10 oz) penne pasta
450 ml (12 fl oz) cheese sauce (see page 233,
   or use ready-made)
4 tablespoons single cream or crème fraîche
a knob of butter, plus extra for greasing
225 g (8 oz) baby leaf spinach
2 plum tomatoes, peeled, seeded and cut into strips
4 tablespoons freshly grated Parmesan cheese
2 tablespoons dried white breadcrumbs, from a packet
salt and freshly ground black pepper
mixed green salad, lightly dressed, to serve (see page 228)

1 Pre-heat the oven to 190°C/375°F/Gas Mark 5. Plunge the penne into a large pan of boiling, salted water; stir once, then cook for 8–10 minutes until almost but not quite *al dente*, as it will finish cooking in the oven.

2 Place the cheese sauce in a pan with the cream and heat gently. Heat the butter in a small pan, add the spinach and season to taste, then quickly sauté until wilted. Drain well in a sieve, then squeeze dry.

3 Grease a shallow ovenproof dish. Drain the pasta, then return it to the pan and fold in the cheese sauce, spinach and tomato strips. Season to taste and tip into the prepared dish.

4 Mix the Parmesan cheese and breadcrumbs in a small bowl and scatter over the pasta. Bake for about 20 minutes until the top is crisp and golden. Serve at once with the salad.

how to make pizzas

These authentic pizzas are fantastic vehicles for all sorts of toppings, but don't overload them or the base will become soggy. I have listed my family's favourites below, which always go down a treat. If you don't want to make your own pizza bases, there is now a selection of ready-made bases available.

basic neapolitan pizza

serves 4 • preparation 1 hr 30 mins • cooking 15 mins

Energy 510 kcals • Protein 22.8 g • Carbohydrate 69.7 g • Fat 17.5 g
Saturated fat 7.4 g • Fibre 2.8 g • Salt 2.29 g • Added sugars 0.5 g

350 g (12 oz) strong white plain flour, plus extra for dusting
1 × 7-g (¼-oz) sachet easy-blend yeast
1 teaspoon salt
2 tablespoons extra virgin olive oil, plus extra for greasing
225 ml (8 fl oz) warm water
2 teaspoons semolina or dried white breadcrumbs

FOR THE TOPPING
8 tablespoons passata rustica
few fresh basil leaves, torn
25 g (1 oz) freshly grated Parmesan cheese
1 × 150-g (5-oz) mozzarella, drained and roughly chopped
salt and freshly ground black pepper

1 Place the flour, yeast and teaspoon of salt in a food processor fitted with a dough attachment, or use a bowl and a wooden spoon if you don't have a processor. Mix the oil and warm water in a jug.

2 With the motor running, slowly pour in the oil mixture through the feeder tube, or stir by hand and mix until you have a soft, stretchy dough. Knead for 5 minutes in the machine or for 10 minutes by hand on a lightly floured work surface.

3 Transfer the dough to a lightly oiled bowl, rub the top with a little more oil, then cover with a clean, damp tea towel. Set aside at room temperature for 1 hour or until the dough has doubled in size.

4 Punch the dough down with a clenched fist. Remove from the bowl and knead for a couple of minutes until smooth, then cut in half and roll each half out on a lightly floured surface to a 25-cm (10-inch) circle. Sprinkle the semolina onto two large baking sheets and place the pizza bases on top.

5 Season the passata to taste, then spread over the pizza bases, leaving a 1-cm (½-inch) border around the edges. Scatter over the basil, drizzle with a little olive oil and scatter the Parmesan and mozzarella on top. Bake for 10–12 minutes until the base is crisp and the cheeses are bubbling and lightly golden. Remove from the oven and drizzle over a little more olive oil. Cut into wedges and serve with a green salad.

VARIATIONS

AMERICAN HOT
Prepare the bases with the passata, basil and olive oil, then scatter over 50 g (2 oz) sliced pepperoni sausage and 50 g (2 oz) drained, sliced jalapeño chillies (from a jar). Finish and serve as described above.

GARLIC MUSHROOM AND PARMA HAM WITH ROCKET
Heat a little olive oil and sauté 50 g (2 oz) sliced mushrooms with a crushed garlic clove for 1–2 minutes. Prepare the bases with the passata, basil and oil. Scatter over the mushrooms. Tear 3 slices of Parma ham and sprinkle on top. Finish and bake as above. Scatter over a little rocket and finish with a drizzle of olive oil and some Parmesan.

summer seafood marinara

This recipe is perfect for lazy summer evenings when you want something light.

serves 4 • preparation 10 mins • cooking 20 mins

Energy 587 kcals • Protein 40.3 g • Carbohydrate 73.4 g • Fat 15.7 g
Saturated fat 2.3 g • Fibre 2.9 g • Salt 3.88 g • Added sugars 1.1 g

- 1.75 kg (4 lb) mussels and/or clams
- 4 tablespoons dry white wine
- 450 g (1 lb) spaghetti
- 4 tablespoons olive oil
- 2 garlic cloves, very finely chopped
- 1 medium-hot red chilli, seeded and finely chopped
- 225 g (8 oz) peeled raw prawns
- 300 ml (½ pint) passata rustica
- a handful of basil leaves, torn into pieces
- the leaves from ½ x 20-g (¾-oz) packet flat-leaf parsley, chopped
- salt and freshly ground black pepper

1 To clean the mussels, wash them under cold running water and discard any that are open and won't close when lightly squeezed or tapped on the work surface. Then pull out the fibrous beards from between the closed shells. The clams just need to be washed. Place the mussels and/or clams in a pan and pour in the wine. Cover tightly and cook over a high heat for a few minutes, shaking the pan occasionally until all the shellfish have opened – discard any that do not open. Strain through a sieve, reserving 150 ml (5 fl oz) of the cooking liquor, leaving behind any grit. Remove the meat from the shells and reserve.

2 Meanwhile, lower the spaghetti into a pan of boiling, salted water, stir once, then cook for 10–12 minutes until *al dente* or according to the packet instructions.

3 Heat the oil in a heavy-based frying pan, add the garlic and chilli, then sauté for about 20 seconds. Tip in the prawns and sauté for another minute or so until just sealed. Pour in the passata and add the reserved cooking liquor. Bring to a gentle simmer, then stir in the cooked shellfish plus the basil and parsley. Season to taste and allow to just warm through.

4 When the pasta is cooked, drain, rinse briefly if necessary (see page 84) and return to the pan. Pour in the seafood sauce and fold together until well combined. Serve at once.

chicken pasta salad with pine nuts

This pasta salad is also good served cold, and appeals to children and adults alike. Omit the chicken if you prefer a vegetarian option.

serves 4 • preparation 10 mins • cooking 20 mins

Energy 923 kcals • Protein 36.7 g • Carbohydrate 68.7 g • Fat 57.7 g
Saturated fat 9.8 g • Fibre 3.5 g • Salt 0.73 g • Added sugars none

- 100 g (4 oz) pine nuts
- 450 g (1 lb) farfalle pasta (bows)
- 50 g (2 oz) fresh basil leaves
- 2 garlic cloves, finely chopped
- 50 g (2 oz) freshly grated Parmesan cheese
- 150 ml (5 fl oz) extra virgin olive oil
- 2 skinless chicken breast fillets, cut widthways into 1-cm (½-inch) strips
- 50 g (2 oz) wild rocket
- salt and freshly ground black pepper

1 Pre-heat the oven to 180°C/350°F/Gas Mark 4. Spread out the pine nuts on a baking sheet and roast for 8–10 minutes until toasted and golden brown. Remove from the oven and leave to cool completely.

2 Plunge the farfalle into a large pan of boiling, salted water, stir once and cook for 8–10 minutes until *al dente* or according to the instructions on the packet.

3 Place the basil in a food processor with a teaspoon of salt and half the garlic, then blend until finely chopped. Add half the pine nuts and all the Parmesan and whizz again briefly; then, with the machine running, pour in all but one tablespoon of the olive oil through the feeder tube until the pesto is thickened and emulsified. Season to taste.

4 Heat a frying pan until very hot. Place the remaining tablespoon of oil in a bowl with the chicken and the rest of the garlic, season well and mix together. Add the chicken to the pan and cook for 2–3 minutes on each side until cooked through and golden brown. Remove from the heat and fold in the rocket, allowing it just to wilt with the heat of the chicken.

5 When the pasta is cooked, drain, rinse briefly if necessary (see page 84), then return to the pan and pour in the pesto, stirring until well coated. Fold in the chicken and rocket mixture with the remaining pine nuts, season to taste and serve.

pasta

Pasta is a great stand-by for those evenings when you have absolutely no time to cook. After a long day few of us have either the energy or the desire to cope with complicated recipes. With this in mind I have made sure that all of the pasta dishes here are quick to prepare, easy to cook, delicious to look at and most importantly, wonderful to eat. Traditionally in Italy pasta is eaten after antipasti (starters) and before a main dish, although as appetites are getting smaller and demands for big long meals rarer, very often pasta is now served just with a salad as an entire meal. Depending on whether the main ingredient in a sauce is oil, cheese, vegetable or meat, it should be combined with a certain shape of pasta to obtain the correct balance of textures and flavours.

WHICH SHAPE?

Of course the pasta shape you choose is entirely up to you, but as a general guide:

Long round pasta: such as spaghetti, spaghettini, vermicelli or capelli d'angelo, need an olive oil- or tomato-based sauce to keep the long strands slippery and separate.

Long flat pasta: such as fettuccine, tagliatelle, linguine, lasagnette or lasagne, should be accompanied by a heavier sauce based on cheese, eggs and/or cream or butter. They also work with ones that contain pieces of meat such as prosciutto.

Short pasta: shaped and tubular pasta are best served with a juicy sauce that will penetrate the pasta hollows. Shaped and medium-sized tubular pasta such as farfalle, rigatoni or fusilli is excellent with vegetable-based sauces, and larger types, such as penne or macaroni, are perfect for baked dishes or with rich meat sauces.

Filled pasta: can be stuffed with a variety of delicious ingredients. I haven't included any recipes in this section, as it is best to keep the sauce simple so as not to mask the flavour of the filling – a little melted butter and perhaps a sprinkling of cheese is all you need.

FRESH OR DRIED?

There's an ongoing debate about which pasta is better – fresh or dried. I think the dried Italian brands are best. They are made with durum wheat, which, when cooked, gives that lovely 'bite' that we talk about when cooking pasta.

HOW MUCH?

For a main course, I normally allow 75–100 g (3–4 oz) of pasta per person.

HOW TO COOK

Always add pasta to a large pan of well-salted boiling water – 3.4 litres (6 pints) water and 6 teaspoons salt is about right for a recipe to serve four people. It's important to remember to stir it once to separate the pasta and cook at a rolling boil to prevent it from sticking. If you don't have a large enough pan to cook the pasta in the correct amount of water, use a smaller pan with less water but, once the pasta is cooked, drain it, then briefly rinse in a kettleful of boiling-hot water to get rid of the extra starch.

READY MADE PASTA SAUCES

There is now a wide range of ready-made pasta sauces available and sometimes the huge array can be confusing. As a rule I would never invest in the cream-based sauces, such as a carbonara, as I feel that they can be knocked-up at home using readily available, fresh ingredients. However, you can buy cartons of béchamel sauce, or some that are flavoured with four different kinds of cheese. These are a good buy as if you pick up some pancetta (Italian streaky bacon) and some fresh spinach or mushrooms, you can very quickly transform good old macaroni cheese into something really special.

One wonderful way to use up fresh tomatoes that are slightly over-ripe and are too soft for a salad, is to make a fresh-tomato sauce for pasta. And if you add a tablespoon or two of sun-dried tomato paste you'll end up with the best home-made tomato sauce imaginable. And don't forget that you don't have to serve pasta with a sauce. Most supermarkets now sell jars of roasted peppers in oil. Slice and toss them with cooked pasta and then serve with shavings of Pecorino cheese. Delicious!

chargrilled tuna with thai butter

The fragrant, Thai-inspired butter is very versatile and would also work well on salmon or swordfish steaks, or even lamb, pork or sirloin steaks. The fish can be cooked on a barbecue, if you like (see page 197).

serves 4 • preparation 20 mins • cooking 10 mins

Energy 380 kcals • Protein 47.8 g • Carbohydrate 0.6 g • Fat 20.8 g
Saturated fat 9.7 g • Fibre 0.1 g • Salt 0.49 g • Added sugars none

> 1 lime
> 50 g (2 oz) unsalted butter, at room temperature
> 1 lemon grass stalk, tough outer leaves removed and the tender core finely chopped
> $\frac{1}{2}$ x 20-g ($\frac{3}{4}$-oz) packet coriander, roughly chopped
> 2 spring onions, finely chopped
> 1 garlic clove, crushed
> 1 small medium-hot green chilli, seeded and finely chopped
> 4 tuna loin steaks, each at least 2.5 cm (1 inch) thick
> sunflower oil, for cooking
> salt and freshly ground black pepper
> steamed rice, to serve

1 Finely grate the rind from half the lime, then cut the fruit in half and squeeze the juice of one half into a mini blender. Cut the remaining half into four wedges and set aside to use as a garnish. Add the butter to the mini blender with the lemon grass, coriander, spring onions, garlic, chilli and lime rind. Season to taste and whizz until well combined.

2 Transfer the Thai butter to a rectangle of baking parchment with a spatula and shape into a roll about 4 cm (1$\frac{1}{2}$ inches) thick. Wrap up tightly and either place in the freezer for 10 minutes if you are short of time, or chill until firm enough to slice.

3 Heat a griddle pan until searing hot. Season the tuna fillets, smear each one with a little oil, then add to the pan. Sear for 1–2 minutes on each side until just sealed and lightly browned. Garnish each serving with two discs of the Thai butter and a lime wedge. Serve with rice.

crispy salmon fingers with sun-blushed dipping sauce

A twist on the humble fish finger. The secret is to cook them over a fairly high heat to seal the outside and create a crisp exterior, while the salmon remains moist and tender. Ooh, now you're talking!

serves 4 • preparation 10 mins • cooking 10 mins

Energy 646 kcals • Protein 34.5 g • Carbohydrate 46.4 g • Fat 37.2 g
Saturated fat 7.4 g • Fibre 1.4 g • Salt 1.78 g • Added sugars none

> 175 g (6 oz) fresh white breadcrumbs
> 2 eggs
> 6 tablespoons milk
> 50 g (2 oz) seasoned flour
> 450 g (1 lb) skinless and boneless salmon fillet
> 4 tablespoons sunflower oil
> 4 tablespoons half-fat crème fraîche
> 2 tablespoons mayonnaise (see page 230, or use ready-made)
> 1 tablespoon sun-dried tomato purée
> a small bunch of chives, snipped
> salt and freshly ground black pepper
> lemon wedges, to garnish
> green salad, lightly dressed, to serve (see page 228)

1 Place the breadcrumbs in a shallow dish, add some seasoning and mix together. Place the eggs and milk in a separate shallow dish, season generously and whisk well. Place the flour on a flat plate.

2 Cut the salmon into fingers, about 7.5 cm (3 inches) × 2 cm ($\frac{3}{4}$ inch) and coat in the flour, shaking off any excess. Dip into the egg mixture, then cover with the breadcrumbs.

3 Heat the oil in a large frying pan over a moderate heat. Add the coated salmon fingers and cook for a minute or two on each side until crisp and golden brown. Drain well on kitchen paper.

4 Meanwhile, make the dipping sauce. Place the crème fraîche in a bowl and mix in the mayonnaise, tomato purée and chives. Season to taste. Arrange stacks of the crispy salmon fingers on warmed plates and add a large spoonful of the dipping sauce on the side. Garnish with lemon wedges and serve at once with the salad.

chicken and broccoli gratin

This recipe is great for using up left-over roast chicken, but a shop-bought cooked chicken also works well.

serves 4 • preparation 10 mins • cooking 30 mins

Energy 600 kcals • Protein 43.2 g • Carbohydrate 30.8 g • Fat 34.6 g
Saturated fat 16.1 g • Fibre 3.9 g • Salt 2.33 g • Added sugars none

1 cooked chicken
450 g (1 lb) broccoli, cut into florets
450 ml (15 fl oz) béchamel or cheese sauce
  (see page 233, or use ready-made)
150 ml (5 fl oz) chicken stock (see page 231)
4 tablespoons double cream or crème fraîche
25g (1 oz) butter, plus extra for greasing
1 small onion, finely chopped
75 g (3 oz) fresh white breadcrumbs
the leaves from ½ x 20-g (¾-oz) packet flat-leaf parsley,
  chopped
2–3 sage leaves, finely chopped
salt and freshly ground black pepper
crusty bread, to serve

1 Pre-heat the oven to 190°C/375°F/Gas Mark 5. Strip the meat off the bones of the chicken and shred or cut into bite-sized pieces – you'll need 450 g (1 lb) in total. Place in a bowl and set aside. Blanch the broccoli in a pan of boiling, salted water for 2–3 minutes, then drain and refresh under cold running water. Tip onto kitchen paper to drain completely.

2 Heat the béchamel sauce in a large pan and whisk in the stock and cream. Bring to a simmer, then cook for a few minutes, stirring occasionally, until you have achieved a thick pouring sauce. You should have about 600 ml (1 pint) in total. Season to taste.

3 Grease a shallow ovenproof dish. Melt the butter in a small pan and sauté the onion for a few minutes, then stir in the breadcrumbs and herbs and season to taste. Arrange the chicken and broccoli in the prepared dish and spoon over the sauce to cover completely. Sprinkle the breadcrumb mixture on top and bake for 20 minutes until bubbling and golden brown. Serve at once with some crusty bread.

pot-roasted chicken with herby garlic butter

Pot-roasting is a great way to keep chicken succulent, and the bed of vegetables in the pot imparts loads of flavour. I like this with a dollop of creamy mash.

serves 4 • preparation 10 mins • cooking 30 mins

Energy 519 kcals • Protein 29.3 g • Carbohydrate 3.4 g • Fat 42.3 g
Saturated fat 10.1 g • Fibre 1.5 g • Salt 0.63 g • Added sugars none

- 75 g (3 oz) unsalted butter, at room temperature
- 2 garlic cloves, crushed
- 2 tablespoons chopped mixed herbs
  (flat-leaf parsley, tarragon and basil)
- 1 tablespoon olive oil
- 4 corn-fed chicken breast fillets (skin on)
- 1 small leek, cleaned and finely chopped
- 1 carrot, peeled and diced
- 2 celery sticks, diced
- the leaves from 3 sprigs of thyme
- 4 tablespoons dry white wine
- 2 tablespoons chicken stock (see page 231)
- salt and freshly ground black pepper
- mashed potatoes, to serve (see page 218)

1 Pre-heat the oven to 160°C/325°F/Gas Mark 3. Place the butter in a food processor with the garlic, herbs and seasoning. Blend briefly and transfer to a small bowl with a spatula. Chill until needed.

2 Heat a flameproof casserole dish over a medium-high heat. Add the oil, then add the chicken breasts, skin-side down. Cook for a few minutes on each side until golden brown. Transfer to a plate.

3 Add the leek, carrot, celery and thyme to the casserole and sauté for about 5 minutes until just starting to soften but not colour. Pour in the wine and chicken stock and allow to bubble down a little, then arrange the chicken breasts on top. Cover with a lid and bake for another 20 minutes, or until the chicken is tender.

4 Transfer the chicken breasts to a warm plate. Whisk two-thirds of the herby garlic butter into the vegetable mixture and spoon onto warmed plates. Arrange the chicken breasts on top and place a scoop of the remaining butter on each one. Add the mash and serve at once.

pork parcels with mushrooms

Individual parcels can be made and served unopened to your guests. However, I find that making one family-sized parcel is the handiest, and gives excellent results.

serves 4 • preparation 5 mins • cooking 1 hr

Energy 262 kcals • Protein 23.6 g • Carbohydrate 8.0 g • Fat 15.3 g
Saturated fat 6.9 g • Fibre 0.9 g • Salt 0.8 g • Added sugars none

    25 g (1 oz) seasoned flour
    4 × 100-g (4-oz) lean pork chops, well trimmed of excess fat
    1 tablespoon olive oil
    a knob of butter
    1 onion, finely chopped
    100 g (4 oz) button mushrooms, wiped clean and thinly sliced
    4 tablespoons double cream or crème fraîche
    1 teaspoon Dijon mustard
    salt and freshly ground black pepper

    TO SERVE
    mashed potatoes (see page 218)
    sautéed green beans (see page 222)

1 Pre-heat the oven to 180°C/350°F/Gas Mark 4. Take a large piece of foil, fold in half and place on a baking sheet.

2 Place the flour on a plate and use to coat the pork chops. Heat the oil in a frying pan and quickly sear the chops on both sides until golden brown, then place side by side inside the folded foil. Season to taste.

3 Melt the butter in the pan, stir in the onion and mushrooms, then sauté for a few minutes until tender. Season to taste and spoon on top of the chops. Mix the cream with the mustard in a small bowl and drizzle over each chop.

4 Seal the edges of the foil together with a double fold, making sure that there will be plenty of room for expansion. Bake for 45–50 minutes, or until the parcel has puffed up. Open at the table for maximum effect and serve, spooning over all those delicious juices. Serve with the mash and beans.

pastrami and new potato salad

Pastrami is brisket of beef that has been cured in a mixture of sugar, spices and garlic, then smoked.

serves 4 • preparation 10 mins • cooking 15 mins

Energy 404 kcals • Protein 21.0 g • Carbohydrate 34.6 g • Fat 21.2 g • Saturated fat 2.8 g • Fibre 2.7 g • Salt 3.02 g • Added sugars 1.0 g

750 g (1¾ lb) baby new potatoes

1 tablespoon white wine vinegar

1 teaspoon clear honey

1 teaspoon wholegrain mustard

1 teaspoon Dijon mustard

2 tablespoons extra virgin olive oil

4 tablespoons groundnut oil

1 small garlic clove, crushed

1 shallot, finely chopped

the leaves from ½ x 20-g (¾-oz) packet flat-leaf parsley, chopped

2 dill pickles (large gherkins), halved and sliced

1 curly lettuce, separated into leaves

350 g (12 oz) pastrami, cut into strips

salt and freshly ground black pepper

1 Steam the potatoes, or boil them in a pan of boiling salted water for 10–12 minutes, or until tender. Meanwhile, place the vinegar in a screw-topped jar with the honey, mustards and seasoning. Shake until the salt has dissolved, then add the oils, garlic, shallot and parsley. Shake again until well combined. Season to taste.

2 When the potatoes are cooked, halve or slice them, then toss in half the dressing. Stir in the dill pickles and season to taste. Arrange the lettuce leaves in a bowl and scatter over the potatoes and pastrami. Drizzle with the remaining dressing and serve at once.

unbelievably easy puddings

Dessert isn't just for dinner parties – pamper yourself after a hard day's work with these easy but perfectly formed puddings. All of them take less than 15 minutes from start to finish, so go on, you know you want to …

chocolate mousse in minutes

These are great served topped with a dollop of Cointreau-flavoured whipped cream and a dusting of cocoa powder.

serves 4 • preparation 10 mins • cooking 5 mins

Energy 465 kcals • Protein 3.6 g • Carbohydrate 22.2 g • Fat 39.1 g
Saturated fat 23.4 g • Fibre 1.5 g • Salt 0.16 g • Added sugars 14.8 g

100 g (4 oz) plain chocolate (60% cocoa solids)
1 × 250-g (9-oz) carton mascarpone cheese
about 2 tablespoons sifted icing sugar
Cognac, to taste
biscotti, to serve

1 Melt the chocolate in the microwave or in a heatproof bowl set over a pan of simmering water. Quickly beat in the mascarpone and enough icing sugar and Cognac to taste. Spoon into small cups or ramekins and chill for at least 10 minutes until cool and set. Serve with the biscotti for dipping.

butterscotch whip in a whirl

This dessert is a fantastic idea for instant indulgence. It could also be turned into a delicious ice-cream sundae with a couple of scoops of vanilla ice-cream and a layer of your favourite crumbled chocolate biscuits.

serves 4 • preparation 10 mins • cooking none

Energy 665 kcals • Protein 4.9 g • Carbohydrate 38.1 g • Fat 55.8 g
Saturated fat 35.0 g • Fibre 0.1 g • Salt 0.31 g • Added sugars 27.0 g

300 ml (½ pint) double cream
1 × 300-ml (½-pint) carton fresh custard
150 ml (5 fl oz) toffee sauce (see page 94, or use ready-made)
1 small chocolate flake, crumbled

1 Whip the cream and custard in a bowl until soft peaks have formed. Fold in the toffee sauce and divide between cocktail glasses. Sprinkle over the crumbled chocolate flake and either serve at once or chill until needed.

✪ iced mixed-fruit platter with passion-fruit cream

I like to leave the skin on the dipping fruits for this dessert so that they're easier to hold when you dip them in the cream.

serves 4 • preparation 15 mins • cooking none

Energy 251 kcals • Protein 4.0 g • Carbohydrate 35.5 g • Fat 11.4 g
Saturated fat 6.9 g • Fibre 2.9 g • Salt 0.07 g • Added sugars 7.8 g

2 passion-fruit
6 tablespoons crème fraîche
6 tablespoons Greek yoghurt
finely grated rind and juice of ½ small orange
about 2 tablespoons sifted icing sugar
2 ripe peaches or nectarines
2 red-skinned apples
1 bunch of red or green seedless grapes
4 ripe figs
plenty of crushed ice, to serve

1 Cut the passion-fruits in half and scoop the pulp into a bowl. Add the crème fraîche, yoghurt, orange rind and juice and enough icing sugar to taste. Beat until well combined and spoon into two serving bowls.

2 Cut the fruits into bite-sized pieces. Cover a large, round serving plate or tray with lots of crushed ice and nestle a bowl of the passion-fruit cream at each end. Arrange the prepared fruits attractively over the ice and serve immediately.

brilliant banana desserts

Bananas can easily be jazzed up into these simple puddings. You'll find most of the ingredients in a well-stocked kitchen. There's something very comforting about these puds, especially on a cold evening.

⭐ baked bananas with greek yoghurt

If you like, these can be cooked on the barbecue for about 15 minutes after the first heat has died down.

serves 4 • preparation 5 mins • cooking 25 mins

Energy 183 kcals • Protein 3.5 g • Carbohydrate 37.4 g • Fat 3.1 g
Saturated fat 1.8 g • Fibre 1.4 g • Salt 0.06 g • Added sugars 7.8 g

> 4 large ripe bananas, left unpeeled
> 8 tablespoons Greek yoghurt
> about 2 tablespoons demerara sugar

1 Pre-heat the oven to 200°C/400°F/Gas Mark 6. Arrange the bananas on a baking sheet and bake for 20–25 minutes until the skins are completely blackened but haven't split.

2 Place the bananas in individual warmed dishes and split them down the middle. Add a dollop of Greek yoghurt to each one, then sprinkle over the sugar to taste. Serve at once.

griddled bananas with toffee sauce

Make sure your griddle pan is spotlessly clean for this recipe, and, if possible, use tongs to turn the bananas.

serves 4 • preparation 5 mins • cooking 15 mins

Energy 361 kcals • Protein 1.7 g • Carbohydrate 47.8 g • Fat 19.4 g
Saturated fat 12.1 g • Fibre 1.4 g • Salt 0.07 g • Added sugars 18.6 g

> 25 g (1 oz) unsalted butter
> 4 large ripe bananas
>
> FOR THE TOFFEE SAUCE
> 50 g (2 oz) unsalted butter
> 50 g (2 oz) light muscovado sugar
> 2 tablespoons golden syrup or clear honey
> 2 tablespoons double cream
> vanilla ice-cream, to serve

1 Heat a griddle pan until searing hot. Melt the butter in a small pan or in the microwave. Peel the bananas and brush all over with the butter. Arrange on the griddle pan, reduce the heat a little and cook for 4–5 minutes on each side until cooked through and lightly charred.

2 Meanwhile, make the toffee sauce. Place the butter in a pan with the sugar and syrup. Bring to the boil, stirring until the sugar has dissolved. Reduce the heat and simmer for 2–3 minutes until thickened. Stir in the cream and allow to bubble down, then remove from the heat. Serve the bananas drizzled with toffee sauce and a scoop of the vanilla ice-cream.

banana custard

Be careful not to let the custard boil, or it will curdle.

serves 4 • preparation 25 mins • cooking 20 mins

Energy 335 kcals • Protein 11.5 g • Carbohydrate 46.5 g • Fat 12.8 g
Saturated fat 4.4 g • Fibre 1.1 g • Salt 0.26 g • Added sugars 15.8 g

> 600 ml (1 pint) milk
> 6 egg yolks
> 4 tablespoons caster sugar
> a few drops of vanilla extract
> 4 over-ripe bananas
> raspberry jam, to serve

1 Pour the milk into a small pan and bring to a gentle simmer. Meanwhile, place the egg yolks in a bowl with the sugar and whisk until light and fluffy. Whisk in the milk and add the vanilla extract to taste. Rinse the pan and pour in the custard. Cook over a low heat for about 10 minutes, stirring until the mixture thickens and coats the back of the spoon.

2 Peel the bananas, cut into thin slices and stir into the custard. Leave for 5 minutes to allow the flavours to combine. Re-heat gently, then serve with a swirl of raspberry jam on top.

FRIENDS FOR DINNER

bruschetta

Don't be tempted to make these too far in advance, as the bread goes soggy. Pre-heat the grill or a griddle pan and use to toast 6 thick slices country bread, preferably sourdough, on both sides. Remove from the heat and immediately rub one side with a halved garlic clove. Drizzle over a little olive oil and serve, or add one of the following delicious toppings.

PARMA HAM WITH BASIL DRESSING
Arrange slices of **Parma ham** on the bruschetta. Whizz 1 small **garlic clove** with 4 tablespoons of **toasted pine nuts** and a good handful of **fresh basil leaves** in a mini blender. Pour in enough **extra virgin olive oil** to make a smooth, thickish dressing and fold in a handful of **freshly grated Parmesan** or **Pecorino cheese**. Season to taste and drizzle over the Parma ham to serve.

GUACAMOLE
Halve 1 **avocado**, remove the stone and scoop the flesh into a bowl. Mash until smooth, then season with a teaspoon of **onion salt** and plenty of **freshly ground black pepper**. Stir in a handful of **diced semi-sun-dried tomatoes** and a couple of **finely chopped spring onions**, spread thickly on the bruschetta and serve.

CHERRY TOMATO, MOZZARELLA AND BASIL
Mix 1 teaspoon **balsamic vinegar** into a bowl with 3 tablespoons **extra virgin olive oil** and season to taste. Stir in 300 g (10 oz) cubed **mozzarella** or halved **mini mozzarella cheeses** with 175 g (6 oz) halved **cherry** or **baby plum tomatoes** and a handful of torn **fresh basil leaves**. Arrange **wild rocket leaves** on the bruschetta, spoon the mozzarella and tomato mixture on top and serve.

ITALIAN BUTTER BEAN
Mash the **butter beans** in a bowl with a crushed **garlic clove** and enough **extra virgin olive oil** to make a rough paste. Add a squeeze of **lemon juice** and fold in 2 chopped, **roasted red peppers** (from a jar or can) with a good handful of chopped, **pitted black olives** and a small handful of roughly chopped **flat-leaf parsley leaves**. Season to taste, spoon onto the bruschetta and serve.

ready-made nibbles

There's no doubt, whether you are planning an informal family lunch or a quick, after-work dinner for friends, that everyone likes to have something to nibble on while you are putting the finishing touches to the meal. Lots of tasty ready-made snacks are now available, listed opposite.

Make them look pretty by arranging them in attractive bowls or on platters, or even layering them in glass vases. If you have more time at your disposal, make your own nibbles from some of the recipes above.

bagel chips a tasty alternative to the more everyday crisp
bombay mix crisp noodles, nuts and fruits, blended with spices
breadsticks I like to serve these wrapped in a thin slice of Parma ham
crisps these always go down a storm, especially with the kids
crostini serve these little Italian toasts with Parma ham or cheese
olives these can be delicious, but they need to be good quality
pretzels these knot-shaped snacks are very popular in America
salted nuts try cashews or almonds as a change from peanuts
tortilla chips great for a Mexican evening, served with salsa dips

how to make risotto

Risotto is a peasant dish that originates from the rice-growing areas of northern Italy. The secret of making a perfect risotto every time is to use a good-quality, heavy-based, shallow pan that distributes the heat evenly – a sauté pan is perfect. Also essential for success is to use proper risotto rice – arborio and Carnaroli are the most widely available in the UK – and a well-flavoured home-made stock.

✦ lemon risotto

serves 4 • preparation 5 mins • cooking 30 mins

Energy 560 kcals • Protein 16.4 g • Carbohydrate 93.1 g • Fat 10.8 g
Saturated fat 3.6 g • Fibre 2.7 g • Salt 1.85 g • Added sugars none

2 tablespoons olive oil

1 large onion, finely chopped

2 garlic cloves, crushed

450 g (1 lb) arborio (risotto) rice

finely grated rind and juice of 1 lemon

about 1.5 litres/2½ pints chicken or vegetable stock

300 ml (½ pint) dry white wine

1 x 20-g (¾-oz) packet chives, snipped

50 g (2 oz) freshly grated Parmesan cheese

salt and freshly ground black pepper

1 Melt the olive oil in a large sauté pan. Add the onion and garlic and cook gently for 4-5 minutes until softened but not coloured, stirring occasionally.

2 Increase the heat, stir in the rice and lemon rind and cook gently for 1 minute, stirring continuously, until the rice is opaque and perfumed.

3 Meanwhile, pour the stock into a separate pan and bring to a gentle simmer. Pour the wine into the rice mixture and allow to bubble away, stirring. Add a ladleful of stock and cook gently, stirring, until absorbed. Continue to add the simmering stock a ladleful at a time, stirring frequently. Allow each stock addition to be almost completely absorbed before adding the next ladleful, until the rice is *al dente* – tender on the outside, but still with a slight bite in the centre of the grain. This should take 15–20 minutes.

4 Stir enough lemon juice to taste into the risotto with the chives and Parmesan and season to taste. Leave to rest and swell a little more for 3 minutes. Ladle into wide-rimmed serving bowls and serve at once.

VARIATION

MIXED MUSHROOM

Soak 25 g (1 oz) dried cep or porcini mushrooms in a bowl with 300 ml (½ pint) of boiling water. Use 50 g (2 oz) of butter instead of the olive oil and omit the lemon rind. Pour the mushroom liquid instead of the wine into the rice. Chop the cep mushrooms and add them too. Slice 450 g (1 lb) mixed fresh mushrooms and sauté in a knob of butter and a tablespoon of oil for 3–4 minutes. Fold into the risotto with a squeeze of lemon juice, chopped parsley and Parmesan cheese.

warm griddled pumpkin and spinach salad

Very stylish, very easy to make and very delicious: the perfect salad. The pumpkin can be replaced with butternut squash, depending on availability.

serves 4 • preparation 10 mins • cooking 40 mins

Energy 494 kcals • Protein 14.0 g • Carbohydrate 7.2 g • Fat 45.6 g
Saturated fat 13.9 g • Fibre 3.0 g • Salt 1.32 g • Added sugars 1.5 g

1 small pumpkin (about 1 kg/2¼ lb), halved, seeded, peeled and cut into 2.5-cm (1-inch) cubes
6 tablespoons extra virgin olive oil
50 g (2 oz) pine nuts
1 tablespoon balsamic vinegar
1 teaspoon golden syrup or maple syrup
1 teaspoon wholegrain mustard
a pinch of muscovado sugar
175 g (6 oz) baby leaf spinach
225 g (8 oz) dolcelatte cheese, at room temperature, cubed
salt and freshly ground black pepper

1 Pre-heat the oven to 200°C/400°F/Gas Mark 6. Place the pumpkin in a roasting tin, drizzle over 2 tablespoons of the oil, then season generously. Toss until evenly coated and roast for 35–40 minutes until tender and lightly caramelized.

2 Meanwhile, put the pine nuts in a small roasting tin and place in the oven for 8–10 minutes until golden brown. Leave to cool.

3 Place the remaining 4 tablespoons of olive oil in a large bowl with the vinegar, golden syrup, mustard, sugar and seasoning. Whisk until well combined and thickened.

4 When the pumpkin is cooked, tip it into the dressing and stir to coat. Fold in the spinach leaves, crumble in the dolcelatte and scatter with the pine nuts.

oven-baked chicken with chorizo and artichokes

This one-pot wonder gives loads of flavour for minimum effort and is guaranteed to wake up your taste buds. If you don't have a suitable casserole dish, use a large frying pan, then transfer the contents to a roasting tin and cover loosely with foil.

serves 4 • preparation 5 mins • cooking 1 hr

Energy 701 kcals • Protein 45.5 g • Carbohydrate 84.7 g • Fat 19.6 g
Saturated fat 7.4 g • Fibre 2.2 g • Salt 2.03 g • Added sugars none

1 × 300-g (11-oz) jar artichoke hearts preserved in olive oil
25 g (1 oz) butter
4–6 chicken breast fillets (skin on)
1 large onion, finely chopped
2 garlic cloves, crushed
100 g (4 oz) chorizo sausage, sliced
350 g (12 oz) long-grain rice
150 ml (5 fl oz) dry white wine
600 ml (1 pint) chicken stock (see page 231)
the leaves from ½ x 20-g (¾-oz) packet flat-leaf parsley, roughly chopped
salt and freshly ground black pepper

1 Pre-heat the oven to 180°C/350°F/Gas Mark 4. Drain the oil from the jar of artichokes and add 1 tablespoon to a flameproof casserole dish. Add half the butter, then place on the hob to heat. Season the chicken breasts, add to the dish, skin-side down, and cook for 2–3 minutes until lightly browned. Turn over and cook for another minute or so until sealed. Transfer to a plate and set aside.

2 Add another tablespoon of the artichoke oil to the dish with the remaining butter, then tip in the onion and garlic. Sauté for 2–3 minutes until softened but not coloured. Add the chorizo and rice and cook for another 2 minutes, stirring until the chorizo has begun to release its oil and all the rice grains are well coated.

3 Pour the wine into the pan, stirring to combine, then add the stock and fold in the artichokes. Arrange the chicken on top, pushing the breasts down into the rice. Cover and bake for 35–40 minutes until all the liquid has been absorbed and the chicken and rice are cooked through and tender. Scatter over the parsley and serve.

✪ thai-style ginger fish

The fresh zingy flavour of the ginger complements the steamed fish perfectly. Take care not to overcook the fish: it should still be very moist and tender when served.

serves 4 • preparation 10 mins • cooking 20 mins

Energy 148 kcals • Protein 28.6 g • Carbohydrate 3.6 g • Fat 1.3 g
Saturated fat 0.2 g • Fibre 0.5 g • Salt 2.62 g • Added sugars 1.5 g

> 4–6 × 150-g (5-oz) firm white fish fillets, such as lemon
>   sole, sea bass or brill, skinned
> 1 teaspoon Maldon sea salt
> 1 bunch spring onions
> 2 tablespoons dry sherry
> 2 teaspoons dark soy sauce
> 2 garlic cloves, finely chopped
> 2 cm (³/₄ inch) fresh root ginger, peeled and shredded
> 1 medium-hot red chilli, seeded and finely chopped
> juice of 1 lime
> 1 teaspoon caster sugar
> 1 tablespoon Thai fish sauce (nam pla)
> **fresh coriander sprigs, to garnish**
> **plain boiled rice, to serve**

1 Set up a steamer or put a rack into a wok or deep-sided pan with a lid (preferably clear glass so that you can keep an eye on the fish while it is cooking). Pour in enough water to come 5 cm (2 inches) up the sides and bring to the boil. Dry the fish fillets with kitchen paper and sprinkle with the salt, rubbing it in with your hands. Trim the onions. Finely chop 2 of them for the dressing and set aside. Arrange the remainder on a heatproof plate and add the sherry and soy sauce. Place the fish fillets on top and scatter with the garlic and ginger. Put the plate of fish on the rack, cover tightly and steam for 5–15 minutes, depending on the thickness of the fillets: they should turn opaque and be flaking slightly but still moist.

2 Meanwhile, place the reserved onions in a small serving bowl with the chilli, lime juice, sugar and Thai fish sauce, stirring until the sugar dissolves. When the fish is cooked, remove the plate from the rack and transfer the fish fillets to serving plates. Drizzle over some of the Thai dressing and garnish with the coriander sprigs. Serve at once with boiled rice and hand the rest of the dressing separately.

✪ sichuan chilli seafood stir-fry

Sichuan peppercorns are the dried aromatic berries of the prickly ash tree, which is native to Sichuan province in western China. Look for them in Chinese or Asian food shops, or on the speciality shelves in supermarkets.

serves 4 • preparation 10 mins • cooking 15 mins

Energy 267 kcals • Protein 40.6 g • Carbohydrate 7.5 g • Fat 8.5 g
Saturated fat 0.9 g • Fibre 0.5 g • Salt 4.85 g • Added sugars 1.5 g

> 1 tablespoon Sichuan peppercorns
> 1 tablespoon Maldon sea salt
> 350 g (12 oz) cleaned squid, cut into 1-cm (¹/₂-inch) slices
> 350 g (12 oz) peeled raw tiger prawns
> 225 g (8 oz) queen scallops, thawed if frozen
> 2 tablespoons sunflower oil
> 4 garlic cloves, crushed
> 2.5 cm (1 inch) fresh root ginger, peeled and grated
> 2 spring onions, finely chopped
> 8 tablespoons sweet chilli sauce
> **steamed rice, to serve**

1 Heat a wok until very hot and toast the peppercorns for a minute or two, tossing occasionally, until fragrant. Tip into a spice grinder, food processor or mortar, add the sea salt, then grind together until coarsely cracked. Tip onto a plate and use to coat the seafood, shaking off any excess.

2 Heat half the oil in the wok until very hot. Add half the garlic, ginger and spring onions and stir-fry for 20 seconds, then tip in half the coated seafood and continue to stir-fry for 1–2 minutes until the seafood is cooked through and just tender. Tip onto a plate and repeat with the remaining garlic, ginger, onions and seafood.

3 Return all the seafood to the wok and pour in the chilli sauce. Continue to stir-fry for a minute or so until the sauce is thick and syrupy, then serve with fragrant rice.

stuffed pork fillet with prunes

The salty flavour of Parma ham combines well with the sweetness of prunes to enhance the succulent pork in this recipe. Don't be too precious when stuffing the prunes – a bit of the soft cheese smeared on the outside is fine.

serves 4 • preparation 15 mins • cooking 45 mins

Energy 464 kcals • Protein 50.4 g • Carbohydrate 14.6 g • Fat 23.1 g
Saturated fat 11.3 g • Fibre 2.4 g • Salt 1.93 g • Added sugars none

2 pork tenderloins (fillets), about 750 g (1½ lb) in total
14 ready-to-eat prunes (Agen, if possible)
100 g (4 oz) Boursin (full-fat garlic and herb soft cheese)
8–10 slices Parma ham
freshly ground black pepper
celeriac and parsnip mash, to serve (see page 221)

1 Pre-heat the oven to 200°C/400°F/Gas Mark 6. Trim away any fat and membrane from the pork tenderloins and split lengthways, without cutting right through. Open each one out flat and season generously with black pepper.

2 Cut the prunes lengthways along one side and remove the stones, then fill with teaspoonfuls of Boursin. Lay the prunes along the middle of each tenderloin, then close up and wrap with the Parma ham. Tie loosely with string at 2.5-cm (1-inch) intervals and arrange in a large roasting tin, seam-side down.

3 Cover with foil and bake for 15 minutes, then remove the foil and cook for another 30 minutes, or until the pork is cooked through and the Parma ham is crispy. Remove from the oven and leave to rest for 5 minutes in a warm place, then carve into slices and serve with the celeriac and parsnip mash.

braised oxtail with butter beans

My late mum's favourite treat, and I hope it becomes yours too. You can use dried butter beans, but soak them overnight and cook them before adding them to the casserole. This dish is fantastic served just as it is, but I also like to have it with some crisp buttered green cabbage (see page 223) and chunks of crusty bread.

serves 4 • preparation 15 mins • cooking 3 hrs

Energy 670 kcals • Protein 44.5 g • Carbohydrate 52.7 g • Fat 27.1 g
Saturated fat 8.0 g • Fibre 12.9 g • Salt 2.20 g • Added sugars 0.2 g

50 g (2 oz) seasoned flour
1.5–1.75 kg (3–4 lb) oxtail pieces
4 tablespoons olive oil
2 onions, chopped
2 carrots, peeled and chopped
2 celery sticks, chopped
2 garlic cloves, finely chopped
the leaves from 3 sprigs of thyme
2 bay leaves
300 ml (½ pint) red wine
1 litre (1¾ pints) chicken stock (see page 231)
1 × 400-g (14-oz) can chopped tomatoes
1 tablespoon tomato purée
1 tablespoon Worcestershire sauce
2 x 400-g (14-oz) cans butter beans, or 1 x 800-g (1¾-lb) jar, drained and rinsed
the leaves from ½ x 20-g (¾-oz) packet flat-leaf parsley, chopped
salt and freshly ground black pepper

1 Place the seasoned flour in a plastic bag and add the oxtail pieces. Shake until well coated, then remove, dusting off any excess flour. Heat the oil in a large flameproof casserole and brown the oxtail pieces in batches. Using a slotted spoon, transfer to a colander and allow the excess oil to drain off.

2 Add the onions, carrots and celery to the pan and sauté for 10 minutes until softened but not coloured. Add the garlic, thyme and bay leaves and continue to cook for a minute or two. Deglaze the pan with a little of the red wine, scraping the bottom of the pan to release the caramelized juices, then pour in the remainder with the stock, tomatoes, tomato purée and Worcestershire sauce. Season to taste.

3 Return the oxtail to the pan, bring to the boil, then cover and simmer gently for about 1½ hours, skimming off any fat that bubbles to the surface. Gently stir in the butter beans and continue to cook over a low heat for a further 45 minutes–1 hour until the meat starts to come away from the bone. Season to taste, scatter with the parsley and serve.

herb-stuffed leg of lamb

Ask your butcher to bone the leg of lamb for you, but to leave the shank end intact. This not only improves the flavour, but also makes carving much easier.

serves 4 • preparation 45 mins • cooking 2 hrs 40 mins

Energy 989 kcals • Protein 93.1 g • Carbohydrate 45.4 g • Fat 49.5 g
Saturated fat 25.2 g • Fibre 2.0 g • Salt 2.20 g • Added sugars 1.6 g

50 g (2 oz) butter

1 large onion, finely chopped

the leaves from 6 sprigs of thyme

the leaves from 1½ x 20-g (¾-oz) packet flat-leaf parsley, chopped

175 g (6 oz) fresh white breadcrumbs

1 leg of lamb, 2.25–2.75 kg (5–6 lb), boned with shank end left intact

50 g (2 oz) fresh rosemary, thyme and sage sprigs

1 tablespoon plain flour

300 ml (½ pint) lamb stock (made with a cube) or chicken stock (see page 231)

1 tablespoon redcurrant jelly

salt and freshly ground black pepper

TO SERVE

crispy roast potatoes (see page 219)

honey-roast carrots and parsnips (see page 224)

1 Pre-heat the oven to 190°C/375°F/Gas Mark 5. To make the stuffing, melt the butter in a large frying pan and sauté the onion for 3–4 minutes until softened but not coloured. Stir in the thyme leaves, parsley and breadcrumbs and season to taste. Press the stuffing inside the boned-out leg of lamb and season the joint all over. Arrange the herb sprigs around the outside of the lamb and then tie it up neatly with string.

2 Place the lamb in a roasting tin, cover loosely with foil and roast for 2 hours. Remove the foil and baste well, then roast for another 30 minutes until just tender. If you like your lamb more well done, give it another 30 minutes in the oven. To check that it is cooked to your liking, insert a skewer into the thickest part of the meat and watch the juice run out: the pinker the juice, the rarer the meat. When it is cooked to your liking, transfer the lamb to a carving platter and leave to rest in a warm plate for 30 minutes.

3 To make the gravy, place the roasting tin directly on the hob and stir the flour into the fat and juices. Cook for 1 minute, stirring continuously, then gradually add the stock, whisking until smooth after each addition and scraping the bottom of the tin to remove any caramelized juices. Transfer to a small pan and whisk in the redcurrant jelly, then simmer gently until you have achieved the desired consistency. Carefully strain into a gravy boat.

4 When the lamb is rested, carefully cut away the herbs and string, then carve into slices, holding the shank end of the bone. Serve at once with the potatoes, carrots, parsnips and gravy.

chilli cornbread pie

There are many different recipes for chilli, and many opinions as to which is 'correct'. Well, this is a very simple recipe, but it's pretty damn good, thanks to the addition of canned beans in smoky chilli sauce.

serves 4 • preparation 10 mins • cooking 50 mins

Energy 770 kcals • Protein 51.6 g • Carbohydrate 94.2 g • Fat 23.3 g
Saturated fat 5.2 g • Fibre 12.6 g • Salt 5.14 g • Added sugars 4.2 g

4 tablespoons sunflower oil

1 large onion, finely chopped

2 garlic cloves, finely chopped

450 g (1 lb) lean minced beef

2 × 400-g (14-oz) cans chopped tomatoes

2 × 400-g (14-oz) cans chilli beans

150 g (5 oz) cornmeal or quick-cook polenta

150 g (5 oz) self-raising flour

2 teaspoons baking powder

2 eggs, lightly beaten

300 ml (½ pint) buttermilk or Greek yoghurt

salt and freshly ground black pepper

mixed green salad, lightly dressed, to serve (see page 228)

1 Heat half the oil in a large frying pan. Add the onion and garlic and sauté for 5 minutes, or until softened but not coloured. Add the beef and sauté for about 5 minutes until lightly browned, breaking up any lumps with a wooden spoon. Pour in the tomatoes and chilli beans, then season to taste. Bring to the boil, then reduce the heat and simmer gently for 30 minutes, or until the beef is tender and the sauce has slightly reduced.

2 Pre-heat the oven to 180°C/350°F/Gas Mark 4. Place the cornmeal in a bowl with the flour, baking powder and a teaspoon of salt. Stir to combine, then make a well in the centre and quickly whisk in the remaining 2 tablespoons of oil, the eggs and buttermilk until you have a smooth batter. Spoon the chilli into the bottom of a deep ovenproof dish and pour over the cornmeal mixture in an even layer. Bake for 35–40 minutes until golden brown and an inserted skewer comes out clean. Serve with the salad.

caribbean beef and red bean stew with dumplings

This is a variation on the traditional Jamaican recipe that I can clearly remember from my childhood. It probably even enticed me to be a chef.

serves 4 • preparation 15 mins • cooking 1 hr 30 mins

Energy 935 kcals • Protein 61.4 g • Carbohydrate 77.6 g • Fat 44.2 g
Saturated fat 1.1 g • Fibre 7.0 g • Salt 0.13 g • Added sugars 8.6 g

2 tablespoons sunflower oil
1 large onion, finely chopped
1–2 Scotch bonnet chillies, seeded and finely chopped
2 garlic cloves, finely chopped
the leaves from 3–4 sprigs of thyme
50 g (2 oz) pancetta or smoked streaky bacon lardons
750 g (1½ lb) rib-eye steak, cut into bite-sized pieces
2 tablespoons tomato purée
300 ml (½ pint) beef stock (see page 231, or use
    ready-made)
1 × 500-g (1 lb 2-oz) carton passata
1 × 250-ml (8-fl oz) carton coconut cream
2 bay leaves
2 × 400-g (14-oz) cans red kidney beans
100 g (4 oz) cornmeal
100 g (4 oz) plain flour, plus extra for dusting
salt and freshly ground black pepper
West Indian hot pepper sauce, to serve

1 Heat the oil in a large, heavy-based pan with a lid. Add the onion and sauté for about 5 minutes until softened. Tip in as much chilli as you like (Scotch bonnets are v-e-r-y hot) with the garlic and 2 teaspoonfuls of the thyme leaves and continue to sauté for another minute or two.

2 Add the pancetta to the onion mixture and cook for 2–3 minutes until lightly golden and sizzling. Add the beef and sauté until lightly browned all over, then stir in the tomato purée and cook for another minute, stirring. Pour in the stock, passata and coconut cream, stirring until the coconut cream has melted.

3 Add the bay leaves and kidney beans to the beef mixture and season to taste. Bring to the boil, then reduce the heat, cover and simmer for 1 hour, stirring occasionally, until the sauce has slightly reduced and the beef is tender.

4 Meanwhile, make the dumplings. Place the cornmeal in a bowl with the flour, pinch of thyme and ½ teaspoon of salt and stir to combine. Add enough cold water to make a soft dough, then turn out onto a lightly floured surface and, using floured hands, roll into 12–16 finger-shaped pieces. Lower them into the beef mixture and simmer gently for another 15 minutes until the dumplings are cooked through.

5 Serve at once and allow people to help themselves to the pepper sauce – if they can take the heat.

spaghetti bolognese

This recipe makes 1.5 kg (3 lb) sauce, which is enough to serve 8 generously. If, however, there are only 4 people to feed, reduce the quantity of pasta to 450 g (1 lb) spaghetti, and you'll have enough sauce left to make the lasagne (see right).

serves 8 • preparation 15 mins • cooking 2 hrs 30 mins

Energy 571 kcals • Protein 33.7 g • Carbohydrate 73.8 g • Fat 15.0 g
Saturated fat 5.3 g • Fibre 3.9 g • Salt 0.63 g • Added sugars none

   2 tablespoons olive oil
   25 g (1 oz) pancetta or rindless, smoked streaky
      bacon, diced
   1 onion, finely chopped
   1 carrot, peeled and finely diced
   1 celery stick, finely diced
   2 garlic cloves, finely chopped
   the leaves from 3 sprigs of thyme
   1 bay leaf
   750 g (1½ lb) lean minced beef
   2 tablespoons tomato purée
   300 ml (½ pint) red wine
   1 × 400-g (14-oz) can chopped tomatoes
   1 teaspoon anchovy essence
   1 kg (2¼ lb) spaghetti
   a knob of butter
   salt and freshly ground black pepper
   freshly grated Parmesan cheese, to serve

1 Heat a heavy-based pan. Add the oil and sauté the pancetta for a minute or two until it has begun to crisp up and release some of its fat. Add the onion, carrot, celery, garlic, thyme and bay leaf. Cook for 8–10 minutes until the vegetables have softened and taken on a little colour, stirring occasionally.

2 Add the minced beef to the pan, mix until well combined, then sauté until well browned, breaking up any lumps with a wooden spoon. Stir in the tomato purée and continue to cook, stirring, for another minute or two.

3 Deglaze the pan with a little of the wine, scraping up any sediment. Pour in the remaining wine with the tomatoes, then add the anchovy essence and season to taste. Bring to the boil, then reduce the heat to the lowest setting and simmer for at least 2 hours, preferably up to 4 hours, until the beef is meltingly tender and the sauce has slightly reduced.

4 When ready to serve, bring a large pan of water to a rolling boil. Add a good pinch of salt and swirl in the spaghetti. Stir once, then cook for 8–10 minutes, or according to the instructions on the packet, until the pasta is *al dente*. Drain, rinse briefly if neccesary (see page 84), then return to the pan and add the butter and bolognese sauce. Toss until well combined and serve with the Parmesan.

luxury lasagne

You'll need to make up the bolognese sauce from the recipe, left, in order to cook this dish. However, you'll only need two thirds of it. The rest can be frozen, or you could of course serve it up as spaghetti bolognese the next day.

serves 4 • preparation 10 mins • cooking 1 hr

Energy 1046 kcals • Protein 82.9 g • Carbohydrate 44.9 g • Fat 55.2 g
Saturated fat 25.2 g • Fibre 4.0 g • Salt 4.21 g • Added sugars none

   7–8 lasagne sheets
   900 g (2 lb) home-made bolognese sauce (see left)
   450 g (1 lb) cottage cheese
   1 egg
   the leaves from 1½ x 20-g (¾-oz) packet flat-leaf parsley,
      chopped
   1½ x 20-g (¾-oz) packet chives, snipped
   75 g (3 oz) freshly grated Parmesan cheese
   450 ml (15 fl oz) cheese sauce (see page 233, or use
      ready-made)
   salt and freshly ground black pepper
   mixed green salad, lightly dressed, to serve (see page 228)

1 Pre-heat the oven to 180°C/350°F/Gas Mark 4. Line a 2.25-litre (4-pint) ovenproof dish with a layer of lasagne sheets, breaking them to fit as necessary. Spread half the bolognese sauce on top, levelling it with the back of a spoon.

2 Place the cottage cheese in a bowl and add the egg, parsley, chives and 50 g (2 oz) of the Parmesan. Season to taste and beat until well combined, then spread over the bolognese layer. Cover with the remaining lasagne sheets.

3 Spread the rest of the bolognese sauce on top, then pour the cheese sauce over it. Scatter the rest of the Parmesan on top and bake for 1 hour, or until the lasagne is bubbling and lightly golden. Serve at once with the salad.

girls'night in

The beauty of this menu is that it can all be prepared in advance, so you'll have to be home only half an hour before your guests arrive. This gives you time for a few last-minute tasks, and even a few moments to relax.

menu

Marinated olives

Mixed platter of bruschetta
(see page 98)

Luxury lasagne
(see page 112)

Mixed green salad with balsamic and honey dressing
(see pages 228 and 230)

Rhubarb and strawberry pudding
(see page 118)

Pouring custard
(see page 235)

TIPS

• Leave everything ready before you go out in the morning – even the table can be set the night before. Once you're home, put the final touches to the nibbles. Draw the curtains, set the music and the lighting to low, then relax with a drink until your guests arrive.

• If you are out at work all day, the lasagne can be prepared up to 2 weeks in advance and frozen until needed. It's best to thaw it out in the fridge overnight, but 4 hours at room temperature will suffice.

SHOP-BOUGHT SHORTCUTS

When time is really short, take advantage of any shop-bought shortcuts available: buy your marinated olives from a deli; use ready-made guacamole and hummus on the bruschetta, and top with Parma ham and Parmesan shavings; buy packets of mixed salads and cartons of custard.

time plan

The day before
Make the lasagne, cover with cling film and leave in the fridge ready to bake.
Make the balsamic dressing and keep in a screw-topped jar in the fridge.
Choose your wines and chill any white ones.

In advance on the day
Prepare the basil dressing and the butter bean topping for the bruschetta.
Make the custard, if using home-made (see shop-bought shortcuts).

time plan for an 8 p.m. start
7.30 p.m.   Prepare the mixed salad and cover with cling film. Place in the fridge.
7.45 p.m.   Open any red wines and allow to breathe at room temperature.
Prepare the rhubarb and strawberry pudding.
Make the bruschetta. Arrange on platters or trays ready to serve.
Drain off any excess oil from the olives and put into serving bowls.
8 pm   Put the lasagne into the oven on the top shelf to bake for 1 hour.
Place the rhubarb and strawberry pudding on the middle shelf to bake for 40 minutes. Set aside at room temperature until ready to serve.
8.55 p.m.   Dress the salad and warm plates in the oven.

deep apple sour-cream pie

A little indulgence is a wonderful thing and it doesn't come much better than this – crisp, buttery pastry filled with creamy apples and luscious prunes, and topped with melt-in-the-mouth crumble. What more could you ask for?

serves 4 • preparation 45 mins • cooking 1 hr 15 mins

Energy 768 kcals • Protein 7.9 g • Carbohydrate 102 g • Fat 39.3 g
Saturated fat 22 g • Fibre 4.8 g • Salt 0.29 g • Added sugars 39.8 g

- 175 g (6 oz) sweet shortcrust pastry (see page 236, or use ready-made)
- 75 g (3 oz) plain flour, plus 1 tablespoon and extra for dusting
- 4 Granny Smith apples
- juice of 1 lemon
- 100 g (4 oz) ready-to-eat prunes, stoned and halved
- 2 pieces stem ginger preserved in syrup, drained and finely chopped
- 100 g (4 oz) caster sugar
- 1 egg
- 120 ml (4 fl oz) double cream
- 1 teaspoon ground cinnamon
- 50 g (2 oz) light muscovado sugar
- 50 g (2 oz) unsalted butter, diced and chilled
- pouring custard (see page 235, or use ready-made), cream or ice-cream, to serve

1 Pre-heat the oven to 200°C/400°F/Gas Mark 6. Roll out the pastry as thinly as possible on a lightly floured surface and use it to line a lightly greased loose-bottomed flan tin, 20-cm (8-inch) wide and 4 cm (1½ inches) deep (see page 164). Prick the base here and there with a fork and chill for 20 minutes to rest the pastry and reduce shrinkage during cooking.

2 Line the pastry case with a crumpled sheet of greaseproof paper and cover the base with a layer of baking beans . Bake for 15 minutes until the pastry case looks cooked, then remove the paper and beans and return the case to the oven for 5 minutes or so until the pastry is crisp and biscuit-coloured around the edges. Remove and lower the oven temperature to 180°C/350°F/Gas Mark 4.

3 Peel, core and cut the apples into wedges. Place in a large bowl and toss in the lemon juice to prevent discoloration, then stir in the prunes and stem ginger. Whisk the caster sugar and egg until thickened, then gently whisk in 1 tablespoon flour and stir in the cream. Fold into the apple mixture.

4 To make the crumble topping, sieve the remaining flour and the cinnamon into a bowl, then stir in the muscovado sugar and rub in the butter until the mixture resembles fine breadcrumbs.

5 When the pastry case has cooled, carefully pour in the apple mixture, piling it high in the centre as the apples will shrink as they cook. Sprinkle the crumble on top in an even layer and bake for 45–50 minutes until the apple mixture is set and the crumble is lightly golden. Leave to cool in the tin for at least 5 minutes. Serve with custard, cream or ice-cream.

alternatives to cream
There is now an enormous choice of dairy produce available, and working out the differences can be confusing. Here's a quick guide.

Crème fraîche is a winner as far as I'm concerned, because it has a much longer shelf life than double cream. I've usually got a carton open in the fridge and use a spoonful here and there. Now you can also buy half-fat crème fraîche, which has all of the creaminess of the full-fat version but doesn't taste as rich. Both are brilliant to use in cooking as they never curdle or separate, no matter what you do.

Fromage frais is a French form of low-fat cream cheese, although it has a texture similar to yoghurt. It's a good substitute for cream in sweet or savoury recipes.

Greek yoghurt is another favourite of mine, as it is much creamier and thicker than ordinary plain yoghurt, having a fat content of 8–10 per cent as opposed to 1–2 per cent. It's great if you want to lighten and reduce the calories of any dairy-based dessert.

Quark is a German version of fromage frais, which is drier and firmer, more like a soft cheese. It's also a good substitute for cream in sweet or savoury recipes.

rhubarb and strawberry pudding

Traditional sponge puddings make excellent comfort food and are, I'm sure, on most people's list of favourite desserts. You can vary the fruit in this delicious pudding according to the time of year, or try using a bag of mixed frozen summer berries.

serves 4 • preparation 15 mins • cooking 40 mins

Energy 856 kcals • Protein 11.1 g • Carbohydrate 117.2 g • Fat 41.3 g
Saturated fat 24.2 g • Fibre 3.0 g • Salt 1.40 g • Added sugars 78.8 g

300 g (10 oz) fresh rhubarb, trimmed and cut into chunks
225 g (8 oz) large strawberries, hulled and quartered
300 g (10 oz) caster sugar
175 g (6 oz) plain flour
1 teaspoon baking powder
175 g (6 oz) butter, at room temperature
3 eggs
pouring custard, to serve (see page 235, or use ready-made)

1 Pre-heat the oven to 180°C/375°F/Gas Mark 4. Arrange the rhubarb and strawberries in a large pie dish and sprinkle over 100 g (4 oz) of the sugar.

2 Sift the flour into a bowl with the baking powder. Place the butter in a separate bowl with the remaining sugar and beat until lightly and fluffy. Beat in the eggs, then fold into the flour.

3 Carefully spread the sponge mixture over the fruit and bake for about 40 minutes, or until the sponge is risen and golden and an inserted skewer comes out clean. Serve with custard.

chilli-glazed mango with yoghurt

The combination of flavours in this dessert will revive even the most jaded palate, so put some spice into your life! You'll need roughly 550 g (1¼ lb) of mango chunks in total.

serves 4 • preparation 15 mins • cooking 15 mins

Energy 300 kcals • Protein 6.0 g • Carbohydrate 32.9 g • Fat 17.1 g
Saturated fat 10.6 g • Fibre 4.5 g • Salt 0.39 g • Added sugars 6.5 g

1 × 285-ml (9½ fl-oz) carton Greek yoghurt
the leaves from ½ x 20-g (¾-oz) packet mint, chopped
2 large mangoes, peeled and flesh cut away from the stone
50 g (2 oz) butter
25 g (1 oz) icing sugar
¼ teaspoon hot chilli powder

1 Pre-heat the grill. Place the yoghurt in a serving bowl and stir in the mint until well combined. Cut the mango into large chunks.

2 Melt the butter in a small pan or in the microwave. Place the mango in a large bowl and pour over the melted butter, tossing to coat evenly.

3 Line the grill rack with foil and arrange the buttered mango on top in an even layer. Sift the icing sugar and chilli powder into a small bowl, then tip into an icing-sugar duster or sieve. Sprinkle over the mango and then cook for 8–10 minutes, turning occasionally, until the mango is heated through and has caramelized.

4 Leave the mango pieces to 'set' for about 5 minutes, then serve with the minted yoghurt.

SPICE IT UP

coconut-and-cumin-spiced prawns with chapatis

Buy large cooked, peeled North Atlantic prawns for this curry. And if you are buying them frozen, you will need to buy a few more, as they lose quite a lot of their weight when they defrost. About 550 g (1¼ lb) will give you 450 g (1 lb) once they have thawed out.

serves 4 • preparation 5 mins • cooking 11–12 mins

Energy 340 kcals • Protein 29.6 g • Carbohydrate 11.0 g • Fat 19.9 g
Saturated fat 8.7 g • Fibre 2.8 g • Salt 4.94 g • Added sugars none

3 tablespoons sunflower oil

1 medium onion, finely chopped

2.5 cm (1 inch) fresh root ginger, peeled and finely grated

3 garlic cloves, crushed

1 teaspoon minced red chilli (sambal oelek, see page 12)

4 teaspoons hot paprika

2 tablespoons garam masala or korma curry paste

2 teaspoons lemon juice

150 ml (5 fl oz) hot water

1 × 200-g (7-oz) can chopped tomatoes

450 g (1 lb) cooked peeled prawns

50 g (2 oz) creamed coconut, chopped

1 × 20-g (¾-oz) packet fresh coriander, chopped

salt and cayenne pepper

1 packet ready-made chapatis, to serve

1 Heat the oil in a large frying pan, add the onion, ginger, garlic and chilli paste and fry for 3–4 minutes until soft and very lightly browned. Add the paprika and garam masala and fry for 2 minutes. Then add the lemon juice and water and simmer for 2 minutes more.

2 Add the tomatoes and prawns and simmer for 2 minutes. Stir in the creamed coconut and cook for a further minute. Season to taste, stir in the coriander and serve with warmed chapatis.

beef kofta kebabs with mango and mint raita

You can make these with minced lamb instead of beef if you prefer, and they are great cooked on the barbecue, too. Just remember, don't use extra-lean mince for these kebabs. The extra fattiness of ordinary mince will help keep them nice and moist during cooking.

serves 4 • preparation 10–15 mins + 20 mins' soaking for skewers • cooking 4–5 mins

Energy 546 kcals • Protein 42.2 g • Carbohydrate 18.2 g • Fat 34.3 g
Saturated fat 14.6 g • Fibre 2.8 g • Salt 0.80 g • Added sugars none

1 small onion, cut into chunks
750 g (1½ lb) minced beef
1 tablespoon ground coriander
1 tablespoon ground cumin
½ teaspoon ground turmeric
1 teaspoon garam masala
2 garlic cloves, crushed
2.5 cm (1 inch) fresh root ginger, peeled and grated
2 tablespoons whole-milk natural yoghurt
a little sunflower oil, for brushing
salt and cayenne pepper

FOR THE MANGO AND MINT RAITA
1 small ripe but firm mango
175 g (6 oz) whole-milk natural yoghurt
1 tablespoon sieved mango chutney
the leaves from 1 x 20-g (¾-oz) packet mint, chopped

1 Cover 12 bamboo skewers with cold water and leave them to soak for 20 minutes.

2 Put the onion into a food processor and blend until very finely chopped. Tip into a bowl and add the rest of the ingredients (apart from the oil), ½ teaspoon of salt and some cayenne pepper and mix together really well with your hands.

3 Divide the mixture into 12 equally sized pieces, then shape roughly into sausages. Push a soaked skewer up through the middle of each sausage and squash it more firmly onto the sticks.

4 For the raita, peel the mango, then slice the flesh away from the stone. Cut it into small pieces and mix with the rest of the ingredients and a little salt to taste.

5 Heat a ridged or heavy-based frying pan over a high heat until smoking hot. Reduce the heat to medium-high, brush the kebabs with a little oil and cook for 4–5 minutes, turning now and again until nicely browned and cooked through. Serve with the mango and mint raita.

creamy cardamom chicken

This is a mildly spiced Persian dish of tender chicken in an almond and cream sauce. It is quick and easy to make, and re-heats very easily if you want to make it ahead of time.

serves 4 • preparation 15 mins • cooking approx. 18 mins

Energy 587 kcals • Protein 49.5 g • Carbohydrate 8.5 g • Fat 39.6 g
Saturated fat 17.1 g • Fibre 1.4 g • Salt 0.88 g • Added sugars none

150 ml (5 fl oz) Greek yoghurt
½ teaspoon cornflour
4 large skinned chicken breasts
1½ teaspoons green cardamom pods
1 tablespoon sunflower oil
25 g (1 oz) butter
½ teaspoon ground turmeric
½ teaspoon ground cinnamon
½ teaspoon ground coriander
150 ml (5 fl oz) chicken stock (see page 231)
4 cm (1½ inches) fresh root ginger, peeled and
    finely grated
2 tablespoons lemon juice
150 ml (5 fl oz) double cream
75 g (3 oz) ground almonds
salt and freshly ground black pepper
coriander sprigs, to garnish

1 Mix the yoghurt with the cornflour and set to one side. Cut each of the chicken breasts into 3 or 4 chunky pieces. Lightly crush the cardamom pods so that the green husks split open, then remove all the little brownish-black seeds from inside. Grind these into a fine powder.

2 Heat the oil and butter in a flameproof casserole dish, add the chicken and cook over a medium heat until lightly browned all over. Add the turmeric, cinnamon, coriander and ground cardamom seeds and cook for a further minute.

3 Remove the pan from the heat and stir in the stock, grated ginger, lemon juice and the yoghurt mixture. Return the pan to the heat, bring to a simmer and leave to cook gently for 15 minutes until the chicken is tender. (You can now set the dish aside until later if you wish.)

4 Mix the cream with the ground almonds, stir into the chicken and simmer for 2–3 minutes. Season to taste and serve, garnished with sprigs of coriander.

chicken tikka masala

No wonder this is Britain's best-loved curry – it's a delicious combination of tender grilled chicken in a mildly spiced and creamy tomato sauce.

serves 4 • preparation 45 mins • cooking 15 mins

Energy 553 kcals • Protein 47.0 g • Carbohydrate 10.5 g • Fat 36.2 g
Saturated fat 13.3 g • Fibre 1.4 g • Salt 1.65 g • Added sugars none

700 g (1½ lb) skinned and boned chicken breasts
juice of 1 small lemon
7 tablespoons tikka masala curry paste
4 cm (1½ inches) fresh root ginger, peeled and grated
5 garlic cloves, crushed
4 tablespoons natural whole-milk yoghurt
1 large onion, finely chopped
3 tablespoons sunflower oil
2 tablespoons tomato purée
1 tablespoon ground almonds
150 ml (5 fl oz) double cream
½ x 20-g (¾-oz) packet coriander, chopped
salt and freshly ground black pepper
pilau rice (see page 232), to serve

1 Cut the chicken into 4-cm (1½-inch) chunks. Place ½ teaspoon of salt, 2 tablespoons of the lemon juice, 3 tablespoons of the curry paste, half the ginger, 3 crushed garlic cloves and the yoghurt in a bowl and mix together. Stir in the chicken and leave to marinate for 20 minutes.

2 For the sauce, fry the onion in 2 tablespoons of the oil for 5 minutes. Add the rest of the ginger and garlic and cook for another 2–3 minutes until soft. Add the rest of the curry paste and fry for 2 minutes. Add the tomato purée, the remaining lemon juice, the ground almonds, 300 ml (10 fl oz) boiling water and some salt and pepper. Simmer for 10 minutes.

3 Pre-heat the grill to high. Thread the pieces of chicken onto metal skewers and place on the lightly oiled rack of the grill pan. Brush with the remaining oil and cook for 10 minutes, turning them now and then, until lightly browned and cooked through. Meanwhile, add the cream to the sauce and simmer for a further 10 minutes.

4 Pour the sauce into a liquidizer and blend until smooth. Return it to the pan and push the pieces of chicken off the skewers into the sauce. Add the coriander and season to taste. Simmer for 2–3 minutes. Serve with the pilau rice.

lamb rogan josh

Curries always taste better when they have been made for a day or two. This one will keep quite happily in the fridge for two days, and also freezes very well. If you wish, replace the ground spices with 4 tablespoons of ready-made rogan josh curry paste.

serves 4 • preparation 20 mins • cooking 30–40 mins

Energy 548 kcals • Protein 40.5 g • Carbohydrate 11.0 g • Fat 38.3 g
Saturated fat 16.1 g • Fibre 1.4 g • Salt 0.75 g • Added sugars none

3 tablespoons sunflower oil
700 g (1½ lb) lamb neck fillet, cut into bite-sized pieces
6 cloves
1 small cinnamon stick
2 bay leaves
1 large onion, chopped
5 cm (2 inches) fresh root ginger, peeled and finely grated
4 garlic cloves, crushed
1 tablespoon ground coriander
2 teaspoons ground cumin
1½ teaspoons paprika, sweet or hot
½–1 teaspoon cayenne pepper
   (depending on how hot you like it)
¼ teaspoon ground cardamom
200 g (7 oz) Greek yoghurt
10 cardamom pods
1 × 200-g (7-oz) can chopped tomatoes
salt and freshly ground black pepper

1 Heat 2 tablespoons of the oil in a large pan, add half the lamb and fry until nicely browned all over. Transfer to a plate and fry the rest of the meat. Set aside.

2 Add another tablespoon of oil to the pan, then fry the cloves, cinnamon and bay leaves for a few seconds. Add the onion and fry for 6–7 minutes until nicely browned. Add the ginger and garlic and fry for 2 minutes, then add the ground spices and fry for another 1 minute. Add the yoghurt, a tablespoon at a time, frying for about 30 seconds between each addition.

3 Return the lamb to the pan and stir in the tomatoes, 150 ml (5 fl oz) boiling water, ½ teaspoon salt and some black pepper. Part cover and simmer gently for 30–40 minutes until the lamb is tender and the sauce has reduced and thickened and is clinging to the meat. Serve with either Bombay spiced potatoes (see page 220) or pilau rice (see page 232).

aubergine and potato dhansak

A dhansak is a mild curry thickened with red lentils.

serves 4 • preparation 15 mins • cooking 1 hr 20 mins

Energy 571 kcals • Protein 19.8 g • Carbohydrate 50.8 g • Fat 33.4 g
Saturated fat 16.6 g • Fibre 8.1 g • Salt 1.50 g • Added sugars none

4 tablespoons sunflower oil
2 teaspoons black mustard seeds
2 teaspoons cumin seeds
1 small cinnamon stick
8 cloves
2 large onions, finely chopped
4 garlic cloves, crushed
5 cm (2 inches) fresh root ginger, peeled and finely grated
1 × 400-g (14-oz) can chopped tomatoes
1 tablespoon ground cumin
1 tablespoon ground coriander
1 tablespoon ground turmeric
1 tablespoon sweet paprika
1 teaspoon chilli powder
1 × 200-ml (7-fl oz) carton coconut cream
600 ml (1 pint) water
100 g (4 oz) red lentils
225 g (8 oz) peeled potatoes, cut into bite-sized pieces
1 aubergine, about 275 g (10 oz), cut into bite-sized pieces
225 g (8 oz) cauliflower florets, broken into bite-sized pieces
1 × 225-g (8-oz) bag baby leaf spinach
leaves from 1 small pot of coriander, chopped
¾ teaspoon salt
chapatis or naan bread, to serve

1 Heat the oil in a pan, add the mustard seeds, cumin seeds, cinnamon and cloves and leave to sizzle for 30 seconds. Add the onion, garlic and ginger and cook for 10 minutes until soft.

2 Add the tomatoes, spices, coconut cream, water and lentils and simmer for 45 minutes until the lentils are quite soft and have disintegrated into the sauce.

3 Remove the cinnamon stick and add the potatoes, aubergine, salt and another 150 ml (5 fl oz) of water if necessary. Cover and simmer for 15 minutes. Add the cauliflower, cover and simmer for a further 15–20 minutes until the vegetables are soft but not breaking apart.

4 Stir in the spinach and cook for 2 minutes. Stir in the coriander and serve with chapatis or warm naan bread.

caribbean lamb and sweet potato curry with clap-hand roti

Roti are the Caribbean equivalent of Indian paratha, traditionally served wrapped around a mild, dry West Indian curry and eaten with your hands. Step 7 below reveals where the name 'clap-hand' comes from.

serves 4 • preparation 20 mins • cooking 1 hr 20 mins for the curry, 20 mins + 30 mins' resting for the roti

Energy 824 kcals • Protein 49.1 g • Carbohydrate 69.6 g • Fat 40.6 g
Saturated fat 15.0 g • Fibre 5.5 g • Salt 3.27 g • Added sugars none

3 tablespoons sunflower oil
800 g (1¾ lb) diced leg of lamb,
    trimmed of excess fat
1 onion, finely chopped
2 garlic cloves, crushed
¼ teaspoon ground cloves
½ teaspoon ground turmeric
½ teaspoon ground cinnamon
2 teaspoons mild curry powder
2 teaspoons garam masala
1 × 200-g (7-oz) can chopped tomatoes
juice of ½ lime
300 ml (10 fl oz) chicken stock (see page 231)
2 small sweet potatoes, about 350 g (12 oz),
    peeled and cut into small dice
½ teaspoon salt

FOR THE CLAP-HAND ROTI
225 g (8 oz) plain flour
1 teaspoon baking powder
1 teaspoon salt
40 g (1½ oz) chilled butter
vegetable oil or ghee, for cooking

1 Heat 1½ tablespoons of the oil in a large pan, add half the lamb and cook, turning, until nicely browned all over. Transfer to a plate and repeat with the rest of the oil and lamb.

2 Add the onion to the pan and cook until a rich golden brown. Return the meat to the pan with the garlic, spices, tomatoes and lime juice. Cover and cook gently for 5 minutes.

3 Add the stock, bring to the boil and simmer, part-covered, for 1 hour.

4 Meanwhile, make the roti. Sift the flour, baking powder and salt into the bowl of a food processor, add the butter and process until the mixture looks like fine breadcrumbs. Transfer to a bowl and stir in 5 tablespoons water to make a stiff, but soft dough. Cover and leave in a warm place for 30 minutes.

5 Uncover the curry, add ½ teaspoon salt and the sweet potatoes and cook uncovered for a further 15–20 minutes until they are tender and the sauce has reduced and thickened.

6 When ready, knead the dough on a lightly floured surface until smooth, then form into 4 balls, flatten slightly and roll out into 23-cm (9-inch) rounds about 5mm (¼ inch) thick. Brush with the oil or ghee, fold in half, then into quarters, roll back into balls, and then roll out again.

7 Heat a dry, heavy-based frying pan or flat griddle over a medium heat. Brush each one in turn with a little more oil or ghee, add a roti to the pan and cook for 3–4 minutes, turning frequently and brushing with oil each time you do. Remove from the pan, place in your palm and clap your hands together 3–4 times, taking care not to burn yourself. Wrap the roti in a tea towel and keep warm while you cook the rest.

8 To serve, spoon some of the curry down the centre of each roti, roll up and serve hot.

jamaican curried snapper with coconut and lime

This is a very simple curry, which you could make even more simple, if you wish, by using a ready-made mild curry powder instead of grinding your own spices as suggested below. However, the flavour won't be quite as subtle. This curry is also good made with monkfish, salmon or large raw prawns.

serves 4 • preparation 20 mins • cooking 10 mins

Energy 569 kcals • Protein 48.0 g • Carbohydrate 13.3 g • Fat 36.7 g
Saturated fat 20.2 g • Fibre 1.3 g • Salt 1.28 g • Added sugars 1.3 g

1 teaspoon coriander seeds
1 teaspoon cumin seeds
1 teaspoon black mustard seeds
1 teaspoon black peppercorns
½ teaspoon cayenne pepper
½ teaspoon ground turmeric
3 tablespoons sunflower oil
40 g (1½ oz) butter
1 large onion, finely chopped
2 garlic cloves, crushed
5 cm (2 inches) fresh root ginger, peeled and
   finely grated
1 teaspoon light soft brown sugar
1 × 200-g (7-oz) can chopped tomatoes
2 tablespoons lime juice or juice of 1 lime
1 × 400-ml (14-fl oz) can coconut milk
2 bay leaves
4 × 225-g (8-oz) pieces red snapper fillet
salt and freshly ground black pepper

TO SERVE
mango chutney
pilau rice (see page 232) or roti (see page 128)

1 Grind the whole spices into a powder and mix with the cayenne pepper and turmeric.

2 Heat the oil and butter in a large shallow pan, add the onion and fry gently until soft and just beginning to brown. Add the garlic, ginger, sugar and spices and cook for another 2–3 minutes. Add the tomatoes, lime juice, coconut milk, bay leaves and some salt and pepper and simmer gently for 10 minutes, stirring now and then, until slightly thickened.

3 Add the snapper fillets, skin-side down, and spoon some of the sauce over them. Simmer uncovered for 10 minutes, carefully turning the fish over halfway through. Remove the bay leaves and serve with pilau rice or roti and mango chutney.

southern-style sausage jambalaya

This is a delicious Cajun dish of rice flavoured with spicy sausages, peppers and peeled prawns. Perfect fork-food for a night in front of the telly.

serves 4 • preparation 15 mins • cooking 25 mins

Energy 641 kcals • Protein 31.8 g • Carbohydrate 64.2 g • Fat 30.3 g
Saturated fat 9.9 g • Fibre 3.0 g • Salt 5.01 g • Added sugars 1.5 g

2 tablespoons sunflower oil

100 g (4 oz) chorizo sausage, thickly sliced

1 × 225-g (8-oz) smoked pork sausage ring, thickly sliced

4 garlic cloves, crushed

1 medium onion, chopped

1 red pepper, seeded and cut into chunky strips

1 green pepper, seeded and cut into chunky strips

2 celery sticks, sliced

1 teaspoon chilli powder

1 teaspoon hot paprika

225 g (8 oz) long-grain rice

leaves from 2 sprigs of fresh thyme

2 bay leaves

400 ml (14 fl oz) passata

300 ml (10 fl oz) chicken stock (see page 231)

225 g (8 oz) large cooked, peeled prawns

leaves from 1 × 20-g (³/₄-oz) packet parsley, chopped

4 spring onions, trimmed and thinly sliced

salt and cayenne pepper

1 Heat the oil in a large, deep frying pan. Fry the chorizo and smoked pork sausage slices on both sides until golden. Lift out and set aside.

2 Add the garlic, onion, red pepper, green pepper and celery and fry for 5 minutes until they are all lightly browned.

3 Add the chilli powder and paprika and cook for 1 minute. Stir in the browned sausages, rice, thyme, bay leaves, passata, chicken stock, 1 teaspoon salt and some cayenne pepper. Bring to the boil, cover and simmer gently for 20 minutes.

4 Uncover the pan and sprinkle over the prawns. Re-cover and cook for another 4–5 minutes. Uncover and fork the prawns and the chopped parsley into the rice. Scatter over the spring onions and serve.

how to make thai curries

Thai curries are very quick and easy to prepare, especially now that many supermarkets sell authentic ready-made curry pastes flavoured with chilli, ginger, garlic, lemongrass and spices. Other traditional flavourings include coconut milk, kaffir lime leaves, Thai fish sauce, lime juice and sugar.

thai red vegetable curry with basil

serves 4 • preparation 5 mins • cooking approx. 16 mins

Energy 308 kcals • Protein 5.2 g • Carbohydrate 17.0 g • Fat 24.9 g
Saturated fat 14.16 g • Fibre 2.8 g • Salt 2.29 g • Added sugars 2.7 g

350 g (12 oz) prepared squash, such as butternut or kabocha
100 g (4 oz) fine green beans, trimmed and halved
100 g (4 oz) baby sweetcorn, halved lengthways
1 small red pepper, stalk and seeds removed, cut into strips

FOR THE CURRY BASE
2 tablespoons sunflower oil
5 cm (2 inches) fresh root ginger, peeled and cut into
   thin matchsticks
3 garlic cloves, thinly sliced
2 heaped tablespoons good-quality Thai red curry paste
1 × 400-g (14-oz) can coconut milk
2 teaspoons light soft brown sugar
juice of 1 lime

2 tablespoons light soy sauce
   (or Thai fish sauce for non-vegetarians)
150 ml (5 fl oz) vegetable stock (see page 231)
   (or chicken stock for non-vegetarians, see page 231)
leaves from 1 small pot of basil

1 For the curry base, heat the oil in a large pan. Add the ginger and garlic and cook gently for 1 minute without browning. Add the curry paste and cook, stirring, for 2 minutes. Add the coconut milk, sugar, lime juice, soy sauce and stock and simmer for 2 minutes.

2 Stir in the squash and beans and simmer for 6 minutes. Add the sweetcorn and red pepper and simmer for a further 5–6 minutes until all the vegetables are tender. Stir in the basil leaves and serve with some steamed rice.

VARIATIONS

THAI YELLOW CHICKEN CURRY

Replace the red curry paste with yellow. Add 350 g (12 oz) chicken breast-fillet strips to the base and cook for 4 minutes, followed by 100 g (4 oz) sugar snap peas or mangetout and 1 drained 200-g (7-oz) can bamboo shoots and cook for a further 4 minutes. Stir in the basil.

THAI GREEN PRAWN CURRY

Replace the red curry paste with green. Add 175 g (6 oz) halved baby new potatoes and cook for 15 minutes until tender. Add 350 g (12 oz) peeled raw prawns and 100 g (4 oz) halved cherry tomatoes and cook for a further 2–3 minutes. Stir in the basil.

mexican beef fajitas

This is great for a Friday-night supper. You can just put everything into the centre of the table and let everyone help themselves.

serves 4 • preparation 15 mins • cooking approx. 12 mins

Energy 712 kcals • Protein 39.1 g • Carbohydrate 78.1 g • Fat 29.1 g
Saturated fat 8.7 g • Fibre 7.1 g • Salt 3.73 g • Added sugars 2.3 g

450 g (1 lb) rump, sirloin or fillet steak
1 red pepper
1 green pepper
1 small yellow pepper
2 large onions
150 ml (5 fl oz) soured cream
1 cos lettuce heart, finely shredded
3 tablespoons sunflower oil
8–12 soft flour tortillas
salt and cayenne pepper

FOR THE SPICY TOMATO SALSA
1 medium-hot green chilli, deseeded and finely chopped
1 small red onion, very finely chopped
1 × 200-g (7-oz) can chopped tomatoes
juice of 1 lime
1 × 20-g (³⁄₄-oz) packet fresh coriander, chopped

1 Cut the steak into long thin strips. Season well with salt and some cayenne pepper and set to one side. Deseed and thickly slice the red, green and yellow peppers. Peel and thickly slice the onions. Pre-heat the grill to high.

2 Mix all the salsa ingredients together with a little salt to taste. Transfer to a serving bowl. Spoon the soured cream into another bowl and put the shredded lettuce into a small salad bowl.

3 Heat half the oil in a large frying pan. Add the onions, peppers and some seasoning and stir-fry over a high heat for 5 minutes until soft and slightly browned. Tip onto a plate and set aside.

4 Add half the remaining oil to the pan and, when really hot, add half the steak and stir-fry for 3–4 minutes until well browned. Set aside with the peppers while you cook the remainder.

5 Return everything to the pan and toss together briefly over a high heat. Warm the tortillas under the grill for 10 seconds. Wrap in a napkin and take to the table with the pan of steak and peppers and the bowls of salsa, lettuce and soured cream.

6 To eat, lay a tortilla on a plate and spoon some of the beef and peppers down the centre. Spoon a little spicy tomato salsa and soured cream on top, sprinkle with lettuce, then roll up tightly and eat with your hands.

home-made indian take-away
Hot and spicy food always seems to fit the bill in our house on a Friday night. Not only is it quick and easy to prepare, but it also suits an informal style of dining which I particularly like after a heavy week at work.

menu

Coconut-and-cumin-spiced prawns
(see page 122)

Chicken tikka masala
(see page 124)

Lamb rogan josh
(see page 127)

Aubergine and potato dhansak
(see page 127)

Pilau rice
(see page 232)

Plus whatever other accompaniments you fancy
(see opposite)

Mango kulfi
(see page 138)

TIPS

- Indian food is nicest if everything is served at the same time, in serving dishes from which people can help themselves. Cast-iron or stainless-steel balti-style dishes are ideal and give the meal an authentic Indian feel.
- I think beer is nicest with curries, but for a non-alcoholic drink, salted lassi (see opposite) is great as it helps to cool down the heat of the food.

ready-made accompaniments for your curry menu

STARTERS

Onion bhajis – onion and chick-pea flour fritters. Serve with mango chutney and raita.

Pakoras – little mixed-vegetable fritters dipped in a chick-pea flour batter. Re-heat and serve as a starter with raita.

Poppadoms – available plain or spicy, and great served with raita, mango chutney and a spicy tomato salsa.

Samosas – small, triangular-shaped parcels stuffed with spiced meat or vegetables. Heat and serve with raita and mango chutney.

SIDE DISHES

Bombay aloo – a mildly spiced potato dish.

Pilau rice – basmati rice cooked with whole mild spices, such as cardamom, cumin and cinnamon. All you need to do is heat it.

Saag bhaji – a mildly spicy spinach dish.

Tarka dhal – a mildly spiced dish made with red lentils.

BREADS

Chapati – a very thin, disc-shaped bread made with wholemeal flour and cooked on a flat griddle.

Naan – a large, flat, tear-shaped white bread, sometimes flavoured with garlic or chillies, and sometimes stuffed with dried fruit and coconut (peshwari naan), spiced minced beef or lamb (keema naan), or spiced vegetables.

Paratha – a thin, disc-shaped wholemeal bread, slightly richer than chapati, made with butter and cooked on a flat griddle.

Poori – a thin, round bread, which is shallow-fried and puffs up to look like a flying saucer.

RELISHES & CHUTNEYS

Lime pickle – a sour, salty and very spicy pickle,

Mango chutney – a sweet, spicy chutney, which can be mild or quite spicy,

Raita – a mint-flavoured yoghurt.

DRINKS

Beer – try Cobra or Kingfisher beers. Serve them icy cold.

Lassi – a cold drink made from natural yoghurt. Available salty or sweet (flavoured with mango).

time plan

The day before
Make the chicken tikka masala.
Make the rogan josh.
Make the mango kulfi and freeze.
Chill the beers.

In advance on the day
Make the aubergine and potato dhansak.
Prepare the ingredients for the coconut-and-cumin-spiced prawns.
Thaw the prawns, if necessary, on lots of kitchen paper.

time plan for an 8 p.m. supper

7.45 p.m.   Put the curries into separate pans, cover and leave to warm through over a low heat. Bring a kettle full of water to the boil and lightly fry the spices for the pilau rice in a little oil. Turn off the heat and set aside.

7.50 p.m.   Wash the basmati rice and leave it to soak for 7 minutes. Cook the cumin-spiced prawns. Warm the chapatis just before serving.

8 p.m.   Put the rice on to cook as soon as you sit down to eat your starter.

mango kulfi

Kulfi is an Indian-style ice-cream traditionally made with long-simmered milk, which takes on a lovely rich and creamy consistency. Although very simple, it takes quite a long time to make, so I have cheated by making it with evaporated milk.

serves 6 • preparation 5 mins + churning or freezing • cooking 5 mins

Energy 353 kcals • Protein 9.4 g • Carbohydrate 49.6 g • Fat 14.3 g
Saturated fat 8.9 g • Fibre 1.3 g • Salt 0.50 g • Added sugars 30.6 g

    1 tablespoon cornflour
    600 ml (1 pint) evaporated milk
    175 g (6 oz) caster sugar
    1 ripe mango
    a pinch of ground cardamom
    150 ml (5 fl oz) single cream

    TO SERVE
    1 ripe but firm mango
    4 ripe and wrinkly passion-fruit

1 Mix the cornflour with 1 tablespoon of cold water and set to one side. Quickly bring the evaporated milk to the boil in a non-stick saucepan. Add the cornflour mixture and simmer for 2 minutes until it is the consistency of pouring custard. Stir in the sugar until dissolved, then transfer to a bowl and leave to go cold.

2 Peel the mango and slice the flesh away from the stone. Place in a food processor and blend to a smooth purée.

3 Stir the mango purée, ground cardamom and cream into the custard, then press the mixture through a sieve into a clean bowl. Now you can either churn the mixture in an ice-cream maker or pour it into a plastic container, cover with a lid and freeze until firm but not rock solid – about 2 hours. If using the latter method, transfer the ice-cream to a food processor and blend until smooth, then freeze for another hour. Repeat this process twice more, then spoon it into six tall, freezer-proof moulds – clean, small yoghurt pots are ideal. Freeze for at least 8 hours, or until firm.

4 To serve, peel the second mango and slice the flesh away from the stone. Halve the passion-fruit and scoop out the pulp with a teaspoon. Cut the mango flesh into small, neat pieces and mix with the passion-fruit pulp.

5 Remove the kulfi containers from the freezer, leave them at room temperature for 5 minutes, then turn them out onto serving plates. Spoon some of the mango and passion-fruit salsa alongside and serve straight away.

✪ fresh pineapple with lime and mint sugar

To check if a pineapple is ripe, give one of the leaves in the centre a very gentle tug. It should come away really easily.

serves 4 • preparation 7–8 mins • cooking none

Energy 138 kcals • Protein 1.0 g • Carbohydrate 34.7 g • Fat 0.4 g
Saturated fat none • Fibre 2.6 g • Salt 0.01 g • Added sugars 13.1 g

    1 large ripe pineapple
    50 g (2 oz) caster sugar
    finely grated zest of 1 lime
    the leaves from 1 × 20-g (³/₄-oz) packet of mint

1 Slice the top and bottom off the pineapple, sit it upright on a board and slice away the skin and all the little brown 'eyes'. Cut the fruit lengthways into quarters, then cut away about 2.5 cm (1 inch) of the sharper edges of each wedge to remove the core, which can be quite woody.

2 Now cut the pineapple across each wedge into thin slices and arrange on a serving plate. Cover with cling film and chill in the fridge until needed.

3 Shortly before serving, put the caster sugar, lime zest and mint leaves into a food processor and blitz for about 30 seconds until the mint is finely chopped and you have a bright green mixture. Sprinkle over the pineapple and serve.

FAMILY FAVOURITES

cheesy haddock and prawn pie

Use small, cooked, peeled prawns for this pie. I think they are better for this dish than the larger tiger prawns. Add a few chopped hard-boiled eggs to the sauce if you wish.

serves 4 • preparation 40 mins • cooking 35–40 mins

Energy 1096 kcals • Protein 59.2 g • Carbohydrate 72.3 g • Fat 65.4 g
Saturated fat 40.2 g • Fibre 4.6 g • Salt 4.32 g • Added sugars none

> 600 ml (1 pint) full-cream milk
> 300 ml (10 fl oz) double cream
> 450 g (1 lb) haddock fillet
> 225 g (8 oz) undyed smoked haddock fillet
> 175 g (6 oz) cooked peeled prawns
> 100 g (4 oz) butter
> 40 g (1½ oz) plain flour
> leaves from 1 x 20-g (¾-oz) packet curly parsley, chopped
> 1.25 kg (2½ lb) peeled floury potatoes, such as Maris
>   Piper, cut into chunks
> 50 g (2 oz) Cheddar cheese, coarsely grated
> salt and freshly ground black pepper

1 Put 450 ml (15 fl oz) of the milk into a large pan, add the cream and bring to the boil. Add the haddock and smoked haddock and simmer for 5–6 minutes until the fish is just cooked through. Transfer the fish to a plate to cool slightly, and strain the liquid into a jug.

2 When the fish is cool, break it into large flakes, discarding the skin and any bones. Put into a 1.75-litre (3-pint) shallow ovenproof dish and scatter over the prawns.

3 Melt half the butter in a pan, add the flour and cook, stirring, for 1 minute. Off the heat, gradually stir in the reserved cooking liquid, return to the heat and slowly bring back to the boil, stirring. Simmer for 5 minutes, season, stir in the parsley and pour over the fish. Leave to go cold.

4 Put the potatoes into a pan of cold salted water, bring to the boil and simmer for 20 minutes until tender. Drain well, pass through a potato ricer, or mash until smooth. Stir in the remaining butter, the cheese and enough milk to make a spreadable mash. Season to taste with salt and pepper.

5 Pre-heat the oven to 200°C/400°F/Gas Mark 6. Spoon the mash over the top of the pie and spread it out. Rough up the surface with a fork and bake for 35–40 minutes until golden on top and bubbling underneath.

fishcakes with lemon crème fraîche

Fishcakes are always a favourite, and with the addition of the lemon crème fraîche these are even more yummy.

serves 4 • preparation 50 mins • cooking 7–8 mins

Energy 799 kcals • Protein 44.4 g • Carbohydrate 51.0 g • Fat 47.6 g
Saturated fat 17.0 g • Fibre 3.2 g • Salt 0.99 g • Added sugars none

> 750 g (1½ lb) floury potatoes, peeled and cut into chunks
> 700 g (1½ lb) skinned salmon fillet
> 15 g (½ oz) butter
> 2 tablespoons double cream
> the leaves from ½ x 20-g (¾-oz) packet parsley, chopped
> 15 g (½ oz) seasoned plain flour
> 1 egg, beaten
> 75 g (3 oz) fresh white breadcrumbs
> sunflower oil, for frying
> salt and freshly ground black pepper
>
> FOR THE LEMON CRÈME FRAÎCHE
> 4–5 heaped tablespoons crème fraîche
> 2 teaspoons lemon juice
> finely grated zest of ½ lemon
> 3 tablespoons mixed chopped parsley, chives and tarragon

1 Put the potatoes into a pan of cold salted water, bring to the boil and cook for 20 minutes. Meanwhile, bring some water to the boil in another pan. Add the salmon and simmer for 6 minutes, or until just cooked. Transfer to a plate and, when cool enough to handle, break it into flakes, removing any bones.

2 Drain the potatoes well and press through a potato ricer or mash until smooth. Beat in the butter, cream, parsley and some salt and pepper, followed by the flaked salmon. Divide the mixture into 8 and shape into round patties about 4 cm (1½ inches) thick. Cover and chill for 20 minutes.

3 For the lemon crème fraîche, simply mix all the ingredients together with a little salt and pepper to taste.

4 You can now either deep-fry or shallow-fry the fishcakes. Coat them in the seasoned flour, then the beaten egg and finally the breadcrumbs, pressing them on well. If deep-frying, heat some oil to 180°C/350°F; if shallow-frying, heat about 1 cm (½ inch) oil in a deep frying pan. Fry the fishcakes 4 at a time for 7–8 minutes, turning them over halfway through, until golden. Lift them out onto kitchen paper and keep hot while you cook the rest. Serve with the lemon crème fraîche.

spinach and ricotta pancakes

The beauty of this dish is that it can be made well in advance and takes only 30 minutes to cook. If you really want to cheat, you can buy ready-made sauces as well as pancakes – two tubs of tomato and two tubs of creamy three-cheese sauce for the top.

serves 6 • preparation 40 mins • cooking 30–35 mins

Energy 721 kcals • Protein 24.1 g • Carbohydrate 45.4 g • Fat 50.4 g
Saturated fat 21.5 g • Fibre 124.3 g • Salt 1.92 g • Added sugars none

12 ready-made savoury pancakes or crêpes

FOR THE TOMATO SAUCE
2 tablespoons olive oil
1 medium onion, finely chopped
1 fat garlic clove, crushed
1 × 400-g (14-oz) can chopped tomatoes
1 × 200-g (7-oz) can chopped tomatoes
leaves from 2 sprigs of thyme
2 bay leaves

FOR THE SPINACH AND RICOTTA FILLING
2 tablespoons olive oil
1 garlic clove, crushed
450 g (1 lb) fresh spinach, washed and large stalks removed
250 g (9 oz) ricotta cheese
25 g (1 oz) Parmesan cheese, finely grated
a pinch of freshly grated nutmeg

FOR THE PARMESAN CHEESE SAUCE
50 g (2 oz) butter
35 g (1¼ oz) plain flour
600 ml (1 pint) milk
50 ml (2 fl oz) double cream
50 g (2 oz) Parmesan cheese, finely grated
salt and freshly ground white pepper

1 For the tomato sauce, heat the oil in a medium-sized pan, add the onion and fry gently for 7–8 minutes until soft but not browned. Add the garlic, fry for a few seconds, then add all the chopped tomatoes, the thyme and bay leaves and simmer for 20–25 minutes, stirring now and then, until well reduced and thickened. Discard the bay leaves.

2 Meanwhile, for the spinach and ricotta filling, heat the oil in a large saucepan. Add the garlic and spinach and stir-fry over a high heat until it has wilted down into the bottom of the pan. Tip into a colander and press out the excess liquid. Coarsely chop, transfer to a mixing bowl and leave to cool. Mix in the ricotta, Parmesan, the nutmeg and some seasoning to taste.

3 For the Parmesan cheese sauce, melt the butter in a medium–sized saucepan, add the flour and cook gently for 30 seconds. Pull the pan off the heat and gradually stir in the milk. Return to the heat and slowly bring to the boil, stirring all the time. Stir in the cream, most of the Parmesan cheese and some seasoning to taste.

4 Pre-heat the oven to 200°C/400°F/Gas Mark 6. Spoon 1 heaped tablespoon of the filling in a short line across the centre of each pancake. Fold the sides of the pancakes over the ends of the filling, and then roll each one up into a neat parcel.

5 Spread the tomato sauce over the base of a large, shallow ovenproof dish. Arrange the pancakes in the dish, seam-side down and pour over the Parmesan cheese sauce. Sprinkle over the remaining Parmesan cheese and bake in the oven for 30–35 minutes until bubbling and golden brown.

root vegetable and nut crumble

This is a real winter-warmer dish that even non-vegetarians will love as it's satisfying too.

serves 6 • preparation 25 mins • cooking 30 mins

Energy 552 kcals • Protein 17.0 g • Carbohydrate 44.0 g • Fat 36.0 g
Saturated fat 17.0 g • Fibre 9.3 g • Salt 1.3 g • Added sugars none

175 g (6 oz) peeled potatoes
175 g (6 oz) peeled carrots
175 g (6 oz) peeled parsnips
175 g (6 oz) peeled and seeded butternut squash
175 g (6 oz) peeled swede
25 g (1 oz) butter
2 leeks, cleaned and sliced
50 g (2 oz) wholemeal flour
300 ml (10 fl oz) vegetable stock (see page 231)
150 ml (5 fl oz) milk
1 × 200-g (7-oz) can chopped tomatoes
the leaves from ½ x 20-g (¾-oz) packet parsley, chopped
salt and freshly ground black pepper

FOR THE CRUMBLE TOPPING
175 g (6 oz) plain wholemeal flour
110 g (4 oz) butter
100 g (4 oz) Cheddar cheese, coarsely grated
75 g (3 oz) mixed shelled nuts (Brazils, almonds and
   cashews), coarsely chopped
1 tablespoon sunflower seeds
1 tablespoon sesame seeds

1 Cut the root vegetables into 2.5-cm (1-inch) chunks. Melt the butter in a large saucepan, add the prepared root vegetables, cover and cook gently for 10 minutes. Add the leeks and cook for a further 3–4 minutes until tender. Stir in the flour and cook for a further minute. Gradually stir in the stock, milk and chopped tomatoes. Cover and simmer for 10 minutes until the vegetables are just tender.

2 Pre-heat the oven to 190°C/375°F/Gas Mark 5. For the topping, work the butter into the flour, by hand or in a food processor, until it looks like coarse breadcrumbs. Stir in the grated cheese, nuts and seeds.

3 Stir the parsley into the filling and season to taste. Spoon it into a 2.25-litre (4-pint) shallow ovenproof dish and spoon over the topping. Bake in the oven for 30 minutes or until golden and bubbling.

italian meatballs in tomato and basil sauce

The addition of smoked bacon to these meatballs makes them even more exciting to the palate.

serves 4 • preparation 20–25 mins • cooking 20 mins

Energy 665 kcals • Protein 57.2 g • Carbohydrate 29.5 g • Fat 36.1 g
Saturated fat 13.2 g • Fibre 2.8 g • Salt 3.87 g • Added sugars 1.3 g

3–4 tablespoons olive oil
1 medium onion, finely chopped
1 fat garlic clove, crushed
1½ teaspoons dried oregano
225 g (8 oz) rindless smoked bacon
750 g (1½ lb) lean minced beef
finely grated zest of ½ lemon
75 g (3 oz) fresh white breadcrumbs
the leaves from ½ x 20-g (¾-oz) packet parsley, chopped
1 medium egg, beaten

FOR THE TOMATO SAUCE
olive oil, if necessary
a small knob of butter
1 medium onion, finely chopped
1 fat garlic clove, crushed
1 red pepper, deseeded and finely chopped
1 × 200-g (7-oz) can chopped tomatoes
350 g (12 oz) passata
leaves from 1 small pot of basil, finely shredded
salt and freshly ground black pepper

1 For the meatballs, heat 1 tablespoon of the olive oil in a small frying pan, add the onion, garlic and oregano and cook over a medium heat for 5–6 minutes until soft. Leave to cool slightly.

2 Put the bacon into a food processor and finely chop using the pulse button. Transfer to a large bowl and add the minced beef, lemon zest, breadcrumbs, parsley and cooked onion mixture and mix together well with your hands. Add the egg, ½ teaspoon salt and plenty of black pepper and mix again. Shape the mixture into walnut-sized balls using slightly wet hands.

3 Heat another 1½–2 tablespoons of oil in a large frying pan. Add the meatballs, a few at a time, and brown all over, then transfer to a flameproof casserole.

4 To make the tomato sauce, add a little more olive oil if necessary to the frying pan and, when hot, add the butter, onion, garlic and red pepper and fry gently until softened. Add the chopped tomatoes, passata, ½ teaspoon salt and some black pepper.

5 Pour the sauce over the meatballs, partly cover and simmer gently for 20 minutes, stirring gently now and then so as not to break up the meatballs. Stir in the basil and serve with some egg tagliatelle pasta or mashed potatoes.

chicken parmigiana with parsley butter tagliatelle

This classic Italian dish can easily be prepared in advance and cooked just before serving.

serves 4 • preparation 20–25 mins • cooking 30 mins

Energy 721 kcals • Protein 61.3 g • Carbohydrate 53.7 g • Fat 30.5 g
Saturated fat 15.8 g • Fibre 2.8 g • Salt 1.92 g • Added sugars none

1 tablespoon olive oil
1 garlic clove, crushed
1 × 400-g (14-oz) can chopped tomatoes
1 tablespoon tomato purée
leaves from 1 × 20-g (¾-oz) packet basil, chopped
50 g (2 oz) finely grated Parmesan cheese
25 g (1 oz) seasoned plain flour
1 egg, beaten
25 g (1 oz) butter
4 skinned, boned chicken breasts
150 g (5 oz) mozzarella cheese, sliced
salt and freshly ground black pepper
fresh basil sprigs, to garnish

FOR THE PARSLEY BUTTER TAGLIATELLE
350 g (12 oz) egg tagliatelle pasta
25 g (1 oz) butter
1 small garlic clove, crushed
leaves from 1 × 20-g (¾-oz) packet flat-leaf parsley,
   chopped

1 Pre-heat the oven to 200°C/400°F/Gas Mark 6. Put the olive oil and garlic into a medium-sized pan and, as soon as it starts to sizzle, add the tomatoes and tomato purée. Simmer for about 10 minutes until thickened. Stir in the basil and some seasoning to taste. Set to one side.

2 Mix half the grated Parmesan cheese into the seasoned flour and tip it into a shallow dish. Tip the egg into another shallow dish.

3 Melt the butter in a medium-sized frying pan. Dip the chicken breasts into the beaten egg, then the flour and cheese mixture, add them to the pan and cook over a medium-high heat for about 3 minutes on each side until lightly golden. Transfer them to a small, shallow ovenproof dish and pour over the tomato sauce.

4 Lay two slices of the mozzarella cheese on top of each chicken breast, sprinkle over the rest of the Parmesan, cover the dish loosely with foil and bake for 15 minutes. Uncover and cook for a further 15 minutes or until the cheese is lightly browned.

5 Meanwhile, bring a large pan of salted water to the boil. Add the tagliatelle and cook for 8–9 minutes. Mix the butter with the garlic, chopped parsley and some seasoning to taste. Drain the pasta, return to the pan with the parsley butter and toss together well. Remove the chicken from the oven and serve with the tagliatelle, garnished with the fresh basil sprigs.

how to make quiches

Once you have mastered the art of the basic quiche, the possibilities for the fillings are endless.

smoked bacon, leek and gruyère quiche

serves 6 • preparation 25–30 mins • cooking 30 mins

Energy 761 kcals • Protein 19.2 g • Carbohydrate 32.3 g • Fat 62.6 g
Saturated fat 34.5 g • Fibre 2.4 g • Salt 2.62 g • Added sugars none

FOR THE PASTRY CASE
1 x quantity basic shortcrust pastry (see page 236)

FOR THE BASIC QUICHE MIXTURE
300 ml (10 fl oz) double cream
3 large eggs
salt and freshly ground black pepper

FOR THE FILLING
1 teaspoon sunflower oil
6 rindless smoked back bacon rashers, cut into thin strips
25 g (1 oz) butter
2 large leeks, about 350 g (12 oz), cleaned and thinly sliced
100 g (4 oz) Gruyère cheese, finely grated
a little freshly grated nutmeg

1 Roll out the pastry thinly on a lightly floured surface and use to line a lightly greased loose-bottomed flan tin 25 cm (10 inches) wide and 4 cm (1½ inches) deep (see page 164). Chill for 20 minutes. Pre-heat the oven to 200°C/400°F/Gas Mark 6. Line the pastry case with a crumpled sheet of greaseproof paper and cover the base with a layer of baking beans. Bake for 15 minutes, then remove the paper and beans and return the case to the oven for 5 minutes until the pastry is crisp. Remove once more and brush the inside of the case with a little of the beaten egg intended for the basic quiche mixture. Bake for a further 2 minutes. Remove and lower the oven temperature to 190°C/375°F/Gas Mark 5.

2 For the basic quiche mixture, beat the cream, eggs and some seasoning together in a jug.

3 For the filling, heat the oil in a frying pan, add the bacon and fry until golden. Tip onto a sheet of kitchen paper and leave to drain. Melt the butter in a pan, add the leeks and a little seasoning. Cook gently for 5 minutes until soft. Spoon them into the pastry case and scatter with the bacon. Beat the cheese and nutmeg into the basic quiche mixture, pour into the pastry case and bake for 30 minutes, or until set and golden.

VARIATION

ROASTED VEGETABLE AND GOATS' CHEESE QUICHE
Mix together 100 g (4 oz) diced aubergine, 2 sliced small courgettes, 1 seeded and diced red pepper, 1 red onion and 1 tomato, each cut into wedges, 1 chopped garlic clove, 2 tablespoons olive oil, ½ teaspoon salt and some pepper. Place in a roasting tin and roast at 220°C/425°F/Gas Mark 7 for 30 minutes. Spread over the base of the pastry case and scatter over 100 g (4 oz) crumbled goats' cheese and 25 g (1 oz) chopped semi-sun-dried tomatoes. Beat the eggs and cream with 25 g (1 oz) grated Parmesan cheese, 20 g (¾ oz) chopped basil and some seasoning. Pour over the filling and bake.

succulent steak and ale pie

If you are going to make a lot of home-made pies like this, it's worth investing in a little china pie funnel. They help to keep the pastry off the surface of the filling so that it can puff up and go nice and crispy and it also lets out the excess steam.

serves 6 • preparation 2 hrs + 30 mins' chilling • cooking 30–35 mins

Energy 692 kcals • Protein 42.3 g • Carbohydrate 43.7 g • Fat 38.9 g
Saturated fat 14.1 g • Fibre 1.3 g • Salt 1.63 g • Added sugars 2.9 g

25 g (1 oz) plain flour
900 g (2 lb) diced stewing or braising steak
5 tablespoons sunflower oil
25 g (1 oz) butter
225 g (8 oz) small chestnut mushrooms, wiped clean
2 onions, halved and thinly sliced
1 tablespoon sugar
4 garlic cloves, crushed
300 ml (10 fl oz) beef stock (see page 231)
300 ml (10 fl oz) brown ale
1 teaspoon tomato purée
leaves from 3 sprigs of thyme
3 tablespoons Worcestershire sauce
1 × 500-g (1 lb 2-oz) packet chilled puff pastry
1 egg, beaten, to glaze
salt and freshly ground black pepper

1 Season the flour with salt and pepper, put into a bowl with the beef and toss together well until all the pieces are coated.

2 Heat 3 tablespoons of the oil in a large, flameproof casserole, add half the beef and fry over a high heat until browned. Transfer to a plate and repeat with the rest of the beef. Set aside.

3 Add half the butter and the mushrooms to the pan and fry briskly over a high heat for 2 minutes. Set aside with the beef. Add the rest of the oil and butter, the onions and sugar to the casserole and cook over a medium-high heat for 20 minutes, stirring frequently, until nicely browned. Add the garlic and cook for 1 minute.

4 Stir any remaining seasoned flour into the onions, followed by the beef stock, brown ale, tomato purée, thyme leaves and Worcestershire sauce and bring to the boil, stirring. Return the beef and mushrooms to the pan, season with salt and pepper, part-cover and simmer for $1\frac{1}{2}$ hours until the beef is just tender and the sauce has reduced and thickened. Leave to go cold.

5 Roll out the pastry on a lightly floured surface and then put a 1.75-litre (3-pint) pie dish upside-down in the centre of it. Cut out a lid which is about 2.5 cm (1 inch) larger than the dish and then cut a small hole in the centre to let out the steam during cooking. Cut off a thin strip from around the edge, brush it with beaten egg and press it onto the rim of the dish.

6 Spoon the filling into the pie dish. Brush the strip of pastry with a little more of the beaten egg and lay the pastry over the filling. Press the edge of the pastry firmly onto the top and underside of the rim to make a really good seal, trim away the excess pastry and crimp the edge to give it an attractive finish. Chill for 30 minutes.

7 Pre-heat the oven to 200°C/400°F/Gas Mark 6. Brush the top of the pie with beaten egg and bake for 30–35 minutes until the top is golden and the filling is bubbling hot.

pork chops baked on tomato and rosemary potatoes

These chops are cooked on boulangère-style potatoes – thinly sliced potatoes, onions and tomatoes cooked slowly with stock and butter until they are meltingly tender.

serves 4 • preparation 15 mins • cooking approx. 1 hr

Energy 650 kcals • Protein 51.9 g • Carbohydrate 45.0 g • Fat 30.4 g
Saturated fat 13.2 g • Fibre 4.5 g • Salt 1.06 g • Added sugars none

> 4 thick, boneless pork chops or steaks, the rind
>   and some of the fat removed
> 1 tablespoon sunflower oil
>
> FOR THE POTATOES
> 300 ml (10 fl oz) chicken stock (see page 231)
> 50 g (2 oz) butter
> 2 garlic cloves, crushed
> the leaves from 1 large sprig of rosemary
> 900 g (2 lb) floury potatoes, such as Maris Piper, peeled
>   and thinly sliced
> 1 onion, halved and very thinly sliced
> 4 vine tomatoes, skinned and thinly sliced
> salt and freshly ground black pepper

1 Pre-heat the oven to 200°C/400°F/Gas Mark 6. Season the chops on both sides with some salt and pepper. Heat the oil in a large frying pan, add the chops and fry over a medium heat for 1–2 minutes on each side until nicely browned. Set aside on a plate.

2 For the potatoes, put the chicken stock, butter, garlic, rosemary leaves, 1/2 teaspoon of salt and some freshly ground black pepper into a pan and bring up to a gentle simmer. Add the potatoes and onion and cook gently for 5–10 minutes, or until just tender when pierced with the tip of a knife but not falling apart. This will depend on your potatoes.

3 Spoon half the potatoes and onions over the base of a lightly buttered 2.25-litre (4-pint) shallow ovenproof dish and cover with the sliced tomatoes and a little seasoning. Spoon the remaining potatoes and onions on top, season lightly and bake in the oven for 40 minutes.

4 Overlap the pork chops on top of the potatoes and return them to the oven for a further 20–25 minutes, until the potatoes are tender and the chops are cooked through.

lamb chops on minted pea purée with crispy pancetta

Take care not to overcook the peas to ensure that the pea purée retains a brilliant green colour.

serves 4 • preparation 2–3 mins • cooking 10 mins

Energy 683 kcals • Protein 51.7 g • Carbohydrate 21.4 g • Fat 43.9 g
Saturated fat 20.6 g • Fibre 11.5 g • Salt 1.66 g • Added sugars none

> 8 lamb chops or 4 × 6–8 oz (175–225 g) leg of lamb steaks
> 2 tablespoons olive oil
> 1 × 100-g (4-oz) packet thinly sliced smoked pancetta
>   or thin-cut rindless streaky bacon
> salt and freshly ground black pepper
>
> FOR THE MINTED PEA PURÉE
> 1 × 900-g (2-lb) bag frozen peas
> the leaves from 1/2 × 20-g (3/4-oz) packet mint, chopped
> 50 g (2 oz) butter
> 2 tablespoons double cream (optional)

1 Bring a large pan of salted water to the boil. Brush the chops on both sides with oil and season with the pepper and a little salt. Heat a ridged cast-iron griddle or a heavy-based frying pan over a high heat until smoking hot. Reduce the heat to medium-high, add the chops or steaks and cook for 3–4 minutes on each side until golden brown on the outside but still pink and juicy in the middle.

2 Meanwhile, drop the peas into the pan of boiling salted water, bring them back to the boil and cook for 1 minute or until tender. Drain well, tip into a food processor and add the chopped mint, butter, cream (if using) and some seasoning. Process into a slightly rough-looking purée.

3 To serve, spoon the pea purée into the centre of 4 warmed plates and rest 2 of the lamb chops on top. Add the pancetta slices to the griddle and cook for 30 seconds on each side, until crisp and golden. Drain briefly on kitchen paper, then pile on top of the chops and serve.

sausages and garlic mash with onion, red wine and rosemary jus

The gravy is quite time consuming to make, but really worth the effort. If you think you may be short of time you can make it well in advance and heat it through at the last minute.

serves 4 • preparation 1 hr for the gravy • cooking 20 mins

Energy 734 kcals • Protein 23.0 g • Carbohydrate 59.2 g • Fat 41.1 g
Saturated fat 19.7 g • Fibre 4.9 g • Salt 3.36 g • Added sugars 0.7 g

450 g (1 lb) meaty pork sausages
a little oil for cooking

FOR THE GARLIC MASH
900 g (2 lb) peeled floury potatoes,
    such as Maris Piper, cut into chunks
50 g (2 oz) butter
3 garlic cloves, crushed
the leaves from ½ x 20-g (¾-oz) packet parsley, chopped
a little milk

FOR THE ONION, RED WINE AND ROSEMARY JUS
40 g (1½ oz) butter
450 g (1 lb) onions, halved and thinly sliced
½ teaspoon sugar
300 ml (10 fl oz) gutsy red wine, such as Cabernet
    Sauvignon
1 tablespoon plain flour
600 ml (1 pint) beef stock (see page 231)
the leaves from 1 large stalk of rosemary
salt and freshly ground black pepper

1 For the jus, melt the butter in a large frying pan, add the onions and sugar and cook over a medium heat for 20–30 minutes, stirring every now and then, until soft and nicely browned. Add the red wine, increase the heat a little and simmer quite rapidly until the wine has almost disappeared. Stir in the flour and cook for a few seconds, then add the beef stock, rosemary and some salt and pepper and simmer for a further 20 minutes.

2 For the garlic mash, put the potatoes into a pan of cold salted water, bring to the boil and simmer for 20 minutes until tender. After 10 minutes, heat a little oil in a frying pan, add the sausages and cook then over a medium-high heat for 10 minutes, turning now and then as they brown.

3 Melt the butter for the mash in a small pan, add the garlic and cook very gently for 2–3 minutes without browning. Keep hot. Drain the potatoes well, pass through a potato ricer, or mash until smooth. Stir in the garlic butter, parsley, salt and pepper and enough milk to make a smooth mash.

4 Spoon the garlic mash into the centre of 4 warmed plates and rest the sausages alongside. Spoon over some of the gravy and serve.

shepherd's pie with irish champ mash topping

Using lamb gravy in the filling gives this pie a lovely flavour.
Just remember to save some next time you do a roast.

serves 4 • preparation 30 mins • cooking 30–35 mins

Energy 782 kcals • Protein 54.7 g • Carbohydrate 63.9 g • Fat 35.7 g
Saturated fat 16.3 g • Fibre 6.6 g • Salt 1.37 g • Added sugars 0.2 g

- **2 tablespoons sunflower oil**
- **1 medium onion, finely chopped**
- **225 g (8 oz) peeled carrots, finely diced**
- **900 g (2 lb) lean minced lamb**
- **the leaves from 4 sprigs of thyme**
- **1 tablespoon Worcestershire sauce**
- **1 teaspoon tomato purée**
- **300 ml (10 fl oz) lamb gravy or meat stock (beef or**
  chicken, see page 231)
- **salt and freshly ground black pepper**

FOR THE IRISH CHAMP MASH
- **1.25 kg (2½ lb) peeled floury potatoes, such as Maris**
  Piper, cut into chunks
- **50 g (2 oz) butter**
- **2 bunches spring onions, trimmed and sliced**
- **3–4 tablespoons milk**

1 Heat the oil in a large pan, add the onion and cook over a medium heat for 5 minutes until soft and lightly browned. Add the carrots and cook for a further 2 minutes. Add the minced lamb, increase the heat to high, and cook for 3–4 minutes, breaking up the meat with a wooden spoon as it browns.

2 Add the thyme leaves, Worcestershire sauce, tomato purée and gravy or stock and simmer for 20 minutes until the liquid has reduced and the mixture has thickened slightly. Season to taste, then spoon into a shallow 2.25-litre (4-pint) ovenproof dish.

3 Meanwhile, put the potatoes into a pan of cold salted water, bring to the boil and simmer for 20 minutes until tender. Drain well, pass through a potato ricer, or mash until smooth.

4 Pre-heat the oven to 200°C/400°F/Gas Mark 6. Melt the butter in another pan, add the spring onions and cook gently for 2 minutes until soft. Stir into the mashed potato with the milk and some seasoning.

5 Spoon the champ mash over the top of the lamb, spread out evenly and then rough up a little with a fork. Bake for 30–35 minutes until bubbling hot and golden brown.

roast chicken with crunchy stuffing and bacon rolls

I don't like cooking my stuffing inside the chicken, because I prefer it to get a little bit crunchy. These little stuffing and bacon rolls do two jobs in one go – you get the crunchy stuffing as well as some slightly crisp (but not overcooked) bacon.

serves 4 • preparation 10 mins • cooking 1½ hrs

Energy 584 kcals • Protein 58.6 g • Carbohydrate 18.3 g • Fat 29.9 g
Saturated fat 13.0 g • Fibre 1.3 g • Salt 3.05 g • Added sugars none

1 × 1.75-kg (4-lb) chicken
a small bunch of thyme
3 bay leaves
½ lemon
olive oil, for rubbing
salt and freshly ground black pepper

FOR THE CRUNCHY STUFFING AND BACON ROLLS
15 g (½ oz) butter
½ onion, finely chopped
1 small leek, cleaned and thinly sliced
1 small celery stick, thinly sliced
100 g (4 oz) thickly sliced smoked ham, finely chopped
50 g (2 oz) Gruyère or Cheddar cheese, coarsely grated
75 g (3 oz) white breadcrumbs, made from day-old bread
½ teaspoon Dijon mustard
1½ tablespoons beaten egg
100 g (4 oz) rindless streaky bacon

FOR THE GRAVY
75 ml (3 fl oz) dry white wine
1 teaspoon plain flour
300 ml (10 fl oz) chicken stock (see page 231)
2–3 tablespoons double cream

1 Pre-heat the oven to 200°C/400°F/Gas Mark 6. Season the cavity of the chicken with salt and pepper, then push in the thyme, bay leaves and lemon. Rub the outside of the chicken with olive oil and season with salt and pepper. Put into a small roasting tin and roast for 1 hour 20 minutes, i.e. 20 minutes per 450 g (1 lb). Cover with a loose piece of foil during cooking if it starts to get a bit too brown.

2 Meanwhile, for the crunchy stuffing and bacon rolls, melt the butter in a pan, add the onion, leek and celery and fry gently for 5 minutes until soft but not browned. Transfer to a bowl and leave to cool. Add the ham, cheese, breadcrumbs and some seasoning and mix together lightly. Beat the mustard with the egg and stir in to bind everything together.

3 Divide the mixture into 8 even-sized pieces and shape them into short, fat little barrels. Stretch each bacon rasher on a board with the back of a sharp knife, then cut in half into 2 shorter pieces. Wrap one piece of bacon around each barrel of stuffing and put seam-side down into a lightly oiled shallow roasting tin. Roast alongside the chicken for the last 20–30 minutes, until crisp and golden.

4 To test if the chicken is cooked, push a skewer into the thickest part of the thigh, where it presses up against the body. If the juices run pink, it is not cooked and needs to be returned to the oven. When the juices run clear, remove it from the oven, drain the cooking juices from the cavity into the roasting tin and put the bird onto a board. Cover with foil and leave somewhere warm for about 10–15 minutes to allow the meat to relax, while you make the gravy. (Relaxing the meat will really make all the difference, and you will end up with a very moist, tender chicken.)

5 Skim off any oil from the surface of the cooking juices, place the roasting tin over a high heat and pour in the wine. Boil until reduced by half, rubbing the base of the tin with a wooden spoon to release all the caramelized juices. Stir in the flour, then the chicken stock and boil once more until the gravy has reduced and is well flavoured. Stir in the cream and adjust the seasoning if necessary.

6 To carve the chicken, cut through the skin between the legs and the body, then gently pull each leg away, cutting through the joint attaching it with the tip of the knife. Cut each leg in half at the joint between the drumstick and the thigh. Now carve away the breast meat from each side in long, thin slices, and cut off the wings if you wish. Serve with the crunchy stuffing and bacon rolls, the gravy and some vegetables of your choice (see pages 218–227).

family **sunday roast** There's nothing better than gathering the whole family around the table to eat together, especially for a leisurely Sunday roast. This is a great summer menu, as it uses lots of fresh seasonal ingredients, and it's easy to prepare by following our time plan.

menu

Roast chicken with crunchy stuffing and bacon rolls
(see page 156)

Crispy roast potatoes
(see page 219)

Braised peas with leeks
(see page 225)

Glazed carrots with lemon
(see page 225)

Apple and berry crumble
(see page 162)

Quick clotted cream ice-cream *(see page 164)* **or pouring cream**

time plan

The day before
If you are serving ice-cream with the crumble, make it the day before, as it takes quite a while to freeze.

In advance on the day
Make the apple and berry crumble.
Make the crunchy stuffing and bacon rolls.
Prepare the potatoes for the roasties and put them in a pan of salted water, ready for cooking.
Clean and slice the leeks.
Prepare the carrots.
Prepare the chicken and set it aside somewhere cool.

Time plan for a 1 p.m. lunch

11.30 a.m.	Pre-heat oven to 200°C/400°F/Gas Mark 6. Bring the pan of potatoes to the boil and cook for just 7 minutes, then drain.
11.40 a.m.	Put the chicken in to roast.
11.55 a.m.	Heat the oil for the roast potatoes.
12.00 p.m.	Add the potatoes to the tin, turn, drain and roast.
12.30 p.m.	Cook the crunchy stuffing and bacon rolls
in 12.45 p.m.	Cook the carrots. Start to cook leeks for the peas.
12.50 p.m.	Transfer the chicken to a board, cover with foil and leave to rest. Make the gravy.
12.55 p.m.	Add the peas to the leeks and finish
1 p.m.	Serve lunch. Put the crumble in to cook.
1.40 p.m.	Remove the ice-cream from the freezer to soften before serving.

TIPS
- Lay the table as soon as you can so that that job is out of the way.
- If you are entertaining guests, think about where you like them to sit beforehand. Split up the girls and boys and the couples, and put place names on the table if you like.
- Serving a starter before a hefty Sunday roast is not always a good idea, but you could offer a few light nibbles, such as olives and nuts, to keep people going while they have a pre-lunch drink.
- Remember to put some plates and serving dishes to warm.
- Chill some white wine.
- Most importantly of all, give yourself some time before the meal to get ready and relax. And have maybe a small glass of wine to get you in the mood.

ROASTING CHART FOR MEAT AND POULTRY

Weigh your meat or poultry and calculate the total cooking time according to the chart below. This includes cooking at both the higher and lower temperatures, where necessary.

BEEF
Start off at: 240°C/475°F/Gas Mark 9 for 20 mins
Lower to: 200°C/400°F/Gas Mark 6
Rare: 13 mins per 450 g (1 lb)
Medium: 18 mins per 450 g (1 lb)
Well-done: 24 mins per 450 g (1 lb)

LAMB
Start off at: 230°C/450°F/Gas Mark 8 for 15 mins
Lower to: 200°C/400°F/Gas Mark 6
Rare: 12 mins per 450 g (1 lb)
Medium: 16 mins per 450 g (1 lb)
Well-done: 20 mins per 450 g (1 lb)

PORK
Start off at: 230°C/450°F/Gas Mark 8 for 20 mins
Lower to: 180°C/350°F/Gas Mark 4 for 30 mins per 450 g (1 lb), plus 30 mins

CHICKEN
Roast at: 200°C/400°F/Gas Mark 6 20 mins per 450 g (1 lb)

DUCK
Start off at: 230°C/450°F/Gas Mark 8 for 20 mins
Lower to: 180°C/350°F/Gas Mark 4 for 15 mins per 450 g (1 lb)

TURKEY
Start off at: 230°C/450°F/Gas Mark 8 for 30 mins uncovered
Lower to: 170°C/325°F/Gas Mark 3 allow 15–18 mins per 450 g (1 lb) covered
Finish at: 200°C/400°F/Gas Mark 6 for about 30 mins uncovered

bread and butter pudding

This is a classic vanilla-flavoured bread pudding, but for a change why not add the finely grated zest of a lemon to the custard and use dried blueberries instead of the sultanas? Alternatively, use the zest of an orange and spread the bread with a little marmalade.

serves 4 • preparation 10 mins • cooking 30 mins

Energy 668 kcals • Protein 11.3 g • Carbohydrate 59.9 g • Fat 44.3 g
Saturated fat 26.0 g • Fibre 1.0 g • Salt 0.97 g • Added sugars 20.3 g

1 small, fresh, tin-shaped white loaf
50 g (2 oz) butter
100 g (4 oz) sultanas
250 ml (8 fl oz) double cream
250 ml (8 fl oz) full-cream milk
3 medium eggs
75 g (3 oz) caster sugar
1 teaspoon vanilla extract

1 Pre-heat the oven to 190°C/375°F/Gas Mark 5. Cut 7 very thin slices from the loaf of bread and remove the crusts. Spread them with the butter, cut each one into 4 triangles and layer half into the base of a buttered 1.5-litre (2½-pint) ovenproof dish that measures about 6 cm (2½ inches) deep. Sprinkle over the sultanas and overlap the rest of the bread triangles, buttered-side up, on top.

2 Mix together the cream, milk, eggs, 50 g (2 oz) of the caster sugar and the vanilla extract. Pour over the bread and leave to soak for 5 minutes.

3 Put the dish into a roasting tin and sprinkle the top with the remaining sugar. Pour enough hot water into the tin to come halfway up the sides of the dish and cook in the oven for about 30 minutes until the top is crisp and golden and the custard is just set. Remove the dish from the tin and serve, with a little extra cream if you wish.

cheat's banoffee pie with chocolate drizzle

Traditionally this pie was made in a pastry case and called for boiling an unopened can of condensed milk in a deep pan of water for 5 hours. But the good news is that you can now buy banoffee toffee ready-made in jars. If you can't find it, drizzle some toffee ice-cream sauce (see page 94) over the bananas instead.

serves 6 • preparation 15 mins + 15 mins' chilling • cooking none

Energy 926 kcals • Protein 9.0 g • Carbohydrate 89.4 g • Fat 61.5 g Saturated fat 34.9 g • Fibre 1.6 g • Salt 1.15 g • Added sugars 40.6 g

- **225 g (8 oz) digestive (wheatmeal) biscuits**
- **100 g (4 oz) butter**
- **1 × 450-g (1-lb) jar banoffee toffee sauce**
- **2 large ripe bananas, peeled and sliced**
- **450 ml (¾ pint) double cream**
- **¾ teaspoon instant powdered coffee**
- **1 tablespoon caster sugar**
- **25 g (1 oz) plain or milk chocolate, melted**

1 Put the biscuits into a plastic bag and crush into fine crumbs using a rolling pin. Melt the butter in a medium-sized pan and stir in the crushed biscuits. Press the mixture onto the base and sides of a lightly oiled, loose-bottomed flan tin 23 cm (9 inches) wide and 4 cm (1½ inches) deep. Chill for 15 minutes.

2 Spread the banoffee toffee sauce over the base of the biscuit case and cover with the sliced bananas.

3 Lightly whip the cream, instant coffee and caster sugar together in a bowl until the mixture just forms soft peaks. Spoon on top of the bananas and spread it out to make a seal with the edge of the biscuit case. Swirl the top attractively and chill for at least 1 hour.

4 To serve, carefully remove the pie from the tin, drizzle with the warm melted chocolate and cut into wedges.

apple and berry crumble

No nuts or oats here, just a proper, delicious, old-fashioned crumble. Simply yum!

serves 8 • preparation 12 mins • cooking 45–50 mins

Energy 416.2 kcals • Protein 3.6 g • Carbohydrate 62.5 g • Fat 18.4 g
Saturated fat 11.4 g • Fibre 4.35 g • Salt 0.44 g • Added sugars 26.2 g

750 g (1½ lb) cooking apples, such as Bramleys
4 dessert apples, such as Cox's or Braeburn
100 g (4 oz) caster sugar
350 g (12 oz) blackberries, raspberries or blueberries
double or extra-thick double cream, to serve

FOR THE CRUMBLE TOPPING
225 g (8 oz) plain flour
175 g (6 oz) chilled butter
100 g (4 oz) caster sugar

1 Peel, core and slice the apples and put them into a pan with the sugar and 3 tablespoons of water. Part-cover and cook gently for 5 minutes, then uncover and cook for a further 5 minutes until the cooking apples have just started to fall apart and go mushy. Stir in the berries, spoon into a 2.25-litre (4-pint) shallow ovenproof dish and leave to go cold.

2 Pre-heat the oven to 190°C/375°F/Gas Mark 5. For the topping, put the flour and butter into a food processor and work together until the mixture looks like coarse breadcrumbs. Stir in the sugar.

3 Sprinkle the topping over the top of the fruit and bake for 45–50 minutes until the top is crisp and golden brown. Serve with some extra cream.

chocolate-pear upside-down pud

I got this idea from my mate, Paul Rankin, a fantastic chef with whom I work on Ready Steady Cook. *It's the ultimate cheat's pud because it uses ready-made muffins, but is none the worse for that. Thanks Paul.*

serves 6 • preparation 20 mins • cooking 10 mins

Energy 427 kcals • Protein 4.5 g • Carbohydrate 55.0 g • Fat 22.5 g
Saturated fat 13.5 g • Fibre 2.9 g • Salt 0.49 g • Added sugars 31.1 g

75 g (3 oz) unsalted butter, softened
75 g (3 oz) caster sugar
4 ripe but firm dessert pears, such as Williams
juice of 1 lemon
6 double-chocolate muffins
crème fraîche, to serve

1 Pre-heat the oven to 200°C/400°F/Gas Mark 6. Thickly smear the bottom of a 20-cm (8-inch) ovenproof frying pan with the butter and sprinkle over the sugar.

2 Peel the pears, cut them into quarters and remove the cores. Place them in a bowl and toss them with the lemon juice to stop them from going brown. Drain off any excess lemon juice, then tip them into the prepared frying pan. Place over a medium heat and cook for 7–10 minutes, shaking the pan occasionally to stop the pears from sticking, until the butter and sugar caramelize and turn toffee-coloured and the pears are just tender. You might need to lower the heat a little, depending on how quickly the pears are cooking.

3 Crumble the chocolate muffins into pieces and scatter them evenly over the pears. Cover with an ovenproof plate or the base of a flan tin, press down gently to bind everything together slightly, and leave the plate in place. Transfer to the oven and bake for 10 minutes, or until the pears are completely tender but still holding their shape.

4 Remove the frying pan from the oven and leave the pudding to cool for 30 minutes so that all the juices have time to be well absorbed and the caramel can set slightly.

5 To serve, remove the plate and loosen the edges of the pudding with a round-bladed knife. Cover the top of the pan with an inverted serving plate, take hold of both the plate and the pan, then turn them over together. Remove the frying pan, checking to see that the pudding is now on the plate, and serve cut into wedges with a spoonful of crème fraîche.

coconut treacle tart with quick clotted cream ice-cream

The amount of water in the pastry will depend on the weather, how cold the fats were and how much you processed the mixture. The less water you use, the shorter your pastry will be. This tart is also fantastic made with finely grated fresh coconut, too. A treat for friends or family.

serves 8 • preparation 2–3 mins + freezing for the ice-cream, 30 mins + chilling time for the tart • cooking 30 mins

Energy 999 kcals • Protein 11.8 g • Carbohydrate 136.1 g • Fat 49.0 g
Saturated fat 29.1 g • Fibre 3.1 g • Salt 1.69 g • Added sugars 91.7 g

1 x quantity basic shortcrust pastry (see page 236)
a little plain flour for rolling out

FOR THE ICE-CREAM
225 g (8 oz) clotted cream
600 ml (1 pint) carton of chilled fresh custard
(or see page 235 to make your own)
½ teaspoon vanilla extract
6 tablespoons icing sugar

FOR THE FILLING
175 g (6 oz) white breadcrumbs,
made from day-old bread
100 g (4 oz) desiccated coconut
Finely grated zest of 1 lemon
750 g (1½ lb) golden syrup
1½ tablespoons lemon juice
½ teaspoon ground ginger

1 If you don't have an ice-cream maker, make the ice-cream the day before it's needed. Put the clotted cream, custard, vanilla extract and icing sugar into a food processor and blend together until smooth. Pour into a plastic container, cover and freeze for 1–2 hours until firm but not rock hard. Scrape into a food processor and blend until smooth, then return to the box and freeze once more. Repeat this process 3 times more, then leave to freeze hard. If you do have an ice-cream machine, simply churn until frozen, then freeze.

2 Roll out the pastry thinly on a little more flour and use to line a lightly greased, loose-bottomed flan tin 23 cm (9 inches) wide and 4 cm (1½ inches) deep (see below). Chill for 20 minutes.

3 Pre-heat the oven to 200°C/400°F/Gas Mark 6. Line the pastry case with a crumpled sheet of greaseproof paper and a thin layer of baking beans and bake for 15 minutes. Remove the paper and beans and return to the oven for 5 minutes. Remove from the oven and lower the temperature to 180°C/350°F/Gas Mark 4.

4 For the filling, mix the breadcrumbs, coconut and lemon zest together, tip them into the warm pastry case and spread out evenly. Put the golden syrup, lemon juice and ground ginger into a pan and warm gently over a low heat until liquid. Spoon evenly over the breadcrumbs and bake in the oven for 30 minutes until lightly browned. Remove and leave to cool slightly before serving with the clotted cream ice-cream.

how to line a flan tin sucessfully
Lift the pastry up on a rolling pin and gently unroll it over the top of the tin. Ease the pastry into the tin all the way around, then go around again, pressing the pastry onto the base, then the sides of the tin and leave the excess overhanging the edges. Run the rolling pin over the top of the tin to cut off the excess pastry, then firm the pastry into the case once more, making sure that it is pressed well into the indentations all the way around the sides. The pastry should now be slighly proud of the top of the tin all the way around. Prick the base lightly with a fork here and there.

AFTER-EIGHT DINNERS

salmon and goats' cheese pâté

A lovely easy starter for a dinner party with gorgeous flavours. Use smoked salmon trimmings for this pâté if you wish. They are available in most supermarkets and are quite a bit cheaper than the slices.

serves 2 • preparation 3–4 mins • cooking 3–4 mins for the melba toast

Energy 358 kcals • Protein 28.4 g • Carbohydrate 13.0 g • Fat 21.7 g
Saturated fat 13.5 g • Fibre 2.0 g • Salt 3.80 g • Added sugars none

2–3 medium-thick slices wholemeal bread
75 g (3 oz) smoked salmon
150 g (5 oz) soft, mild goats' cheese, such as Chavroux
½ teaspoon grated horseradish from a jar
½ teaspoon lemon juice
the leaves from ½ x 20-g (¾-oz) packet dill, chopped
salt and freshly ground black pepper
watercress sprigs and a lemon wedge, to garnish

1 Pre-heat the grill to medium-high. Toast the bread under the grill until lightly golden on both sides. Transfer to a board and slice off the crusts, then put your hand on top of each slice in turn and slice horizontally through the soft bread in the middle. Cut each square into 2 triangles and grill, uncooked-side up, for a few seconds more until crisp and golden. Remove and leave to cool.

2 For the pâté, cut the smoked salmon across into very fine strips. Put the goats' cheese, horseradish and lemon juice into a bowl and mash together with a fork until smooth. Stir in the smoked salmon, chopped dill and some salt and pepper to taste.

3 Spoon the pâté into a serving bowl, sit it on a serving plate and pile the melba toast alongside. Garnish with the watercress sprigs and lemon wedge and serve.

All the recipes in this section serve two, but simply multiply up, according to the number of guests, if necessary.

parmesan baskets with parma ham

These crisp and cheesy little baskets can be made ahead of time and kept crisp in an air-tight tin until needed. For vegetarians, simply leave out the Parma ham.

serves 2 • preparation 5–6 mins • cooking 5–6 mins

Energy 200 kcals • Protein 10.1 g • Carbohydrate 6.1 g • Fat 15.3 g
Saturated fat 7.5 g • Fibre 0.9 g • Salt 1.38 g • Added sugars 0.2 g

25 g (1 oz) finely grated Parmesan cheese
2 small, ripe figs
2 large, thin slices Parma ham
2 tablespoons crème fraîche
wasabi paste or horseradish sauce, to taste
15 g (½ oz) wild rocket leaves
salt and freshly ground black pepper

FOR THE DRESSING
2 teaspoons extra virgin olive oil
½ teaspoon balsamic vinegar

1 Pre-heat the oven to 200°C/400°F/Gas Mark 6. Line a baking sheet with a piece of non-stick baking parchment and have ready two overturned, narrow-based glasses on which to shape the baskets.

2 Put 2 even-sized piles of Parmesan cheese, well spaced apart, onto the paper-lined tray and spread them out into circles about 10 cm (4 inches) across. Bake for 5–6 minutes until golden and bubbling.

3 Remove the tray from the oven and dab the top of each circle with some kitchen paper to remove the excess oil. Leave to cool for a few seconds, then lift them off with a palette knife and drape over the base of the upturned glasses. Shape into baskets with your fingers and leave to go cold.

4 Meanwhile, cut each fig almost into quarters, but leave the pieces attached at the stalk end and open then up slightly, like the petals of a flower. Wrap each fig loosely in a slice of the Parma ham. Mix the crème fraîche with a little wasabi or horseradish sauce and some seasoning to taste. Whisk together the ingredients for the dressing with a little salt and pepper.

5 When the baskets are cold, put them into the centre of each plate. Fill with the rocket. Nestle the ham-wrapped figs in the centre and spoon a little wasabi-flavoured crème fraîche into the centre. Drizzle the dressing around the plate and serve.

baked polenta with creamy mushrooms and parmesan cheese

These triangles of polenta are also lovely baked with home-made tomato sauce, a little mozzarella and the Parmesan cheese, too.

serves 2 • preparation 20 mins + 2 hrs' chilling • cooking 30 mins

Energy 489 kcals • Protein 14.6 g • Carbohydrate 32.0 g • Fat 34.5 g
Saturated fat 18.2 g • Fibre 2.2 g • Salt 1.06 g • Added sugars none

225 g (8 oz) mixed mushrooms, such as
   chestnut and button
1 tablespoon olive oil
1 small garlic clove, crushed
leaves from 1 large sprig of thyme
4 tablespoons double cream
7 g (¼ oz) fresh white breadcrumbs

15 g (½ oz) finely grated Parmesan cheese
salt and freshly ground black pepper

FOR THE POLENTA
450 ml (15 fl oz) water
75 g (3 oz) quick-cook polenta
25 g (1 oz) Parmesan cheese, finely grated
15 g (½ oz) butter

1 For the polenta, bring the water to the boil, pour in the polenta in a slow, steady stream, stirring all the time, then lower the heat and leave it to simmer for 10 minutes, stirring frequently, until the mixture leaves the sides of the pan. Meanwhile, lightly oil an 18-cm (6-inch) square shallow tin and line it with a sheet of cling film.

2 Take the pan of polenta off the heat and stir in the Parmesan, butter and some salt to taste. Pour it into the prepared tin and spread out and press another sheet of cling film on to the surface. Cover and chill for at least 2 hours.

3 Pre-heat the oven to 200°C/400°F/Gas Mark 6. Remove the top sheet of cling film, turn the polenta out of the tin onto a board, cut into 9 squares, then cut each one diagonally in half into 2 triangles.

4 Wipe the mushrooms clean, then slice them. Heat the olive oil in a frying pan, add the mushrooms, garlic, thyme and some seasoning and stir-fry over a high heat for 2–3 minutes until the mushrooms are tender and the excess moisture from them has evaporated. Add the cream and leave to bubble for a few seconds until thickened.

5 Arrange overlapping pieces of the polenta and the mushrooms in 2 lightly buttered, shallow ovenproof dishes. Mix the breadcrumbs with the Parmesan and a little seasoning and sprinkle over the top of each dish. Bake for 25–30 minutes until the tops are crisp and golden. Serve immediately with a salad.

roasted vegetable and chick pea salad with feta, cumin and lemon

The trick to roasting vegetables is not to overcrowd the roasting tin – it should be large enough so that the vegetables can be spread out in a thin layer. Turn them now and then during roasting so that they brown evenly.

serves 2 • preparation 10 mins • cooking 40 mins

Energy 771 kcals • Protein 25.0 g • Carbohydrate 49.6 g • Fat 53.9 g
Saturated fat 11.8 g • Fibre 13.3 g • Salt 2.81 g • Added sugars none

450 g (1 lb) prepared butternut squash
1 small red pepper, stalk and seeds removed
1 courgette, topped and tailed
1 small fennel bulb, first outer layer removed
1 small red onion, cut into thin wedges through the root
3 tablespoons olive oil
1 bunch asparagus, trimmed
1 × 400-g (14-oz) can chick peas, rinsed and drained
100 g (4 oz) feta cheese, crumbled into pieces
25 g (1 oz) rocket leaves
salt and freshly ground black pepper
foccaccia bread, to serve

FOR THE CUMIN AND LEMON DRESSING
1 teaspoon cumin seeds
1 tablespoon lemon juice
4 tablespoons extra virgin olive oil

1 Pre-heat the oven to 220°C/425°F/Gas Mark 7. Cut the butternut squash, red pepper, courgette and fennel into small chunky pieces and put into a large roasting tin with the red onion, oil and some salt and pepper. Toss together well, spread out into a single layer and roast for 20 minutes.

2 Meanwhile, cut the asparagus stalks in half and make the cumin and lemon dressing. Heat a dry frying pan over a high heat, add the cumin seeds and shake them around for a few seconds until lightly toasted. Tip them into a coffee mug or mortar and grind to a powder with a rolling pin or pestle. Tip them into a bowl, add the lemon juice and gradually whisk in the oil. Season with some salt and pepper and set aside.

3 Add the asparagus to the roasting tin, turn everything over a few times and roast for a further 20 minutes until all the vegetables are just tender and slightly caramelized around the edges.

4 Shortly before the roasted vegetables are ready, drop the chick peas into a small pan of boiling salted water and simmer for 5 minutes.

5 Drain the chick peas. Remove the vegetables from the oven and mix in the chick peas, dressing and a little salt and pepper to taste. Leave to cool a little, then spoon onto a large, flat serving dish and sprinkle over the feta cheese. Scatter over the rocket leaves and serve with some foccaccia bread.

monkfish on crispy potato cakes

A perfect combination of flavours and textures for you to enjoy.

serves 2 • preparation 10 mins • cooking 10 mins

Energy 702 kcals • Protein 41.5 g • Carbohydrate 28.4 g • Fat 45.2 g
Saturated fat 19.0 g • Fibre 1.9 g • Salt 2.39 g • Added sugars none

2 × 175-g (6-oz) pieces of monkfish fillet, trimmed
4–6 long, thin slices smoked pancetta
300 ml (10 fl oz) chicken stock (see page 231)
85 ml (3 fl oz) dry white wine
3 tablespoons double cream
25 g (1 oz) butter
the leaves from 1 large sprig parsley, chopped
salt and freshly ground black pepper

FOR THE CRISPY POTATO CAKES
2 potatoes, 100–150 g (4–5 oz) each, peeled
2 small shallots, peeled and finely chopped
1 egg, beaten
1 slightly rounded tablespoon self-raising flour
sunflower oil, for shallow frying

1 Wrap each piece of monkfish in 2–3 slices of pancetta, overlapping the edges slightly. Tie in a couple of places with some fine string and set aside.

2 Pre-heat the oven to 200°C/400°F/Gas Mark 6. Put the stock, wine and cream into a small pan and boil until reduced to 85 ml (3 fl oz).

3 Heat half the butter in an ovenproof frying pan, add the monkfish, seam-side up, and fry for 1–1½ minutes until golden brown. Turn over, transfer to the oven and roast for 10 minutes.

4 Meanwhile, finely grate the potatoes, by hand or in a food processor. Working with small handfuls at a time, squeeze out as much excess liquid from them as you can. Put into a bowl, fork to separate into strands and mix in the shallots, egg, flour, a scant ½ teaspoon salt and some pepper.

5 Heat 5 mm (¼ inch) sunflower oil in a clean frying pan, then reduce the heat to medium. Divide the potato mixture in half and shape into 4 thin circles 7.5 cm (3 inches) wide. Fry in the oil for 3 minutes on each side until golden brown and crisp on the outside and cooked through in the centre. Drain briefly on kitchen paper and keep warm.

6 Remove the monkfish from the oven, turn the oven off, but leave the potato cakes inside. Transfer the fish to a plate and remove the string. Add the reduced chicken stock to the frying pan and bring to the boil, rubbing the base of the pan with a wooden spoon. Whisk in the remaining butter, stir in the parsley and season with a little salt and pepper.

7 Put the potato cakes into the centre of warmed plates and place the monkfish on top. Spoon around the sauce and serve with a green vegetable.

salmon with herby yoghurt dressing

I love this served on a warm Puy lentil salad, tossed with a little mustardy dressing.

serves 2 • preparation 5 mins • cooking 25 mins

Energy 844 kcals • Protein 59.0 g • Carbohydrate 47.0 g • Fat 47.9 g
Saturated fat 7.8 g • Fibre 8.4 g • Salt 0.76 g • Added sugars none

2 × 175-g (6-oz) pieces skinned salmon fillet
olive oil, for brushing
sea salt and freshly ground black pepper
Warm lentil salad (see page 229), to serve

FOR THE HERBY YOGHURT DRESSING
4 tablespoons whole-milk or Greek natural yoghurt
1 small garlic clove, crushed
2 teaspoons extra virgin olive oil
the leaves from 2 sprigs of flat-leaf parsley, chopped
the leaves from 2 sprigs of mint, chopped
small bundle of chives, snipped

1 Prepare the warm lentil salad and mix together the ingredients for the herby yoghurt dressing and season.

2 Brush the pieces of salmon with oil and season. Heat a dry, heavy-based frying pan over a high heat. Add the pieces of salmon, skinned-side down, lower the heat to medium and cook for 3 minutes until lightly golden. Turn the salmon over and cook for another 2 minutes until the salmon is just cooked through. Remove the pan from the heat and set aside.

3 Warm through the lentil salad and spoon onto 2 plates. Put the salmon on top, drizzle over some of the herby yoghurt dressing and serve with a simple green salad.

chicken, pepper and brie puff parcels

Use chicken breasts which weigh about 175 g (6 oz) for these parcels or there won't be enough to wrap around the cheese and peppers once they've been flattened.

serves 2 • preparation 1 hr 55 minutes • cooking 30 mins

Energy 1270 kcals • Protein 58.2 g • Carbohydrate 97.9 g • Fat 74.4 g
Saturated fat 31.3 g • Fibre 1.2 g • Salt 3.33 g • Added sugars none

2 skinned, boneless chicken breasts
2 teaspoons olive oil
1 teaspoon lemon juice
leaves from 2 large sprigs of thyme
1 red pepper
50 g (2 oz) ripe Brie, thinly sliced
1 × 500-g (1 lb 2-oz) packet chilled puff pastry
1 egg, beaten, to glaze
1 tablespoon finely grated Parmesan cheese
salt and freshly ground black pepper

1 Put each chicken breast, skinned-side down, onto a large sheet of cling film and fold back the little fillets. Cover with another sheet of cling film and flatten with a rolling pin, giving it a bit more of a bash on the thicker side, until they are about the size of a large saucer. Mix the olive oil, lemon juice, thyme leaves, salt and pepper in a shallow dish. Add the chicken, turn once and set aside for at least 1 hour.

2 Pre-heat the oven to 220°C/425°F/Gas Mark 7. Roast the pepper for 20 minutes, then remove and leave to cool. Break in half and remove the stalk, skin and seeds. Remove the chicken from the marinade, place half the pepper on one side of each piece and fold over the other side. Heat a dry, non-stick frying pan, add the chicken and pepper 'sandwiches' and fry for 1–1½ minutes on each side until lightly browned. Remove and leave to cool slightly, then slip the sliced Brie in with the red pepper.

3 Cut the pastry in half and roll each piece out on a lightly floured surface and cut out two 25-cm (10-inch) discs. Place the chicken in the centre of each one, brush the edge with beaten egg and bring them together over the top of the chicken. Press together firmly, seal the ends well, then fold them back on themselves to make an even better seal. Place on a greased baking sheet and chill for at least 20 minutes.

4 Lower the oven temperature to 200°C/400°F/Gas Mark 6. Brush the parcels with beaten egg, sprinkle the tops with the cheese and bake for 30 minutes until crisp and golden.

speedy coq au vin

A quick version of the classic French stew.

serves 2 • preparation 7–10 mins • cooking approx. 35 mins

Energy 488 kcals • Protein 43.6 g • Carbohydrate 9.3 g • Fat 25.3 g
Saturated fat 10.7 g • Fibre 2.7 g • Salt 2.22 g • Added sugars none

350 g (12 oz) skinned, boneless chicken thighs (about 4), trimmed of excess fat
50 g (2 oz) rindless thick-cut back bacon
1 tablespoon sunflower oil
75 g (3 oz) small shallots or button onions, peeled
25 g (1 oz) butter
1 tablespoon brandy (optional)
150 ml (5 fl oz) red wine
150 ml (5 fl oz) chicken stock (see page 231)
1 tablespoon tomato purée
1 garlic clove, crushed
100 g (4 oz) carrots, peeled and sliced
1 bay leaf
leaves from 1 sprig of thyme
75 g (3 oz) small button mushrooms, wiped clean
1 teaspoon plain flour
the leaves from ½ x 20-g (¾-oz) packet parsley, chopped
salt and freshly ground black pepper

1 Cut each chicken thigh into 4 pieces and cut the bacon across into short little strips. Heat the oil in a heavy-based frying pan, add the bacon and shallots and fry for 4–5 minutes until beginning to brown. Add half the butter and the chicken to the pan and fry for 4–5 minutes until golden brown. Add the brandy (if using), set alight with a match and cook until the flames die down.

2 Add the wine to the pan and boil until it has reduced by half, rubbing the base of the pan with a wooden spoon to release all the caramelized juices. Add the stock, tomato purée, garlic, carrots, bay leaf, thyme and some salt and pepper, bring to the boil, lower the heat, cover and simmer for 10 minutes.

3 Heat half the remaining butter in another frying pan. Add the mushrooms and fry for 2–3 minutes until lightly browned. Add them to the chicken and simmer for 5 minutes.

4 Blend the remaining butter with the flour into a smooth paste. Remove the bay leaf, stir in the butter paste and simmer for 2–3 minutes until thickened. Season to taste with salt and pepper, stir in the parsley and serve with some steamed rice.

quick rare roast beef with horseradish sauce

It can be difficult to do a roast dinner for just two people without having lots of left-overs. But this way of cooking beef is perfect for small numbers.

serves 2 • preparation 1–2 mins for the beef + 20 mins for the mash • cooking 18–19 mins

Energy 857 kcals • Protein 62.4 g • Carbohydrate 32.0 g • Fat 54.2 g
Saturated fat 23.8 g • Fibre 9.7 g • Salt 1.79 g • Added sugars none

½ **quantity celeriac and parsnip mash (see page 221), to serve**
2 **tablespoons olive oil**
1 **piece unrolled sirloin of beef, 5 cm (2 inches) thick and weighing about 450 g (1 lb)**
sea salt flakes and coarsely ground black pepper

FOR THE HORSERADISH SAUCE
2 **tablespoons crème fraîche**
1 **tablespoon grated horseradish, from a jar**
½ **teaspoon Dijon mustard**
½ **teaspoon white wine vinegar**

1 Make the celeriac and parsnip mash first, as it takes only a few minutes to cook the beef.

2 Pre-heat the oven to 230°C/450°F/Gas Mark 8. Heat the olive oil in an ovenproof frying pan over a high heat until shimmering hot, add the piece of beef and sear it on all sides for 3–4 minutes until nicely browned.

3 Season the beef on both sides with salt and pepper, slide the frying pan into the oven and roast for just 15 minutes.

4 Remove the beef from the oven, tuck a sheet of foil around it and leave it to rest for 5 minutes. Meanwhile, reheat the celeriac and parsnip mash and mix together the ingredients for the horseradish sauce with a little salt and pepper to taste.

5 Carve the beef across into very thin slices and serve with the celeriac and parsnip mash, horseradish sauce and a green vegetable of your choice.

seared sirloin steak with blue cheese butter and shoestring chips

The recipe for the blue cheese butter will make slightly more than you need. The extra will keep well in the freezer, tightly wrapped in lots of cling film, and can be used with chicken too, or on baked potatoes.

serves 2 • preparation 10 mins • cooking 3–4 mins for the steaks, 4–5 mins for the chips

Energy 811 kcals • Protein 44.5 g • Carbohydrate 38.4 g • Fat 54.3 g
Saturated fat 21.8 g • Fibre 2.6 g • Salt 1.80 g • Added sugars none

2 × 175-g (6-oz) sirloin steaks, each cut about 2.5 cm
 (1 inch) thick
salt and freshly ground black pepper

FOR THE SHOESTRING CHIPS
450 g (1 lb) floury potatoes, such as Maris Piper
Sunflower oil, for deep-frying

FOR THE BLUE CHEESE BUTTER
25 g (1 oz) slightly salted butter, at room temperature
15 g (½ oz) full-fat soft cream cheese
1 teaspoon wholegrain mustard
25 g (1 oz) blue cheese, such as Roquefort, Stilton or
 Danish blue
the leaves from 3 sprigs curly parsley, chopped

1 For the blue cheese butter, put the butter, cream cheese and mustard into a small bowl and mix together well. Crumble in the blue cheese, add the parsley and mix with the back of a fork into a coarse paste. Set to one side (or in the fridge if it's a warm day).

2 Peel the potatoes and cut them lengthways into slices about 5 mm (¼ inch) thick. Then cut them once more into long, thin chips. Heat some oil for deep-frying to 190°C/375°F.

3 Deep-fry the chips in 2 batches for 2–3 minutes until soft but not browned. Lift out and drain briefly on kitchen paper. Bring the oil back up to temperature.

4 Brush the steaks on both sides with a little oil and season well with salt and pepper. Heat a ridged cast-iron griddle or a heavy-based frying pan over a high heat until smoking hot. Add the steaks and cook for 1½ minutes on each side for rare, 2 minutes for medium-rare, pressing down on top of them with a fish slice as they cook.

5 While the steaks are cooking on the second side, drop the chips back into the oil and fry for another 1–2 minutes until crisp and golden. Drain well on lots of kitchen paper and sprinkle with salt.

6 Transfer the steaks to warmed plates and spoon some of the blue cheese butter on top. Pile some of the chips alongside and serve with a simple salad of tomatoes and red onion.

five-spiced duck breasts with stir-fried vegetable sticks

This is a delicious way of jazzing up ready-prepared duck breasts. They are best served slightly pink in the centre, but just cook them for a bit longer if you prefer them well done.

serves 2 • preparation 10 mins • cooking 10–11 mins

Energy 566 kcals • Protein 33.0 g • Carbohydrate 18.7 g • Fat 40.3 g
Saturated fat 10.2 g • Fibre 3.4 g • Salt 3.41 g • Added sugars 6.2 g

2 × 175 g (6 oz) duck breasts
½ teaspoon Chinese five-spice powder
1 tablespoon clear honey
2 tablespoons sweet soy sauce (ketchup manis)
1 tablespoon balsamic vinegar
½ medium-hot red chilli, seeded and finely chopped

FOR THE STIR-FRIED VEGETABLE STICKS
50 g (2 oz) French beans, trimmed
100 g (4 oz) carrots, peeled
½ red pepper, seeded
1 small courgette, trimmed
50 g (2 oz) mangetout
1 tablespoon sunflower oil
1 small garlic clove, chopped
1 cm (½ inch) fresh root ginger,
    peeled and finely chopped

1 Cut all the vegetables into thin sticks about the same size as the French beans. Drop the beans into a pan of boiling water and bring back to the boil. Add the carrots and the red pepper and cook for 1 minute. Drain, rinse under cold water, then dry on kitchen paper.

2 Lightly score the skin of each duck breast into a diamond pattern with the tip of a sharp knife, taking care that you don't cut through to the meat.

3 Heat a dry frying pan until it is quite hot. Add the duck breasts, skin-side down, lower the heat to medium and cook for about 3–4 minutes until the skin is crisp and golden brown.

4 Turn the breasts over and cook them for another 5 minutes, or a little longer if you don't like your duck too pink. Meanwhile, mix together the five-spice powder, honey, sweet soy sauce, balsamic vinegar and chilli.

5 Pour away all the excess fat from the pan. Add the honey mixture and leave it to bubble away, turning the duck breasts now and then, until they are nicely glazed.

6 Meanwhile, heat the oil in a wok or another frying pan, add the garlic, ginger and vegetables and stir-fry for 1–2 minutes until they are cooked but still crunchy. Season with some salt and pepper.

7 Pile the vegetable sticks into the centre of 2 warmed plates. Slice each duck breast on the diagonal and carefully lift on top of the vegetables. Spoon over any remaining glaze and serve.

braised osso bucco-style lamb shanks with gremolata

Osso bucco is a slow-cooked Italian dish traditionally made with veal, flavoured with wine, herbs, tomatoes and lemon. Gremolata, the classic garnish of finely chopped garlic, lemon and parsley, adds a lovely fresh taste to the finished dish. If you use stock cubes in dishes like this, which require long, slow cooking in lots of liquid that eventually reduces right down to a thick sauce, always dilute them with twice the amount of water stated on the packet. Stock cubes are very salty and will end up making your finished sauce taste very salty too.

serves 2 • preparation 15 mins • cooking approx. 2 hrs

Energy 686 kcals • Protein 57.6 g • Carbohydrate 19.6 g • Fat 37.2 g
Saturated fat 13.8 g • Fibre 3.9 g • Salt 2.78 g • Added sugars none

2 lamb shanks
15 g (½ oz) plain flour
2 tablespoons olive oil
1 medium onion, finely chopped
leaves from 1 sprig of rosemary
leaves from 1 large sprig of thyme
1 bay leaf
150 ml (5 fl oz) dry white wine
1 × 200-g (7-oz) can chopped tomatoes
1.2 litres (2 pints) lamb stock (made from a cube)
1 strip lemon zest, removed with a potato peeler
1 celery stick, finely chopped
100 g (4 oz) carrots, peeled and finely chopped
salt and freshly ground black pepper
mashed potatoes, to serve (see page 218)

FOR THE GREMOLATA
1 small garlic clove
leaves from 1 × 20-g (¾-oz) packet flat-leaf parsley
1 small strip lemon zest, removed with a potato peeler

1 Season the lamb shanks with salt and pepper, then dust them in the flour. Heat the oil in a deep, flameproof casserole in which the shanks will fit snugly, add the meat and fry until nicely browned on all sides. Lift out onto a plate.

2 Add the onion, rosemary, thyme and bay leaf and fry until lightly browned. Add the wine and cook rapidly until it has reduced by half. Return the lamb shanks to the pan and add the tomatoes, stock, lemon zest and some pepper. Bring to the boil, reduce the heat to low, part-cover and simmer for 30 minutes.

3 Stir in the celery and carrots and simmer, uncovered, for a further hour, turning the shanks over every now and then.

4 Skim the excess fat from the surface of the sauce, increase the heat a little and simmer for another 30 minutes or so, until the sauce has reduced and the lamb shanks are tender.

5 Meanwhile, for the gremolata, chop the garlic, parsley and lemon zest together quite finely on a board. Scatter over the top of the stew and serve with the mashed potatoes.

how to make pavlovas

Pavlovas are meringues with a crisp exterior and delicious, marshmallow-like centres. They are usually made in one large circle, but if you shape the mixture into smaller circles, you can make as many as you like and to whatever size you want (see variations). They will keep for at least one week in an airtight tin. Add the toppings just before serving or the meringues will go very soft.

✪ mini stawberry pavlovas

makes 6 small pavlovas • preparation 5–10 mins • cooking 45 mins

Energy 310 kcals • Protein 12.6 g • Carbohydrate 58.3 g • Fat 4.5 g Saturated fat 1.1 g • Fibre 7.0 g • Salt 0.13 g • Added sugars 8.6 g

3 egg whites
a very small pinch of salt
175 g (6 oz) caster sugar
1 teaspoon cornflour
½ teaspoon white wine vinegar

FOR THE TOPPING
225 g (8 oz) small ripe strawberries, hulled and halved
1 tablespoon icing sugar
finely grated zest of ¼ orange
1 tablespoon orange-flavoured liqueur, such as Cointreau
300 ml (10 fl oz) double cream

1 Pre-heat the oven to 140°C/275°F/Gas Mark 1. Grease a baking tray and line with non-stick baking parchment.

2 Put the egg whites into a large, clean mixing bowl, add the salt and whisk with a hand-held electric mixer until they form stiff peaks. Whisk in the sugar, 1 tablespoon at a time, to make a stiff, glossy meringue. Whisk in the cornflour and vinegar.

3 Drop 6 even-sized spoonfuls of the mixture onto the prepared baking sheet, spacing them well apart, and flatten slightly with the back of the spoon, making a small dip in the centre. Bake for 45 minutes, then turn off the oven and leave them inside to go cold. This will stop them cracking.

4 For the topping, put the strawberries into a bowl and gently mix with the icing sugar, orange zest and the orange-flavoured liqueur. Set aside for 30 minutes.

5 Just before serving, whip the cream into peaks. Spoon some onto the pavlovas, top with the strawberries and serve.

VARIATIONS

MINI PAVLOVAS WITH CHOCOLATE CREAM AND RASPBERRIES
Break 75 g (3 oz) plain chocolate into a heatproof bowl and rest it over a small pan of just-simmering water. Leave to melt, then cool slightly. Fold into 300 ml (10 fl oz) lightly whipped cream. Spoon onto the pavlovas and decorate with 150 g (5 oz) raspberries.

TO MAKE ONE LARGE PAVLOVA
Double the amounts of egg white, sugar, cornflour and vinegar and spread the mixture out on a baking-parchment-lined tray into a 24-cm (9½-inch) circle. Bake at 180°C/350°F/Gas Mark 4 for 5 minutes, then lower the oven to 140°C/275°F/Gas Mark 1 and bake for a further 1¼ hours. Cool as before.

valentine's day supper
Making a fuss of the one you love is great fun, but you don't want to be stuck by the stove all night. Most of this menu can be prepared the night before, including washing the spinach and scrubbing the potatoes, leaving you plenty of time for romance.

menu

Parmesan baskets with Parma ham
(see page 169)

Chicken, pepper and Brie puff parcels
(see page 175)

Steamed spinach

Minted new potatoes
(see page 220)

Lemon posset with raspberries and refrigerator biscuits
(see page 186)

CHAMPAGNE

If you really want to spoil a loved one, why not push the boat out and crack open a bottle of Champagne? If you do decide to go the whole hog, however, remember to make sure the bottle is really well chilled.

time plan

The day before

Marinate the chicken.

Roast the red pepper.

Make the parcels up to the end of step 3, if you wish.

Make the lemon possets, chill and then cover with cling film until needed.

Make the refrigerator biscuit dough, wrap in cling film and chill until needed.

In advance on the day

Make the Parmesan crisp baskets, cool and then store in an airtight tin.

Make the balsamic vinegar dressing.

Clean the new potatoes, if necessary, and set aside in a pan of cold salted water.

Wash and dry the spinach, if necessary.

Bake a few biscuits, leave to go cold, then store in an airtight tin.

time plan for an 8 p.m. supper

7.15 p.m.	Pre-heat the oven to 200°C/400°F/Gas Mark 6.
7.40 p.m.	Transfer the parcels to a lightly oiled baking tray and brush with beaten egg.
7.45 p.m.	Bake the puff parcels.
7.50 p.m.	Make the wasabi or horseradish crème fraîche.
	Assemble the Parmesan crisp baskets.
	Briefly cook the spinach, then drain and press out the excess water.
8 p.m.	Put the potatoes on to boil as you sit down to eat the starter.
8.15 p.m.	Remove the puff parcels from the oven. Drain the potatoes.
	Toss the spinach in some melted butter and season.

TIPS

• Choose some nice background music.

• Subdue the lighting if you can, or light lots of candles.

• Remember to warm your serving dishes and plates.

• Chill the white wine and open the red wine 30 minutes before the meal is to start.

185

amaretti baked peaches with mascarpone cream

This dish is only really worth doing when you can get hold of very ripe, juicy peaches or nectarines. They are at their best during August and September.

serves 2 • preparation 5 mins • cooking 30 mins

Energy 490 kcals • Protein 5.6 g • Carbohydrate 39.7 g • Fat 35.4 g
Saturated fat 20.6 g • Fibre 2.1 g • Salt 0.38 g • Added sugars 15.4 g

> 2 large, ripe peaches or nectarines
> 40 g (1½ oz) amaretti biscuits
> 1 tablespoon caster sugar
> a drop of vanilla extract
> 1 egg yolk
> 1 teaspoon lemon juice
> a little butter, for greasing
>
> FOR THE MASCARPONE CREAM
> 4 tablespoons mascarpone cheese
> 1 teaspoon caster sugar
> 2 drops vanilla extract
> 4 tablespoons double cream

1 Pre-heat the oven to 180°C/350°F/Gas Mark 4. Put the peaches into a bowl and cover with boiling water. Leave for 1 minute, then drain and cover with cold water. Cut each one in half, remove the stones and peel.

2 Put the amaretti biscuits into a plastic bag and crush with a rolling pin into fine crumbs. Tip into a bowl and mix in the sugar, vanilla extract, egg yolk and lemon juice.

3 Put the peach halves into a lightly buttered, shallow ovenproof dish and fill the cavities generously with the amaretti mixture. Bake for 30 minutes until the filling is golden and the peaches are tender, but still holding their shape.

4 Meanwhile, mix the mascarpone with the sugar and vanilla extract, then stir in the cream.

5 Remove the peaches from the oven and leave to cool slightly. Serve warm with the mascarpone cream.

lemon posset with raspberries and refrigerator biscuits

This biscuit dough is great. You can keep it wrapped in the fridge for a week or two, and simply cut off a few slices when you fancy some freshly baked biscuits.

serves 2 • preparation 5 mins for the posset (+ 4 hrs chilling), 5 mins for the biscuits • cooking 8–9 mins for the biscuits

Energy 1343 kcals • Protein 9.5 g • Carbohydrate 114.6 g • Fat 97.2 g
Saturated fat 60.4 g • Fibre 2.3 g • Salt 0.42 g • Added sugars 65.6 g

> 225 ml (7½ fl oz) double cream
> 50 g (2 oz) caster sugar
> finely grated zest and juice of 1 lemon
> 10 or so fresh raspberries and a little icing sugar, to decorate
>
> FOR THE REFRIGERATOR BISCUITS
> 100 g (4 oz) softened unsalted butter
> 75 g (3 oz) caster sugar
> finely grated zest of 1 lemon
> ½ beaten egg
> 115 g (4½ oz) plain flour
> a pinch of salt

1 Put the cream, sugar and lemon zest into a pan and bring to the boil, stirring it now and then to dissolve the sugar. Boil it for exactly 3 minutes, then take the pan off the heat and whisk in the lemon juice. Strain through a fine sieve into a jug, then pour into 2 dessert dishes. Cover and chill for at least 4 hours.

2 For the biscuits, cream the butter and sugar together in a bowl until pale and fluffy. Beat in the lemon zest and egg, then gradually mix in the flour and the pinch of salt to make a soft dough. Shape the mixture into a rectangular block about 3 cm (1½ inches) wide, wrap in cling film and chill for at least 2–3 hours until firm.

3 Pre-heat the oven to 200°C/400°F/Gas Mark 6. Remove the dough from the fridge, unwrap and cut off 4 or 6 slices about 5 mm (¼ inch) thick. Place them 4 cm (1½ inches) apart on a buttered baking sheet and bake for 8–9 minutes until golden around the edges. Remove, allow to cool slightly, then transfer to a cooling rack and leave to go cold.

4 Remove the lemon possets from the fridge and pile a few raspberries into the centre of each. Dust lightly with icing sugar and serve with the biscuits.

rich chocolate, rum and prune pots with crème fraîche

These are the easiest desserts in the world to make.

serves 2 • preparation 35 mins (+ 4 hrs setting) • cooking none

Energy 473 kcals • Protein 5.9 g • Carbohydrate 40.2 g • Fat 29.5 g
Saturated fat 17.1 g • Fibre 1.7 g • Salt 0.65 g • Added sugars 32.4 g

- **2 no-need-to-soak prunes, such as Agen**
- **2 tablespoons dark rum**
- **150 ml (5 fl oz) single cream**
- **2 teaspoons caster sugar**
- **75 g (3 oz) plain chocolate, broken into small pieces**
- **½ teaspoon vanilla extract**
- **a very small pinch of salt**
- **1½ tablespoons beaten egg**
- **2 teaspoons crème fraîche or extra-thick double cream**
- **a little coarsely grated chocolate, to decorate**

1 Put the prunes into a small ramekin, pour over the rum, and set aside for 30 minutes. Lift them out of the rum and drop them into the bottom of 2 dainty teacups or large ramekins. Reserve the remaining rum.

2 Pour the cream into a small pan, add the sugar and leave to get hot, but don't let it boil. Take the pan off the heat and stir in the chocolate until it has completely melted and the mixture is very smooth. Stir in the reserved rum, the vanilla extract, salt and beaten egg.

3 Pour the mixture into the teacups and gently shake until the tops are smooth. Cover loosely and leave somewhere cold, but not in the fridge, for 4 hours or until set.

4 To serve, put the teacups onto saucers and decorate the tops with a spoonful of crème fraîche or cream and a little grated chocolate.

AL FRESCO EATING

roasted red pepper gazpacho

It's difficult to give the exact amount of water that you will need to thin down this summer soup. It will depend on the water content of your tomatoes and cucumber. Add just enough for it to lose that porridge-like look, but it shouldn't be watery. You might need anything up to 300 ml (½ pint).

serves 6 • preparation 45 mins (+ 2 hrs chilling) • cooking none

Energy 360 kcals • Protein 6.5 g • Carbohydrate 21.2 g • Fat 28.1 g
Saturated fat 4.2 g • Fibre 3.6 g • Salt 0.78 g • Added sugars 0.9 g

2 large red peppers
900 g (2 lb) vine-ripened tomatoes, skinned
1 cucumber
½ ciabatta loaf
4 tablespoons sherry vinegar
1 garlic clove, crushed
150 ml (5 fl oz) olive oil
1 teaspoon caster sugar
Maldon salt and freshly ground white pepper

FOR THE GARNISHES
1 tablespoon extra virgin olive oil for the croûtons,
  plus extra to serve
2 vine-ripened tomatoes, skinned, seeded and cut into
  small dice
¼ cucumber, peeled, seeded and cut into small dice
4 spring onions, trimmed and thinly sliced
2 hard-boiled eggs, peeled and cut into small dice
about 12 ice cubes, to serve

1 Pre-heat the oven to 220°C/425°F/Gas Mark 7. Roast the red peppers for 20–25 minutes, turning them now and then, until the skins are quite black.

2 Meanwhile, quarter each tomato and scoop out the seeds into a sieve set over a small bowl. Roughly chop the flesh and rub the juices from the seeds through the sieve. Peel the cucumber, cut it in half lengthways, scoop out the seeds with a teaspoon and roughly chop the flesh. Take 2 thin slices off the piece of ciabatta and set aside for the croûtons. Remove the crusts from the remainder and whizz into breadcrumbs in a food processor. You need about 50 g (2 oz).

3 Remove the roasted red peppers from the oven and leave to go cold. Break them open, pull out and discard the stalks and seeds, then peel and roughly chop the flesh. Lower the oven temperature to 200°C/400°F/Gas Mark 6.

4 Liquidize the red peppers, the tomatoes and their juice, the cucumber and breadcrumbs with the remaining ingredients and some seasoning until smooth. You will probably have to do this in 2 or 3 batches, depending on the size of your liquidizer. Pour into a bowl, thin to the required consistency with cold water, cover and chill for at least 2 hours.

5 For the croûtons, tear the reserved slices of bread into small, rough pieces and toss with 1 tablespoon of the oil until well coated. Spread over a baking sheet and bake in the oven for 4–5 minutes, or until crisp and lightly golden. Remove and leave to cool.

6 To serve, put all the garnishes into small bowls. Ladle the soup into chilled bowls, drizzle with a little olive oil and add a couple of ice cubes to each one. Leave everyone to garnish their own soup.

✿ roasted pumpkin and cumin dip

When pumpkins are out of season, use other types of squash for this dip. Butternut squash is particularly good.

serves 4 • preparation 45 mins • cooking none

Energy 69 kcals • Protein 1.0 g • Carbohydrate 3.1 g • Fat 5.9 g
Saturated fat 0.8 g • Fibre 1.1 g • Salt 0.25 g • Added sugars none

> **450 g (1 lb) prepared pumpkin or squash**
> **2 tablespoons olive oil**
> **³⁄₄ teaspoon ground cumin**
> **3 tablespoons lemon juice**
> **salt and freshly ground black pepper**
> **lemon wedge, to garnish**

1 Pre-heat the oven to 200°C/400°F/Gas Mark 6. Put the peeled pumpkin into a roasting tin. Sprinkle with the oil, cumin, salt and pepper. Turn over a few times until the pieces are well coated, cover with foil and roast for 40 minutes until tender.

2 Remove the pumpkin from the oven and leave to go cold, then transfer to a food processor and add the lemon juice. Process into a smooth purée and season to taste with a little more salt and pepper. Spoon into a serving bowl and garnish with the lemon wedge.

✿ garlic pitta bread

Do these at the last minute if you can. Toasted pitta bread that is left to go cold again can become hard and chewy.

serves 4 • preparation 1–2 mins • cooking 1–2 mins

Energy 294 kcals • Protein 7.2 g • Carbohydrate 44.0 g • Fat 11.1 g
Saturated fat 6.7 g • Fibre 1.8 g • Salt 1.48 g • Added sugars none

> **50 g (2 oz) butter**
> **2 garlic cloves, crushed**
> **6 pitta bread**
> **salt and freshly ground black pepper**

1 Put the butter, garlic and a little salt and pepper into a small pan and heat gently until melted.

2 Warm the pitta bread in a toaster or on the barbecue until golden on both sides. Lift onto a board and brush with the garlic butter. Cut into fingers and serve warm with dips.

butter bean and rosemary hummus

Butter beans tend to be slightly wetter than the more usual chick peas, so add the oil gradually and add just enough to give the hummus a nice creamy texture.

serves 4 • preparation 1 hr 5 mins • cooking none

Energy 252 kcals • Protein 3.5 g • Carbohydrate 8.1 g • Fat 23.1 g
Saturated fat 3.2 g • Fibre 2.7 g • Salt 0.86 g • Added sugars none

> **1 × 400-g (14-oz) can butter beans**
> **the leaves from 1 sprig of rosemary, finely chopped**
> **1 small garlic clove, crushed**
> **2 tablespoons lemon juice**
> **100–120 ml (3¹⁄₂–4 fl oz) olive oil, plus extra to serve**
> **salt and freshly ground black pepper**

1 Drain the butter beans, rinse under cold water and dry well on kitchen paper. Tip them into a food processor and add the chopped rosemary, garlic, lemon juice and some seasoning.

2 Whizz everything until smooth, then, with the machine still running, gradually pour in enough olive oil to make a smooth, creamy dip. Spoon the mixture into a serving bowl and chill for at least 1 hour.

3 Remove the hummus from the fridge and pour a little more olive oil around the edge of the dish. Serve with some garlic pitta bread (see left).

chargrilled chicken on avocado salad

This is a great main-course salad. It requires a little bit of last-minute work but it's worth it, believe me.

serves 6 • preparation 45 mins • cooking 8–10 mins

Energy 406 kcals • Protein 21.5 g • Carbohydrate 4.8 g • Fat 33.6 g
Saturated fat 4.8 g • Fibre 3.5 g • Salt 0.68 g • Added sugars 0.4 g

450 g (1 lb) skinned mini chicken fillets
juice of ¹⁄₂ small lemon
6 tablespoons olive oil
¹⁄₂ teaspoon salt
freshly ground black pepper

FOR THE SALAD
175 g (6 oz) frozen peas
1 × 225-g (8-oz) bag baby leaf spinach, washed and dried
2 small ripe but firm avocados
salt and freshly ground black pepper
a small handful of mint leaves, to garnish

FOR THE SALAD DRESSING
8 tablespoons extra virgin olive oil
2 tablespoons red wine vinegar
a good pinch of caster sugar
2 shallots, halved and thinly sliced
leaves from a 20-g (³⁄₄-oz) packet of mint, chopped

1 Put the chicken fillets into a shallow dish. Whisk together the lemon juice, oil, salt and some pepper, pour over the chicken and mix together. Set aside for at least 30 minutes.

2 If using a charcoal barbecue, light it 30 minutes before you want to start cooking. If using a gas barbecue, light it 10 minutes beforehand. Alternatively, you can use a ridged griddle pan or frying pan.

3 For the salad dressing, whisk together the oil, vinegar, sugar and some salt and pepper to taste in a bowl. Stir in the shallots and set aside.

4 Drop the peas into a pan of boiling salted water, bring back to the boil and drain immediately. Refresh under cold water and drain well. Spread the spinach leaves over the base of 6 serving plates. Halve the avocados, remove the stones, then quarter the fruit and carefully peel. Cut across into slices and scatter on top of the spinach.

5 Lift the chicken fillets out of the marinade and season with a little salt. Barbecue over a medium heat for 4–5 minutes on each side. Transfer to a plate, cool slightly, then arrange over the top of the salads. Stir the peas and chopped mint into the dressing, spoon over the chicken and salad and scatter with a few small mint leaves to garnish.

mozzarella and three-tomato salad

This is my variation on the classic Italian salad, using cherry tomatoes and sun-dried tomatoes as well as vine tomatoes.

serves 6 • preparation 10 mins • cooking none

Energy 333 kcals • Protein 20.2 g • Carbohydrate 5.1 g • Fat 26.0 g
Saturated fat 11.6 g • Fibre 1.6 g • Salt 2.02 g • Added sugars none

6 vine-ripened tomatoes, sliced
3 × 150-g (5-oz) mozzarella cheeses, drained and sliced or
2 × 150-g (5-oz) tubs mini mozzarella cheeses, drained well
175 g (6 oz) yellow cherry tomatoes, halved
25 g (1 oz) sun-dried tomatoes in olive oil, drained and cut into long, thin strips
a handful of small basil leaves, to garnish
sea salt flakes and freshly ground black pepper

FOR THE FRESH BASIL DRESSING
40 g (1¹⁄₂ oz) fresh basil leaves (about 2 small pots)
1 tablespoon lemon juice
¹⁄₂ teaspoon salt
5 tablespoons extra virgin olive oil

1 Overlap the slices of tomato and sliced mozzarella, if using, over the base of 6 serving plates. Scatter over the cherry tomatoes and the strips of sun-dried tomatoes. If using mini mozzarellas, scatter them over the top of the tomatoes. Cover and chill until needed.

2 Just before serving, make the dressing. Discard the larger basil stalks, then pack the leaves into a food processor and add the lemon juice, ¹⁄₂ teaspoon salt and some black pepper. Turn on the machine and gradually add the oil to make a smooth dressing. Season the salad lightly with salt flakes and pepper, then drizzle the dressing over the salad. Serve scattered with a few extra small basil leaves.

tuna steaks with a tomato, caper and mint salsa

Tuna cooks through in a flash, so be careful not to cook it for too long. The barbecue grill will make marks on the steak. These will be initially be red, but when they start to turn pink you need to turn them over.

serves 4 • preparation 5 mins • cooking 2–3 mins

Energy 388 kcals • Protein 42.6 g • Carbohydrate 4.0 g • Fat 22.6 g
Saturated fat 4.7 g • Fibre 1.2 g • Salt 1.32 g • Added sugars none

4 tuna loin steaks, about 175–225 g (6–8 oz) each
a little olive oil
salt and freshly ground black pepper
2 vine-ripened tomatoes, sliced, and ½ a small red onion,
    very thinly sliced, to serve

FOR THE TOMATO AND CAPER SALSA
2 vine-ripened tomatoes
1 small red onion, finely chopped
2 garlic cloves, finely chopped
1 tablespoon lemon juice
2 tablespoons extra virgin olive oil
3 tablespoons small capers, rinsed and drained
the leaves from ½ x 20-g (¾-oz) packet mint, chopped
the leaves from ½ x 20-g (¾-oz) packet flat-leaf
    parsley, chopped

1 If using a charcoal barbecue, light it 30 minutes before you want to start cooking. If using a gas barbecue, light it 10 minutes beforehand. Alternatively, you can use a ridged griddle pan or frying pan.

2 For the salsa, quarter the tomatoes, discard the seeds and cut the flesh into small pieces. Mix in a bowl with the rest of the salsa ingredients (reserving a little of the flat-leaf parsley, to garnish) and some salt and pepper to taste.

3 If using a griddle or frying pan, place over a high heat until very hot. Brush the tuna on both sides with plenty of oil and season well with salt and pepper. Cook over a high heat for 1–1½ minutes on each side, pressing down lightly on the steaks with the back of a fish slice as they cook. Spread a few of the tomato and red onion slices on each plate, place the tuna steaks on top and sprinkle with the reserved parsley. Serve straight away with the salsa.

✪ piripiri prawn and lemon skewers

Piripiri is the name of a classic Spanish chilli-and-lemon-flavoured marinade, traditionally used for chicken, that goes equally well with prawns. This recipe makes 8 skewers, so we've calculated the nutritional information below on a 2-skewer sized portion.

makes 8 skewers (serves 4) • preparation 10–15 mins +
15 mins' marinating • cooking 4 mins

Energy 115 kcals • Protein 14.0 g • Carbohydrate 4.3 g • Fat 4.8 g
Saturated fat 0.6 g • Fibre 0.5 g • Salt 0.80 g • Added sugars 0.1 g

2 small red onions
2 small lemons
3 tablespoons olive oil
1½ tablespoons sweet chilli sauce
2 teaspoons lemon juice
1 garlic clove, crushed
1 medium-hot red chilli, seeded and finely chopped
24 large peeled raw prawns
salt and freshly ground black pepper

1 Peel the onions, leaving the root ends intact. Cut each one into 8 thin wedges through the root so they stay together in one piece. Cut each lemon into 6 thin wedges, then each one across into 2 small, chunky pieces.

2 Mix together the oil, sweet chilli sauce, lemon juice, garlic, red chilli and some salt and pepper in a bowl. Add the prawns and onion wedges, mix well and set aside for at least 15 minutes.

3 If using a charcoal barbecue, light it 30 minutes before you want to start cooking. If using a gas barbecue, light it 10 minutes beforehand. Alternatively, pre-heat your grill to medium-high.

4 Thread 3 prawns, 3 pieces of lemon and 2 onion wedges onto 8 long metal skewers. Barbecue or grill over or under a medium heat for 2 minutes on each side, brushing them with some of the left-over marinade now and then, until the prawns are cooked through and the onions are slightly blackened around the edges.

lemon and thyme chicken with grainy mustard butter

The simple marinade for the chicken does everything you could wish for: the lemon juice tenderizes the meat, the thyme adds flavour and the oil helps to keep it moist.

serves 6 • preparation 5 mins + 1 hr marinating • cooking 14–16 mins

Energy 264 kcals • Protein 34.3 g • Carbohydrate 0.8 g • Fat 13.7 g
Saturated fat 5.5 g • Fibre 0.4 g • Salt 0.75 g • Added sugars none

6 skinned, boneless chicken breasts
8 tablespoons olive oil
leaves from 3 large sprigs of thyme
juice of 1 small lemon
salt and freshly ground black pepper

FOR THE MUSTARD BUTTER
50 g (2 oz) softened butter
finely grated zest of ½ small lemon
2 tablespoons wholegrain mustard
the leaves from 4 sprigs of thyme
2 garlic cloves, crushed
the leaves from 3 sprigs of parsley, chopped

1 Make 3 shallow diagonal slashes on the top of each chicken breast and put them into a baking dish. Add the olive oil, thyme, lemon juice, ½ teaspoon salt and some pepper, mix well and leave to marinate for at least 1 hour or overnight.

2 Mix together the ingredients for the mustard butter with ¼ teaspoon salt and some black pepper. Set aside somewhere cool until needed.

3 If using a charcoal barbecue, light it 30 minutes before you want to start cooking. If using a gas barbecue, light it 10 minutes beforehand. Alternatively, you can use a ridged griddle pan or frying pan.

4 If using a griddle or frying pan, place it over a high heat until very hot. Brush the bars of the barbecue with oil. Shake the excess marinade off the chicken pieces and cook over a medium heat for 7–8 minutes on each side until cooked through. Serve dotted with the mustard butter.

✪ spicy fried tandoori-style chicken

This dish uses a spicy, yoghurt-based marinade, where the acidity of the yoghurt acts as a meat tenderizer. However, don't marinate for much longer than suggested or the meat will get too soft.

serves 6 • preparation 5 mins + 2 hrs 20 mins' marinating • cooking 14–16 mins

Energy 165 kcals • Protein 34.8 g • Carbohydrate 2.1 g • Fat 2.0 g
Saturated fat 0.6 g • Fibre 0.1 g • Salt 0.54 g • Added sugars none

6 skinned, boneless chicken breasts
1 teaspoon salt
1 teaspoon cayenne pepper
4 teaspoons sweet paprika
juice of 1 small lemon
250 g (9 oz) natural yoghurt
½ medium onion, chopped
2 garlic cloves, crushed
2.5 cm (1 inch) piece root ginger, finely grated
1 teaspoon minced red chilli (from a jar)
1½ teaspoons ground cumin
1½ teaspoons ground coriander

1 Make 3 shallow diagonal slashes on the top of each chicken breast and put them into a baking dish. Sprinkle with the salt, cayenne, 2 teaspoons of the paprika and the lemon juice, mix well and leave for 20 minutes.

2 Meanwhile, blend the yoghurt, onion, garlic, ginger, minced red chilli, remaining paprika, cumin and coriander together in a liquidizer until smooth.

3 Drain the lemon juice from the chicken, pour over the yoghurt marinade and mix. Cover and chill for 2–4 hours.

4 If using a charcoal barbecue, light it 30 minutes before you want to start cooking. If using a gas barbecue, light it 10 minutes beforehand. Alternatively, pre-heat the oven to 240°C/475°F/Gas Mark 9, or as high as your oven will go.

5 Brush the bars of the barbecue with oil. Shake the excess marinade off the chicken pieces and cook over a medium heat for 7–8 minutes on each side until cooked through. If baking the chicken in the oven, place the chicken on a rack over a foil-lined roasting tin. Drizzle with oil and bake for 20 minutes, or until cooked through.

how to make burgers

Home-made burgers are a doddle to make, and it's easy to vary the flavours, too. The trick is not to use lean mince – the additional fat of ordinary mince helps to keep them moist and juicy. The nutritional information given below is per burger, so you'll need to multiply up if you have more than one.

tex-mex burgers with guacamole, chilli salsa and soured cream

makes 6 • preparation 15 mins • cooking 10 mins

Energy 514 kcals • Protein 32.4 g • Carbohydrate 6.7 g • Fat 39.9 g
Saturated fat 15.2 g • Fibre 2.1 g • Salt 0.61 g • Added sugars none

900 g (2 lb) minced beef
3 garlic cloves, crushed
1 small onion, finely chopped
2 teaspoons minced red chilli, from a jar (sambal oelek)
1 tablespoon sweet paprika
2 teaspoons dried oregano
salt and freshly ground black pepper

TO SERVE
6 sesame-seed burger buns or crusty rolls, split in half
lettuce leaves
1 x 170 g tub guacamole (or see recipe on page 236)
1 x 170 g tub chilli tomato salsa (or see recipe on page 236)
150 ml (5 fl oz) soured cream

1 If you are using a charcoal barbecue to cook these burgers, light it 30 minutes before you want to start cooking. If using a gas barbecue, light it 10 minutes beforehand. Alternatively, use a heavy-based frying pan or ridged cast-iron griddle.

2 Put the minced beef, garlic, onion, minced chilli, paprika, oregano, 1 teaspoon salt and some black pepper into a bowl and mix together with your hands. Divide the mixture into 6 and shape into burgers about 2.5 cm (1 inch) thick by pressing the mixture into a 9 cm (3½ inch) plain pastry cutter. Cook the burgers over a medium heat for 5 minutes on each side. Toast the burger buns or rolls cut-face down around the burgers for the last 2–3 minutes of cooking.

3 To serve, put a few lettuce leaves on the bottom half of each bun and top with the burger. Spoon on some guacamole, chilli tomato salsa and soured cream, top with the other half of the bun and eat.

VARIATIONS

CHICKEN AND BACON BURGERS
Use minced chicken and mix with 6 rashers finely chopped streaky bacon, the onion, garlic and seasoning. Cook for 7–8 minutes on each side until cooked through. Serve in buns with some blue cheese mayonnaise.

GREEK LAMB AND FETA BURGERS
Use minced lamb and mix with 1 teaspoon ground cumin, 1 teaspoon coriander, the chopped leaves of ½ x 20-g (¾-oz) packet mint, the onion, garlic and seasoning. Shape the burgers around 1 × 2.5-cm (½ × 1-inch) pieces of feta cheese. Cook for 5 minutes on each side and serve with some Greek yoghurt flavoured with chopped mint and a little salt.

cumberland sausages with roasted red pepper chutney

Cumberland sausages are coiled, either as individual sausages, or as one large sausage, which is enough to feed 4–6 people. However, if you can't find them, use 8 good-quality meaty sausages instead.

serves 4 • preparation 5 mins • cooking 10–12 mins for the sausages, 1 hr for the chutney

Energy 500 kcals • Protein 19.0 g • Carbohydrate 52.9 g • Fat 25.1 g
Saturated fat 8.2 g • Fibre 5.0 g • Salt 2.56 g • Added sugars 25.4 g

1 large or 4 individual Cumberland sausages

FOR THE ROASTED RED PEPPER CHUTNEY
6 red peppers
1 tablespoon olive oil
2 red onions, halved and thinly sliced
100 g (4 oz) light soft brown or muscovado sugar
2 teaspoons minced red chilli, from a jar (sambal oelek)
180 ml (6 fl oz) red wine vinegar
1 × 200-g (7-oz) can chopped tomatoes
salt and freshly ground black pepper

1 For the chutney, pre-heat the oven to 220°C/425°F/Gas Mark 7. Roast the red peppers for 15–20 minutes until the skins are black all over and the flesh has softened. Meanwhile, heat the oil in a medium-sized pan, add the onions and cook for 10 minutes until soft and lightly browned. Add the sugar and cook for 2 minutes.

2 Remove the peppers from the oven and leave them to cool, then break in half and remove the seeds, stalks and skin. Cut the flesh into long, thin strips. Add them to the pan with the chilli, vinegar, tomatoes, 1/2 teaspoon salt and some pepper and simmer for 30–40 minutes until the mixture is well reduced and thick, and just beginning to catch on the bottom of the pan. Adjust the seasoning if necessary. This can be made well in advance if you wish.

3 If using a charcoal barbecue, light it 30 minutes before you want to start cooking. If using a gas barbecue, light it 10 minutes beforehand.

4 If you wish to grill the sausages, pre-heat the grill to medium-high. Barbecue or grill the sausages over a medium heat for 5–6 minutes on each side until cooked through. Warm through the chutney and serve with the sausages.

thai pork chops with sweet-and-sour carrot salad

The coconut, chilli and lime marinade used for pork in this recipe works equally well with chicken breasts and large peeled prawns.

serves 4 • preparation 3–4 mins for the chops (+ 6 hrs marinating) + 3–4 mins for the salad • cooking 14 mins

Energy 560 kcals • Protein 45.6 g • Carbohydrate 15.9 g • Fat 35.4 g
Saturated fat 16.4 g • Fibre 2.3 g • Salt 1.73 g • Added sugars 6.7 g

1 × 200-ml (7-fl oz) carton coconut cream

3 garlic cloves, crushed

1 teaspoon minced red chilli (sambal oelek), from a jar

2.5 cm (1 inch) fresh root ginger, peeled and finely grated

3 tablespoons light soy sauce

finely grated zest and juice of 1 lime

2 tablespoons caster sugar

4 thick, boneless spare-rib pork chops, excess fat removed

FOR THE SWEET-AND-SOUR CARROT SALAD

3 large carrots, peeled

2 tablespoons white wine vinegar

1 tablespoon caster sugar

1 medium-hot red chilli, seeded and finely chopped

2 teaspoons Thai fish sauce

1 × 20-g (¾-oz) packet coriander, finely chopped

1 Make the marinade by combining the coconut cream, garlic, minced chilli, ginger, soy sauce, lime zest and juice and sugar in a liquidizer or food processor and blending until smooth. Place the chops in a shallow dish, pour over the marinade and turn once or twice. Cover and chill for 6 hours or overnight.

2 If using a charcoal barbecue, light it 30 minutes before you want to start cooking. If using a gas barbecue, light it 10 minutes beforehand. Alternatively, you can use a hot, ridged cast-iron griddle.

3 Lift the chops out of the marinade and shake off the excess liquid. Brush the bars of the barbecue or griddle with a little oil, add the chops and cook over a medium heat for 7 minutes on each side until cooked through.

4 Meanwhile, grate the carrots on a mandolin or on the coleslaw blade of your food processor into long, very thin strips. You want to be left with 225 g (8 oz). Mix the vinegar, sugar, red chilli and Thai fish sauce together in a bowl. Just before serving, add the grated carrot and coriander and mix well. Serve with the pork chops.

chargrilled lamb steaks with fennel ratatouille

I love ratatouille with any type of roasted or grilled lamb. The addition of some fennel seeds and bulb fennel gives the ratatouille even more of a Mediterranean flavour, and if you have it, a teaspoon of Pernod wouldn't go amiss.

serves 4 • preparation 15 mins (+ 1 hr chilling) • cooking 10–12 mins for the lamb steaks, 50 mins for the ratatouille

Energy 557 kcals • Protein 46.5 g • Carbohydrate 9.7 g • Fat 37.1 g
Saturated fat 12.3 g • Fibre 4.4 g • Salt 1.13 g • Added sugars none

4 × 225-g (8-oz) leg of lamb steaks, cut 2.5 cm
  (1 inch) thick
salt and freshly ground black pepper

FOR THE MARINADE
2 garlic cloves, crushed
1 medium-hot red chilli, seeded and finely chopped
leaves from 1 sprig of rosemary, chopped
leaves from 2 large thyme sprigs, chopped
zest of 1 small lemon
juice of ½ lemon
½ teaspoon coarsely ground black pepper
1 teaspoon salt
6 tablespoons olive oil

FOR THE FENNEL RATATOUILLE
1 small aubergine, weighing about 175 g (6 oz)
1 small red pepper, seeded
1 small green pepper, seeded
2 small fennel bulbs, trimmed
4 tablespoons olive oil
1 small onion, thinly sliced
2 large garlic cloves, sliced
1 teaspoon fennel seeds, lightly crushed
1 courgette, thickly sliced
1 × 400-g (14-oz) can chopped tomatoes
2 tablespoons chopped dill

1 Mix the marinade ingredients together in a large, shallow dish. Add the lamb steaks, turn over a few times until well coated, then cover and chill for at least 1 hour.

2 For the fennel ratatouille, cut the aubergine, peppers and fennel into 2.5-cm (1-inch) chunks. Heat 2 tablespoons of the oil in a large pan, add the aubergine and fry for 4 minutes until golden. Transfer to a plate and set aside. Heat the rest of the oil in the pan, then fry the onion for 5 minutes until lightly browned. Add the garlic and the fennel seeds, fry for 1 minute, then add the peppers and fry for another 5 minutes until soft. Add the courgette and fennel and fry for another 5 minutes. Return the aubergine to the pan with the chopped tomatoes (the Pernod, if you wish) and some seasoning, part-cover and simmer for 30 minutes until all the vegetables are tender and the sauce has reduced and thickened slightly. Stir in the dill and some seasoning to taste. Set aside.

3 If using a charcoal barbecue, light it 30 minutes before you want to start cooking. If using a gas barbecue, light it 10 minutes beforehand. Alternatively, you can use a hot, ridged griddle pan.

4 If using a griddle or frying pan, place it over a high heat until very hot. Brush the bars of the barbecue or the base of the griddle with a little oil. Remove the lamb steaks from the marinade and allow the excess oil to drain away, then season with a little more salt and pepper. Cook over a medium-high heat for 5–6 minutes on each side. Transfer to a board, cover with foil and leave them to rest for 5 minutes. Reheat the ratatouille and serve with the steaks.

field mushrooms with spinach, blue cheese and pine nuts

Try to choose deep field mushrooms with curled-up edges so that they hold the filling in place.

serves 4 • preparation 20 mins • cooking 8–10 mins

Energy 343 kcals • Protein 12.9 g • Carbohydrate 5.8 g • Fat 30.0 g
Saturated fat 7.8 g • Fibre 5.1 g • Salt 1.57 g • Added sugars none

450 g (1 lb) spinach, washed and large stalks removed
6 tablespoons olive oil
1 small onion, finely chopped
2 garlic cloves, crushed
1 × 200-g (7-oz) can chopped tomatoes
1 tablespoon freshly squeezed lemon juice
25 g (1 oz) lightly toasted pine nuts
8 evenly sized large field mushrooms, wiped clean
100 g (4 oz) mild blue cheese, such as Roquefort or
    Danish Blue, coarsely grated
salt and freshly ground black pepper

1 If using a charcoal barbecue, light it 30 minutes before you want to start cooking. If using a gas barbecue, light it 10 minutes beforehand. Alternatively, preheat the oven to 230°C/450°F/Gas Mark 8, or as high as your oven will go.

2 Remove the excess water from the spinach (give it a whizz in a salad spinner if you have one). Heat 2 tablespoons of the olive oil in a large pan, add the spinach and stir-fry it over a high heat until it just wilts into the bottom of the pan. Tip into a colander and press out the excess liquid, then transfer to a chopping board and roughly chop.

3 Add another 2 tablespoons of oil to the pan, followed by the onion and garlic, and cook for 5 minutes until soft. Stir in the tomatoes and lemon juice and cook for 10 minutes until reduced and thick. Stir in the spinach, toasted pine nuts and some seasoning to taste.

4 Discard the stalks from the mushrooms, then brush both sides of the caps with a little olive oil and season well with salt and pepper. Barbecue, gill-side down, over a medium heat for 4 minutes. Transfer to a plate, flip over and top with the spinach mixture, then the blue cheese. Return to the barbecue and cook for another 5–6 minutes until the mushrooms are tender and the cheese has just started to melt. Alternatively, place the mushrooms gill-side up on a lightly oiled baking tray and bake in the oven for 4 minutes, then top with the spinach and blue cheese and bake for a further 6–8 minutes.

halloumi and vegetable skewers on spicy chick-pea couscous

These skewers are best eaten as soon as they come off the grill, otherwise the cheese has a tendency to go rubbery.

makes 8 skewers • preparation 10–15 mins + 30 mins' soaking for the skewers • cooking 9–10 mins for the skewers, 5 mins for the couscous

Energy 787 kcals • Protein 25.3 g • Carbohydrate 63.1 g • Fat 49.6 g
Saturated fat 13.8 g • Fibre 4.3 g • Salt 3.40 g • Added sugars none

250 g (9 oz) halloumi cheese

2 small red peppers

2 × 100-g (4-oz) courgettes

16 large vine-ripened cherry tomatoes

16 small bay leaves

3 tablespoons olive oil

sea salt flakes and coarsely ground black pepper

FOR THE SPICY CHICK-PEA COUSCOUS

2 tablespoons olive oil

1½ teaspoons ground cumin

1½ teaspoons ground coriander

a pinch of ground turmeric

1 × 400-g (14-oz) can chick peas, drained and rinsed

600 ml (1 pint) vegetable stock (see page 231)

350 g (12 oz) couscous

FOR THE GARLIC, MINT AND LEMON DRESSING

2 garlic cloves, crushed

2 tablespoons lemon juice

6 tablespoons extra virgin olive oil

leaves from 1 × 20-g (³⁄₄-oz) packet mint, chopped

1 Cover 8 bamboo skewers with water and leave them to soak for at least 30 minutes. If using a charcoal barbecue, light it 30 minutes before you want to start cooking. If using a gas barbecue, light it 10 minutes beforehand. Alternatively, preheat the grill to medium-high.

2 Cut the halloumi cheese into 16 even-sized pieces and cut the red peppers into similar-sized pieces. Cut the courgettes into slightly chunky slices and drop into a pan of boiling water. Cook for 2 minutes, then drain and refresh under cold water. Put all these prepared ingredients into a bowl with the cherry tomatoes, bay leaves and olive oil and mix together well.

3 Thread the cheese, vegetables and bay leaves onto the skewers and season well with salt and pepper. Barbecue or grill over or under a medium heat for 9–10 minutes, turning them every now and then as they brown.

4 Meanwhile, for the couscous, put the oil and spices into a medium-sized pan and place over a high heat. As soon as they start to sizzle, add the chick peas, stock and ½ teaspoon salt and bring to the boil. Stir in the couscous, cover and remove from the heat. Leave undisturbed for 5 minutes. Mix together the ingredients for the dressing.

5 Uncover the couscous and fluff it up into separate grains with a fork. Season to taste. Spoon some onto each plate and rest the skewers on top. Spoon over a little dressing and serve.

fourth of july barbecue

Americans love to celebrate their special day with a barbecue, so why not do the same and invite your friends, too? With a bit of planning, a lot of the food can be prepared the day before, and there are sure to be plenty of guys on hand to help with cooking.

menu

Butter bean and rosemary hummus
(see page 193)

Roasted pumpkin and cumin dip
(see page 193)

Garlic pitta bread
(see page 193)

Lemon and thyme chicken with grainy mustard butter
(see page 198)

Tex-Mex burgers with guacamole, chilli salsa and soured cream
(see page 200)

Field mushrooms with spinach, blue cheese and pine nuts
(see page 206)

New potato salad
(see page 228)

Crunchy coleslaw
(see page 229)

Quick blueberry and lemon cheesecake
(see page 211)

Long Island iced tea
(see page 215)

time plan

The day before

Marinate the chicken and make the grainy mustard butter.
Shred the vegetables and make the dressing for the
coleslaw, but keep them separate.
Chill the drinks (beers, wine, soft drinks and mixers).
Make lots of ice.

In advance on the day

Make the dips (you could do them the day before, but they
will taste much fresher if made on the day).
Make the burgers.
Make the chilli salsa and refrigerate.
Cook the potatoes for the salad and make the dressing, but
keep them separate.
Make the cheesecake base, fill it and refrigerate.
Make the cheesecake topping but keep it separate.
Prepare the mushrooms, make the spinach filling and slice
the cheese.
Get out the barbecue and all the necessary equipment –
cooking utensils, a large oven glove, kitchen timer, etc. –
and set it up in the garden. Check that you have sufficient
charcoal or gas.

time plan for a 7 p.m. barbecue

6 p.m.	Remove the grainy mustard butter from the fridge and allow it to come back to room temperature somewhere cool. Make the guacamole, put into a serving bowl and refrigerate. Put the tomato salsa and soured cream into bowls and keep chilled. Prepare the lettuce for the burgers.
6.30 p.m.	Light the charcoal barbecue, if using.
6.45 p.m.	Dress the potato salad. Mix the coleslaw ingredients together. Prepare the garlic butter for the pitta bread.
6.50 p.m.	Light the gas barbecue, if using.
6.55/7 p.m.	Make jugs of the Long Island iced tea. Griddle some pitta bread and set out with the dips.
9 p.m.	Remove the cheesecake from the flan tin and spoon over the topping just before serving.

BARBECUE HINTS AND TIPS

- Place your barbecue on a level, firm surface, away from anything that could catch fire (hedges, trees, fences, etc.).
- Never use a barbecue in high winds and never leave it unattended.
- Keep children and animals well away.
- Make sure the bars of the grill are clean before you start. A brisk scrub with a wire brush should do the trick. Ideally, clean it before you put it away so that it's always ready to use.
- Buy the best charcoal fuel that you can. Cheap stuff will just burn away very quickly and not give a very high heat. Lumpwood charcoal is better than charcoal briquettes. Australian Parlour's Heat Beads® are excellent and stay hot for much longer than other fuels.
- Use barbecue lighter fuels sparingly, and don't be tempted to use anything else, such as petrol or white spirit. Not only are these dangerous, but they will give off fumes that will taint the food.
- Always make sure the barbecue is up to temperature before cooking anything. The coals should be covered in a layer of light grey ash. This can take between 30 and 40 minutes, depending on the weather.
- Keep some extra coals handy in case you need to top up the heat before the end of the cooking time. Be sure to add them before the others have cooled down too much so that they have a better chance of coming up to temperature.
- Keep raw food out of the sun before cooking, somewhere cool, but at room temperature.
- Lightly brush the grill bars with a little oil before cooking , to help prevent foods from sticking.
- Remove excess oil and marinades from the food before grilling (ditto excess fat from meats). They cause the coals to flare up, scorching the outside of the food.
- Once the food is on the bars, avoid turning it over until the required cooking time is up. It needs to have time to seal properly on the outside, which makes it much easier to turn over.
- Don't use a fork for turning meats and fish as this pierces the flesh, allowing the juices to run out. Use long-handled tongs or a fish slice instead.
- Always soak wooden skewers before using them on the barbecue, to prevent them burning. And use flat metal ones to prevent the food from spinning around. A good trick is to thread the food onto two parallel skewers (wooden or metal) to make it easier to turn.

quick blueberry, lemon and crème fraîche cheesecake

This cheesecake is extra easy because it does not require any gelatine. The action of the lemon juice on the cream cheese and crème fraîche helps it set all on its own.

serves 8 • preparation 15 mins (+ 2 hrs chilling) • cooking none

Energy 571 kcals • Protein 5.2 g • Carbohydrate 46.9 g • Fat 41.6 g
Saturated fat 24.8 g • Fibre 1.0 g • Salt 0.98 g • Added sugars 26.7 g

2 large lemons
225 g (8 oz) full-fat cream cheese
100 g (4 oz) caster sugar
200 g (7 oz) crème fraîche

FOR THE BASE
100 g (4 oz) butter
225 g (8 oz) digestive biscuits
1½ tablespoons demerara sugar

FOR THE BLUEBERRY TOPPING
3 tablespoons lemon juice
50 g (2 oz) caster sugar
150 g (5 oz) blueberries
1 teaspoon arrowroot

1 For the base, put the butter into a large saucepan and melt over a low heat. Put the biscuits into a large plastic bag, seal the end and crush with a rolling pin into fine crumbs. Stir into the butter with the demerara sugar. Press the mixture firmly onto the base and sides of a lightly oiled 20-cm (8-inch) loose-bottomed flan tin using the back of a spoon. Chill while you make the filling.

2 Finely grate the zest from 1 lemon and squeeze the juice from both – you should get 150 ml (5 fl oz) of juice. Beat the cream cheese, sugar and lemon zest together in a bowl until smooth. Very gradually, beat in the lemon juice until you have a thick, creamy mixture, then gently fold in the crème fraîche. Spoon the filling into the biscuit case, swirl the top with a knife and chill for at least 2 hours.

3 For the topping, put the lemon juice and sugar into a small pan and leave over a low heat until the sugar has dissolved. Add the blueberries, bring to a gentle simmer and cook for 1 minute. Mix the arrowroot with 1 teaspoon of cold water, stir in and cook for about 30 seconds until thickened. Transfer to a small bowl and leave to cool. Then cover and chill alongside the cheesecake.

4 Remove the cheesecake from the flan tin and transfer it to a serving plate. Spoon over the blueberry topping, cut into wedges and serve.

lemon meringue pie

If you are really short of time, you could make this pudding with a ready-baked sweet pastry case, now available in most supermarkets.

serves 8 • preparation 35–40 mins • cooking 15 mins

Energy 467 kcals • Protein 4.5 g • Carbohydrate 69.2 g • Fat 21.0 g
Saturated fat 10.4 g • Fibre 0.9 g • Salt 0.26 g • Added sugars 42.7 g

350 g (12 oz) sweet shortcrust pastry (see page 236)
1 egg yolk, beaten with 1 teaspoon water

FOR THE FILLING
finely grated zest of 1 lemon
300 ml (10 fl oz) lemon juice (about 5 lemons)
225 g (8 oz) caster sugar
3 tablespoons cornflour
2 egg yolks
50 g (2 oz) unsalted butter

FOR THE MERINGUE
2 egg whites
100 g (4 oz) caster sugar

1 Thinly roll out the pastry on a lightly floured surface and use to line a lightly greased, loose-bottomed flan tin about 20 cm (8 inches) wide and 4 cm (1½ inches) deep (see page 164). Prick the base here and there with a fork and chill for 20 minutes.

2 Pre-heat the oven to 200°C/400°F/Gas Mark 6. Line the pastry case with a crumpled sheet of greaseproof paper and a thin layer of baking beans and bake for 15 minutes. Carefully remove the paper and beans and return the case to the oven for 4 minutes. Slide out once more, brush the inside of the case with the egg yolk and water mixture and return to the oven for 2 minutes. Remove and lower the oven temperature to 180°C/350°F/Gas Mark 4.

3 For the filling, put the lemon zest, lemon juice and sugar into a pan and heat gently, stirring now and then, until the sugar dissolves. Mix the cornflour with 2 tablespoons cold water, bring the lemon mixture to the boil, then stir in the slaked cornflour. Cook for 1–2 minutes until thickened. Remove from the heat, cool slightly, then beat in the egg yolks and butter. Pour into the pastry case and leave to go cold.

4 For the meringue, place the egg whites in a large, very clean bowl and whisk into stiff peaks. Gradually whisk in the sugar, a spoonful at a time, to make a stiff, glossy meringue. Spoon it on top of the tart and spread it out, making sure it makes a good seal with the pastry edge. Swirl the top with the tip of a knife and bake for 15 minutes until lightly browned.

5 Carefully remove the tart from the tin and leave to cool slightly. Serve warm or cold, cut into wedges.

✪ watermelon and lime granita

Watermelon, as its name suggests, consists mostly of water, so is ideal for making into a water ice, or granita, *as the Italians call it.*

serves 4 • preparation 2–3 mins + 3–4 hrs' freezing • cooking none

Energy 136 kcals • Protein 0.7 g • Carbohydrate 34.4 g • Fat 0.4 g
Saturated fat none • Fibre 0.2 g • Salt 0.01 g • Added sugars 26.3 g

750 g (1½ lb) wedge of watermelon
100 g (4 oz) caster sugar
150 ml (5 fl oz) freshly squeezed lime juice (about 3 limes)
thin lime wedges, to decorate

1 Slice the watermelon flesh away from the skin and hook out all the little black seeds. Put the flesh into a food processor with the sugar and lime juice and blend until smooth. Pass through a sieve into a shallow plastic container, cover with a lid and leave in the freezer for about 1 hour until some of the mixture has frozen around the edges.

2 Scrape all the frozen ice away from the sides and break it up into smaller crystals with a fork. Return to the freezer and continue to do this every 30 minutes or so until you have a frozen but still grainy mixture. Leave in the freezer until needed.

3 Spoon the mixture into 4 glasses that have been chilled in the freezer and serve straight away, garnished with a thin wedge of lime.

✪ tropical ginger pimm's

Traditional Pimm's is made with lemonade, and flavoured with sliced apples, cucumber and mint, but this one is made with ginger beer and has a vaguely Caribbean twist.

makes 6 glasses • preparation 5 mins • cooking none

Energy 230 kcals • Protein 0.5 g • Carbohydrate 32.0 g • Fat 0.1 g
Saturated fat none • Fibre 0.7 g • Salt 0.09 g • Added sugars 18.5 g

> 12 fresh lychees, peeled
> 1 lime, cut into 6 wedges
> 250 g (9 oz) prepared pineapple pieces
> 6 large mint sprigs
> 1 × 70-cl bottle Pimm's No. 1 cup
> 750 ml (1¼ pints) traditional ginger beer
> plenty of ice, to serve

Thread the lychees, lime wedges and pineapple pieces onto 6 bamboo skewers and put into 6 tall glasses with the mint sprigs and lots of ice. Mix the Pimm's with the ginger beer in a large jug, then pour into the glasses and serve.

✪ mexican sangria

Sangria is actually a Spanish drink, but by using lime instead of lemon juice, and tequila instead of brandy, you can imagine being on a sandy beach on the other side of the Atlantic. Bliss!

makes 6 glasses • preparation 5 mins • cooking none

Energy 115 kcals • Protein 0.5 g • Carbohydrate 9.2 g • Fat 0.1 g
Saturated fat none • Fibre 0.3 g • Salt 0.02 g • Added sugars 7.0 g

> 1 orange, sliced
> 1 lemon, sliced
> 1 lime, sliced
> juice of 2 limes
> 40 g (1½ oz) caster sugar
> 300 ml (10 fl oz) fruity red wine, such as Beaujolais
> 120 ml (4 fl oz) tequila
> 300 ml (10 fl oz) sparkling mineral water
> plenty of ice, to serve

Fill a jug with the sliced fruits and plenty of ice. Mix the lime juice with the sugar until it has dissolved, then add the wine, tequila and water. Pour into the jug and serve.

✪ long island iced tea

Iced tea is once again all the rage, but in my house it's always been the ultimate summer thirst quencher … maybe it's the alcohol that goes down so well.

makes 6 glasses • preparation 5 mins • cooking none

Energy 384 kcals • Protein 0.1 g • Carbohydrate 24.9 g • Fat none
Saturated fat none • Fibre none • Salt 0.03 g • Added sugars 23.6 g

> 175 ml (6 fl oz) lemon juice
> 4 tablespoons icing sugar
> 175 ml (6 fl oz) vodka
> 175 ml (6 fl oz) light rum, such as Mountgay
> 175 ml (6 fl oz) tequila
> 175 ml (6 fl oz) gin
> 85 ml (3 fl oz) orange-flavoured liqueur, such as Triple Sec or Cointreau
> 600 ml (1 pint) Coca-Cola, chilled
> plenty of ice
> sliced lemon
> mint sprigs

1 Mix the lemon juice with the icing sugar, then strain into a jug and mix in the vodka, rum, tequila, gin and orange-flavoured liqueur.

2 Fill 6 tall glasses with ice, pour over the boozy mixture and top each glass up with 85 ml (3 fl oz) Coca-Cola. Decorate with a slice of lemon and a mint sprig.

BACK TO BASICS

potato recipes

mashed potatoes

Once mastered, this recipe can be adapted for different results. Try replacing two tablespoons of the milk with crème fraîche, or quark (skimmed-milk soft cheese) for a lower-calorie version.

serves 4 • preparation 5 mins • cooking 25 mins

Energy 434 kcals • Protein 9.0 g • Carbohydrate 66.2 g • Fat 16.6 g
Saturated fat 10.1 g • Fibre 4.9 g • Salt 0.72 g • Added sugars none

> 1.5 kg (3 lb) King Edward or Maris Piper potatoes, peeled and cut into even-sized chunks
> 75 g (3 oz) butter
> about 120 ml (4 fl oz) milk
> salt and freshly ground black pepper

1 Place the potatoes in a large pan of salted water. Bring to the boil, cover and simmer for 15–20 minutes, or until the potatoes are tender without breaking up. Drain and return to the pan over a low heat to dry out.

2 Mash the potatoes, or pass them through a potato ricer or vegetable mouli if you want a really smooth finish. Using a wooden spoon, beat in the butter until melted, then beat in enough milk to achieve a smooth, creamy mash. Season to taste and serve at once.

chips

If you don't have a deep-fat fryer, use a large, deep saucepan, but avoid filling it more than two-thirds full with oil, and never leave it unattended. If you want to cook a large quantity of chips, please remember that it's safer to fry in batches than to overfill the pan.

serves 4 • preparation 40 mins • cooking 10 mins

Energy 400 kcals • Protein 7.9 g • Carbohydrate 64.5 g • Fat 14.0 g
Saturated fat 1.6 g • Fibre 4.9 g • Salt 0.32 g • Added sugars none

> 1.5 kg (3 lb) Maris Piper or King Edward potatoes
> sunflower oil, for deep-frying
> fine sea salt

1 Peel the potatoes and cut each one lengthways into 1-cm (½-inch) slices. Stack the slices, then cut them into 1-cm (½-inch) sticks. Rinse under cold running water. If time allows, place in a bowl of water and leave to soak for 30 minutes to remove some of the starch, which ensures crisper results.

2 Heat the oil in a deep-fat fryer to 180°C/350°F. Drain the chips, transfer to a clean tea towel and dry well. Dip the frying basket in the hot oil to prevent the chips sticking to the wire, then add the chips and lower into the heated oil. Deep-fry for 3–5 minutes until tender and just starting to colour. Drain well on kitchen paper.

3 When ready to serve, return the chips to the frying basket and fry for 1–2 minutes until crisp and golden brown. Drain well on kitchen paper and season with salt to serve.

sautéed potatoes

I normally make these from left-over potatoes, but you could always use 2.5-cm (1-inch) chunks steamed for about 5 minutes until almost, but not quite, tender. The word 'sauté' is simply the French culinary term for fry. However, it usually refers to food that is cooked, uncovered, in just a few tablespoons of oil in a large shallow pan (where the food has room to cook in a thin, single layer) until it is crisp and has a good golden colour.

serves 4 • preparation 5 mins • cooking 25 mins

Energy 342 kcals • Protein 6.4 g • Carbohydrate 51.6 g • Fat 13.6 g
Saturated fat 6.9 g • Fibre 3.9 g • Salt 0.67 g • Added sugars none

> 1 tablespoon sunflower oil
> 50 g (2 oz) butter
> 1.5 kg (3 lb) left-over cooked potatoes, peeled or unpeeled, and cut into 2.5-cm (1-inch) cubes
> Maldon sea salt

1 Heat the oil in a large, heavy-based pan and add the butter. Once it has stopped foaming, tip in the potatoes and toss until well coated. Season to taste with salt and cook for 2 minutes without moving to allow a crust to form. Reduce the heat and continue to sauté for another 15–20 minutes, shaking the pan now and then and turning the potatoes until crisp and golden brown. Serve at once.

2 Meanwhile, pre-heat a roasting tin containing 1 cm (½ inch) oil, dripping or fat for a few minutes until just smoking. Put the lid on the potatoes and shake vigorously to break up and soften the edges, or roughly prod the outside of them with a fork. Carefully tip into the hot oil, basting thoroughly, and scatter in the garlic cloves, if using.

3 Return the tin to the oven for 40 minutes, then pour off most of the fat before turning the potatoes over. Season to taste with the salt and cook for a further 20 minutes until crispy around the edges and golden brown. Serve at once.

dauphinoise potatoes

The wonderful thing about this potato dish is that it can be made in advance, then reheated in individual portions on a baking sheet for about 30 minutes at the oven temperature specified below.

serves 4 • preparation 10 mins • cooking 1 hr 10 mins

Energy 608 kcals • Protein 10.2 g • Carbohydrate 57.7 g • Fat 38.8 g
Saturated fat 24.1 g • Fibre 4.0 g • Salt 0.50 g • Added sugars none

> 300 ml (½ pint) double cream
> 300 ml (½ pint) full-cream milk
> 1 garlic clove, crushed
> 1.5 kg (3 lb) Maris Piper or King Edward potatoes
> a knob of butter, for greasing
> salt and freshly ground black pepper

1 Pre-heat the oven to 150°C/300°F/Gas Mark 2. Place the cream and milk in a large pan with the garlic and season to taste. Peel and thinly slice the potatoes on a mandolin or using a food processor with an attachment blade.

2 Add the sliced potatoes to the pan and stir well to ensure that they are evenly coated. Bring to the boil, then reduce the heat and simmer for about 15 minutes, stirring gently every 5 minutes or so, until the potatoes are tender and the cream mixture has thickened slightly.

3 Generously butter an ovenproof dish, then tip in the potato mixture, spreading it into an even layer. Bake for about 1 hour until completely tender and lightly golden on top.

crispy roast potatoes *(ABOVE)*

There's no doubt that the fat from roasting beef or pork makes the best roast potatoes. Alternatively, if you ever roast a goose or duck, save every drop of the fat and freeze it in ice-cube trays, then bag it to use at your leisure. Even just a couple of cubes added to the oil will improve the flavour.

serves 4 • preparation 10 mins • cooking 1 hr 10 mins

Energy 389 kcals • Protein 7.9 g • Carbohydrate 64.5 g • Fat 12.7 g
Saturated fat 1.5 g • Fibre 4.9 g • Salt 0.32 g • Added sugars none

> 1.5 kg (3 lb) King Edward or Desirée potatoes, cut into
>   large, even-sized pieces
> vegetable oil, beef dripping or canned goose/duck fat
> 6 garlic cloves, not peeled (optional)
> Maldon sea salt

1 Pre-heat the oven to 220°C/425°F/Gas Mark 7. Place the potatoes in a pan of cold, salted water and bring to the boil. Reduce the heat, then cover and simmer for 8–10 minutes until the outsides have just softened. Drain and return to the pan for a minute or two to dry out.

crushed new potatoes

This recipe makes the kind of textured mash that you see in restaurants, so don't be tempted to make it too smooth. For a professional look, shape each serving into a circle by piling the potatoes into a plain pastry cutter set on each plate.

serves 4 • preparation 10 mins • cooking 20 mins

Energy 362 kcals • Protein 2.9 g • Carbohydrate 27.4 g • Fat 27.5 g
Saturated fat 3.8 g • Fibre 1.7 g • Salt 0.30 g • Added sugars none

> 675 g (1¼ lb) new potatoes, scraped or scrubbed clean
> 120 ml (4 fl oz) extra virgin olive oil
> a handful of fresh basil leaves
> salt and freshly ground black pepper

1 Place the potatoes in a pan of cold water, adding 1 teaspoon of salt for every pint and bring to the boil. Cover and simmer for 12–15 minutes until tender, then drain well.

2 Tip the cooked potatoes into a large bowl. Add the olive oil and, using the back of a fork, gently crush each potato until it just splits. Season, then mix carefully until all the oil has been absorbed. Finely chop the basil and stir through the potatoes, then season to taste and serve at once.

minted new potatoes

Choose small, even-sized new potatoes for this recipe. For me, nothing can beat the pleasure of cooking your first batch of Jersey Royals, so good that I would never dream of doing anything but boiling them with a sprig of mint. They should be bought in small quantities, as new potatoes kept hanging around may look fine, but they will have an unpleasant mouldy taste when eaten.

serves 4 • preparation 5 mins • cooking 20 mins

Energy 176 kcals • Protein 3.9 g • Carbohydrate 36.3 g • Fat 2.7 g
Saturated fat 1.3 g • Fibre 2.3 g • Salt 0.36 g • Added sugars none

> 900 g (2 lb) small, waxy new potatoes, scraped or
>   scrubbed clean
> 2 large mint sprigs
> a knob of butter
> Maldon sea salt

1 Place the potatoes in a pan of cold water, adding 1 teaspoon of salt for every pint of water. Bring to the boil, then simmer for 10 minutes.

2 Add 1 sprig of mint and continue to cook for a further 2–5 minutes, or until the potatoes are tender when pierced with a small, sharp knife.

3 Meanwhile, finely chop the leaves from the remaining mint sprig. Drain the potatoes and return them to the pan with the butter and chopped mint. Toss briefly until the butter has melted, then serve at once.

bombay spiced potatoes

These dry, mildly spiced, sautéed potatoes not only go with all Indian dishes, but are fantastic with roasted and grilled meats, especially roast chicken or grilled lamb chops.

serves 4 • preparation 10 mins • cooking 20 mins

Energy 244 kcals • Protein 4.3 g • Carbohydrate 31.7 g • Fat 12.0 g
Saturated fat 1.5 g • Fibre 2.3 g • Salt 0.29 g • Added sugars none

> 700 g (1½ lb) peeled floury potatoes, cut into 2.5-cm
>   (1-inch) chunks
> 4 tablespoons sunflower oil
> 1 teaspoon cumin seeds
> 1 medium-hot green chilli, seeded and finely chopped
> 1 teaspoon ground cumin
> ½ teaspoon cayenne pepper
> ½ teaspoon ground turmeric
> salt and freshly ground black pepper

1 Drop the potatoes into a pan of boiling salted water and cook for 6–7 minutes until just tender. Drain and leave to cool.

2 Heat the oil in a large frying pan. Add the cooked potatoes and fry for 8–10 minutes until crisp and golden all over. Sprinkle with the cumin seeds and chilli and fry for 3 more minutes. Sprinkle over the ground cumin, cayenne pepper and turmeric and fry for another 5 minutes, turning the potatoes every now and then until they are coated in a spicy crust. Sprinkle with some seasoning and serve.

vegetables

celeriac and parsnip mash

This is fantastic served with fish, beef or game.

serves 2 • preparation 10 mins • cooking 25 mins

Energy 632 kcals • Protein 26.6 g • Carbohydrate 61.1 g • Fat 33.2 g
Saturated fat 19.0 g • Fibre 18.4 g • Salt 2.44 g • Added sugars none

> 1 celeriac, peeled, quartered and cut into 1-cm
> (½-inch) chunks
> 2 parsnips, peeled and cut into 1-cm (½-inch) chunks
> 1.2 litres (2 pints) milk
> 50 g (2 oz) butter
> salt and freshly ground black pepper

1 Place the prepared celeriac and parsnips in a large saucepan. Add the milk, bring to the boil, then simmer for 15–20 minutes until the vegetables are completely tender.

2 Drain in a colander set over a bowl to catch the milk. Transfer to a food processor, add the butter and about 6 tablespoons of the milk and whizz for a few minutes until you have a smooth purée. Season to taste and serve at once.

smashed steamed swede

Small, early-season swedes need only the thinnest layer of skin removing, but once they increase in size, you need to peel away quite a thick layer to get rid of the woody skin.

serves 4 • preparation 5 mins • cooking 15 mins

Energy 147 kcals • Protein 1.7 g • Carbohydrate 11.4 g • Fat 10.9 g
Saturated fat 6.5 g • Fibre 4.3 g • Salt 0.57 g • Added sugars none

> 900 g (2 lb) swede, peeled and cut into 2.5-cm (1-inch) chunks
> 50 g (2 oz) butter
> salt and freshly ground black pepper

1 Place the swede in a steamer set above a pan of simmering water and season with salt. Cover and cook for about 10 minutes until tender, then roughly mash with the butter. Season to taste, and serve at once.

sweet potatoes with marshmallows *(ABOVE)*

This is a Thanksgiving dish that is more often served as a relish than a vegetable because it is very rich.

serves 4 • preparation 10 mins • cooking 1 hr 15 mins

Energy 579 kcals • Protein 4.6 g • Carbohydrate 110.1 g • Fat 16.2 g
Saturated fat 10.0 g • Fibre 5.4 g • Salt 0.95 g • Added sugars 49.1 g

> 900 g (2 lb) orange-fleshed sweet potatoes, scrubbed
> 75 g (3 oz) butter, plus extra for greasing
> 100 g (4 oz) light muscovado sugar
> 175 g (6 oz) miniature marshmallows
> a pinch of ground cinnamon
> a pinch of ground nutmeg
> ¼ teaspoon salt

1 Place the sweet potatoes in a large pan of cold, salted water, bring to the boil, then cover and simmer for 25–30 minutes until just tender. Drain and leave to cool.

2 Pre-heat the oven to 190°C/375°F/Gas Mark 5. Meanwhile, place the butter in a heavy-based pan with the sugar, two-thirds of the marshmallows, the spices and salt. Simmer gently for about 5 minutes until the marshmallows are melted, stirring occasionally.

3 Peel the sweet potatoes and cut them into 2-cm (¾-inch) slices. Arrange them in a single layer in a buttered ovenproof dish and pour over the marshmallow sauce. Bake for about 30 minutes until bubbling and golden, then scatter over the remaining marshmallows and bake for another 15 minutes, or until the marshmallows are golden brown.

boiled green vegetables

This is a great way to ensure that your vegetables are perfect every time. They can be part-cooked and refreshed with cold water a few hours in advance.

serves 4 • preparation 5 mins • cooking 10 mins

Energy 158 kcals • Protein 7.6 g • Carbohydrate 11.3 g • Fat 9.5 g
Saturated fat 5.4 g • Fibre 7.5 g • Salt 0.45 g • Added sugars none

> **675 g (1½ lb) fresh or frozen peas or tailed French beans or trimmed and sliced runner beans or fresh or frozen broad beans, podded**
> **40 g (1½ oz) butter**
> **salt and freshly ground black pepper**

1 Bring 1.75 litres (3 pints) water to the boil in a large pan with 1 tablespoon of salt. Cook the vegetable of your choice for 3–4 minutes, according to size. Taste for readiness, then drain and plunge into a bowl of cold water for 5 minutes to prevent further cooking. Drain again and reserve.

2 Heat the butter in the pan with 2 tablespoons water until emulsified (when the butter and water become one liquid). Add the drained vegetables and season to taste. Sauté gently for 1 minute until just heated through. Serve at once.

sautéed green beans *(BELOW)*

These would also be delicious if two seeded and diced vine tomatoes were added to the pan, but only in the summer when tomatoes are at their best.

serves 4 • preparation 5 mins • cooking 10 mins

Energy 118 kcals • Protein 3.4 g • Carbohydrate 5.9 g • Fat 9.1 g
Saturated fat 1.2 g • Fibre 3.9 g • Salt 0.25 g • Added sugars none

> **675 g (1½ lb) French beans, tails removed**
> **3 tablespoons extra virgin olive oil**
> **1 shallot, finely chopped**
> **1 garlic clove, crushed**
> **1 tablespoon chopped fresh flat-leaf parsley**
> **salt and freshly ground black pepper**

1 Plunge the beans into a large pan of boiling, salted water, return to the boil, then boil for a further 2 minutes until just tender. Drain and refresh under cold running water.

2 Return the pan to the heat with the olive oil. Tip in the shallot and garlic and sauté for 2–3 minutes until softened. Add the beans and continue to sauté for a minute or two until just heated through. Sprinkle in the parsley and toss until well coated. Season to taste and serve at once.

crisp buttered green cabbage

Even those who don't like cabbage will enjoy this recipe.

serves 4 • preparation 10 mins • cooking 5 mins

Energy 118 kcals • Protein 2.9 g • Carbohydrate 7.1 g • Fat 8.9 g
Saturated fat 5.2 g • Fibre 4.1 g • Salt 0.46 g • Added sugars none

- 40 g (1½ oz) butter
- 750 g (1½ lb) green cabbage, trimmed, stalks removed and cut across the grain into 1-cm (½-inch) slices
- salt and freshly ground black pepper

1 Three minutes before you wish to serve this dish, place the butter and 3 tablespoons water in a large, heavy-based pan with a lid over a high heat.

2 When the butter has melted and everything is boiling, add the cabbage all at once with a pinch of salt, cover, shake vigorously and cook over a high heat for 1½ minutes. Shake the pan again, cook for another 1½ minutes, then remove from the heat. Season with pepper and serve at once.

spinach with garlic

This would also be delicious if a few handfuls of sliced mushrooms were added with the garlic and cooked until tender, or even a few tablespoons of double cream.

serves 4 • preparation 5 mins • cooking 10 mins

Energy 107 kcals • Protein 6.5 g • Carbohydrate 4.2 g • Fat 7.1 g
Saturated fat 3.6 g • Fibre 4.8 g • Salt 1.17 g • Added sugars none

- 900 g (2 lb) fresh spinach
- 25 g (1 oz) butter
- 1 garlic clove, crushed
- a pinch of freshly grated nutmeg
- salt and freshly ground black pepper

1 Wash the spinach and remove any large stalks, then dry well. Heat a heavy-based pan and add fistfuls of the spinach, waiting for each one to wilt before adding another. Cook for 1 minute, then tip into a colander and press out the excess moisture.

2 Melt the butter in the pan and sauté the garlic for 30 seconds, then add the spinach, season to taste and add a little nutmeg. Toss until heated through and serve at once.

cauliflower au gratin *(ABOVE)*

This recipe also works brilliantly with broccoli cooked in exactly the same manner.

serves 4 • preparation 10 mins • cooking 40 mins

Energy 477 kcals • Protein 24.6 g • Carbohydrate 31.1 g • Fat 29.2 g
Saturated fat 17.6 g • Fibre 2.6 g • Salt 2.27 g • Added sugars none

- 1 cauliflower, broken into even-sized florets
- 900 ml (1½ pints) cheese sauce (see page 233, or use ready-made)
- 25 g (1 oz) butter, plus extra for greasing
- 2 tablespoons dried white breadcrumbs
- 1 tablespoon freshly grated Parmesan or Grùyere cheese
- salt and freshly ground black pepper

1 Pre-heat the oven to 200°C/400°F/Gas Mark 6. Place the cauliflower in a steamer set over a pan of boiling water and sprinkle with salt to taste. Cover and cook for 5–10 minutes until tender – check by piercing a stem with a sharp knife.

2 Spread 2 tablespoons of the cheese sauce in the bottom of a buttered ovenproof dish. Add the cauliflower in an even layer, then cover with the remaining cheese sauce. Melt the butter in a small pan or in the microwave, stir in the breadcrumbs, then fold in the cheese and season to taste. Sprinkle this mixture over the cauliflower and bake for 25–30 minutes, or until bubbling and golden. Serve at once.

honey-roast carrots and parsnips

The sweetness of the carrots and parsnips is picked up by the honey, and the result makes the perfect accompaniment for my herb-stuffed leg of lamb (see page 108).

serves 4 • preparation 10 mins • cooking 50 mins

Energy 173 kcals • Protein 2.8 g • Carbohydrate 26.0 g • Fat 7.1 g
Saturated fat 0.8 g • Fibre 7.9 g • Salt 0.35 g • Added sugars 2.9 g

2 tablespoons olive oil
450 g (1 lb) carrots, trimmed, peeled and cut into chunks
450 g (1 lb) parsnips, trimmed, peeled, quartered, cored
  and cut into chunks
the leaves from 2 sprigs of thyme
1 tablespoon clear honey
salt and freshly ground black pepper

1 Pre-heat the oven to 180°C/350°F/Gas Mark 4. Place the oil in a large roasting tin and add the carrots and parsnips. Sprinkle over the thyme and toss everything together until well coated. Season generously. Roast for 30–40 minutes until tender and just beginning to caramelize.

2 Drizzle the honey over the carrot and parsnip mixture and toss until evenly coated. Roast for another 10 minutes, or until the vegetables are just beginning to catch and caramelize around the edges. Serve at once.

roasted balsamic beetroot

Although delicious hot, this beetroot dish would also be wonderful served at room temperature as a salad with some orange segments, or alongside smoked mackerel with a dollop of horseradish cream.

serves 4 • preparation 5 mins • cooking 30 mins

Energy 106 kcals • Protein 2.4 g • Carbohydrate 11.8 g • Fat 5.9 g
Saturated fat 0.8 g • Fibre 2.4 g • Salt 0.47 g • Added sugars none

6 large, raw beetroot
3 tablespoons balsamic vinegar
1 teaspoon cumin seeds
2 tablespoons olive oil
salt and freshly ground black pepper

1 Pre-heat the oven to 200°C/400°F/Gas Mark 6. Peel the beetroot and cut each one into 8 wedges. Tip into a roasting tin, then drizzle over the vinegar. Sprinkle the cumin seeds on top and season generously, then drizzle over the oil. Roast for 25–30 minutes, turning occasionally, until tender but retaining a bit of bite. Serve at once, or allow to cool and serve at room temperature.

braised red cabbage

Any left-overs will keep in the fridge for a couple of days and can be re-heated. Alternatively, they also freeze very well.

serves 4 • preparation 15 mins • cooking 2 hrs

Energy 264 kcals • Protein 4.1 g • Carbohydrate 51.1 g • Fat 6.2 g
Saturated fat 3.3 g • Fibre 7.9 g • Salt 0.45 g • Added sugars 25.4 g

100 g (4 oz) light muscovado sugar
½ teaspoon ground cinnamon
¼ teaspoon ground cloves
a good pinch of freshly grated nutmeg
900 g (2 lb) red cabbage, trimmed, stalks removed and cut
  into 1-cm (½-inch) slices
450 g (1 lb) onions, finely chopped
450 g (1 lb) cooking apples, peeled, cored and finely
  chopped
4 tablespoons red wine vinegar
juice of 1 orange
25 g (1 oz) butter
salt and freshly ground black pepper

1 Pre-heat the oven to 150°C/300°F/Gas Mark 2. Place the sugar in a bowl with the cinnamon, cloves and nutmeg and stir to combine. Arrange a layer of cabbage in the bottom of a large casserole dish and season to taste.

2 Scatter a layer of the onions over the seasoned cabbage, followed by a layer of the apples, and sprinkle some of the flavoured sugar on top. Continue layering in this way, finishing with a layer of the seasoned cabbage, until all the ingredients have been used up.

3 Pour the vinegar and orange juice into the casserole and dot the butter on top. Cover tightly and bake for about 2 hours, stirring every 30 minutes, until the cabbage is meltingly tender. Serve at once.

glazed carrots with lemon *(ABOVE, LEFT)*

This is a version of Vichy-style carrots, which are traditionally cooked in water from the famous spa. Failing that, a pinch of bicarbonate of soda added to ordinary tap water is a good substitute. When cooking, shake the pan occasionally to prevent the bottom catching and the glaze caramelizing.

serves 4 • preparation 10 mins • cooking 20 mins

Energy 121 kcals • Protein 1.1 g • Carbohydrate 17.5 g • Fat 5.6 g
Saturated fat 3.3 g • Fibre 4.1 g • Salt 0.83 g • Added sugars 3.9 g

750 g (1½ lb) carrots, peeled and sliced on the diagonal
pared rind of 1 lemon, removed using a potato peeler
25 g (1 oz) butter
1 tablespoon caster sugar
a good pinch of bicarbonate of soda
the leaves from ½ x 20-g (¾-oz) packet flat-leaf parsley, chopped
salt and freshly ground black pepper

1 Place the carrots in a small pan with the lemon rind, butter and sugar. Season to taste, pour over just enough water to cover, then add the bicarbonate of soda. Bring to the boil and boil fast until the carrots are completely tender and the liquid has evaporated to a small amount of colourless glaze. Remove the pieces of lemon rind, season to taste and sprinkle over the parsley to serve.

braised peas with leeks *(ABOVE, RIGHT)*

This is a great way of serving frozen tiny peas, or petits pois. We always have a bag in the freezer, and I find that they have even more flavour than the fresh peas that you can buy these days (often out of season). Maybe this is because they are frozen within an hour or so of been picked, whereas fresh peas have to get to us via a long chain of middle-men between grower and seller during which time their sugar turns to starch.

serves 4 • preparation 5 mins • cooking 10 mins

Energy 184 kcals • Protein 7.6 g • Carbohydrate 13.0 g • Fat 11.6 g
Saturated fat 6.9 g • Fibre 7.1 g • Salt 0.33 g • Added sugars 0.5 g

50 g (2 oz) unsalted butter
2 small leeks, cleaned, trimmed and shredded
450 g (1 lb) frozen petits pois or garden peas
5 tablespoons chicken stock (see page 231)
a pinch of sugar
salt and freshly ground black pepper

1 Melt the butter in a large pan and gently sauté the leeks for 3–4 minutes until tender but not coloured. Tip in the peas and add the chicken stock and sugar. Season to taste, then cover and simmer gently for 4–5 minutes until the peas are completely tender and most of the liquid has evaporated. Check the seasoning and serve at once.

fried plantains

Plantains belong to the banana family and are ripe when the skins go black. If you have difficulty getting hold of them, try using firm, only-just-ripe bananas instead.

serves 4 • preparation 5 mins • cooking 5 mins

Energy 250 kcals • Protein 1.7 g • Carbohydrate 44.3 g • Fat 8.6 g
Saturated fat 5.4 g • Fibre 1.9 g • Salt 0.46 g • Added sugars none

3 ripe plantains (their skins should be black)
40 g (1½ oz) butter
salt and freshly ground black pepper

1 Peel the plantains, cut across into 2 shorter pieces, then cut each piece in half again, lengthways. Heat a large frying pan and melt the butter, add the plantain pieces and season to taste. Fry over a medium-high heat for about 2 minutes on each side until lightly golden. Drain briefly on kitchen paper and serve at once.

sautéed courgettes with herbs

The delicate flavour of courgettes makes them a perfect accompaniment to chicken or fish, both of which have an affinity with tarragon, which is another ingredient in this recipe.

serves 4 • preparation 5 mins • cooking 5 mins

Energy 106 kcals • Protein 3.2 g • Carbohydrate 3.3 g • Fat 8.9 g
Saturated fat 5.4 g • Fibre 1.6 g • Salt 0.45 g • Added sugars none

40 g (1½ oz) butter
750 g (1½ lb) courgettes, thinly sliced
2 tablespoons chopped, fresh mixed herbs (flat-leaf parsley, chives and tarragon)
salt and freshly ground black pepper

1 Heat a large sauté pan and melt the butter. Once it stops foaming, tip in the courgettes and sauté for 1–2 minutes until almost, but not quite, tender. Sprinkle in the herbs and season to taste, then continue to sauté for another minute or so until tender. Serve at once.

savoy cabbage with bacon

I think I could probably eat a plate of this just on its own, but it would also be wonderful with steamed fish or roast chicken.

serves 4 • preparation 10 mins • cooking 10 mins

Energy 170 kcals • Protein 8.0 g • Carbohydrate 8.1 g • Fat 11.1 g
Saturated fat 3.0 g • Fibre 5.5 g • Salt 1.08 g • Added sugars 0.7 g

1 tablespoon sunflower oil
100 g (4 oz) streaky bacon lardons
4 spring onions, finely chopped
2 garlic cloves, finely chopped
2 tablespoons freshly grated root ginger
750 g (1½ lb) Savoy cabbage, trimmed, stalks removed and finely shredded
2 tablespoons dry sherry
2 teaspoons sesame oil
salt and freshly ground black pepper

1 Heat a wok or large frying pan over a high heat. Add the oil, then tip in the bacon and stir-fry for a few minutes until it begins to crisp up and release its fat. Add the onions, garlic and ginger and continue to stir-fry for another 30 seconds.

2 Add the cabbage, season to taste and stir-fry for a minute, then add the sherry and continue to stir-fry for another 2–3 minutes until tender. Sprinkle over the sesame oil and give the mixture a couple of good stirs. Serve at once.

sweetcorn wheels with harissa

Ideally, sweetcorn should be cooked the moment it is picked, as the sugar soon converts to starch. Failing that, I recommend using frozen cobs. Serve as an accompaniment to roast meat, or as a side order for barbecued food.

serves 4 • preparation 1 hr 10 mins • cooking 10 mins

Energy 201 kcals • Protein 3.8 g • Carbohydrate 17.8 g • Fat 13.2 g
Saturated fat 6.5 g • Fibre 1.6 g • Salt 0.30 g • Added sugars none

50 g (2 oz) unsalted butter, softened
1 tablespoon harissa paste
1 teaspoon freshly grated root ginger
1 x 20-g (¾-oz) packet coriander, chopped
4 large corn on the cob, cut into 2.5-cm (1-inch) pieces
Maldon sea salt and freshly ground black pepper

1 Place the butter in a bowl with the harissa, ginger, coriander and some seasoning. Mix until well combined, then spoon onto a sheet of cling film in the shape of a log or sausage. Roll up the cling film to enclose the butter completely, then twist the ends to secure. Chill for at least 1 hour, or up to 2 days, to become firm.

2 When you are ready to serve, arrange the wheels of sweetcorn in a steamer set over a pan of simmering water and sprinkle with salt to taste. Cover and cook for about 5 minutes, or until tender. (When it is in season it normally takes less time to cook.) Arrange the wheels on a warmed serving plate, top with thin slices of the flavoured butter and serve at once, just as the butter is beginning to melt.

bok choi with thai-style dressing

Bok choi *is a crunchy vegetable with a distinctive flavour. If you can't get hold of it you could also use Chinese cabbage. This dish (shown below) is a good accompaniment to roast duck because it provides a much-needed sauce.*

serves 4 • preparation 5 mins • cooking 10 mins

Energy 66 kcals • Protein 3.8 g • Carbohydrate 6.4 g • Fat 3.2 g
Saturated fat 0.4 g • Fibre 0.1 g • Salt 3.96 g • Added sugars 0.2 g

- 750 g (1½ lb) bok choi
- 1 teaspoon salt
- 1 tablespoon sunflower oil
- 2.5 cm (1 inch) fresh root ginger, peeled and finely grated
- 1 medium-hot red chilli, seeded and finely diced
- 2 garlic cloves, finely chopped
- 2 tablespoons light soy sauce
- 2 teaspoons Thai fish sauce (nam pla)

1 Place the bok choi in a steamer set over a pan of boiling water and sprinkle over the salt. Cover and cook for 3–5 minutes until tender, then tip into a warmed serving dish.

2 Meanwhile, heat a wok or large frying pan until hot. Add the oil, ginger, chilli and garlic and stir-fry for 1 minute. Add the soy sauce and Thai fish sauce, just heat through, then dribble over the bok choi to serve.

salads

three-tomato salad with basil

This tomato salad is visually enticing, and the different varieties of tomato each have their own individual textures and flavours.

serves 4 • preparation 5 mins • cooking none

Energy 135 kcals • Protein 1.4 g • Carbohydrate 6.8 g • Fat 11.6 g
Saturated fat 1.6 g • Fibre 1.8 g • Salt 0.29 g • Added sugars 0.5 g

    2 beef tomatoes, thinly sliced
    4 vine-ripened tomatoes, cut into wedges
    100 g (4 oz) Sungold or baby plum tomatoes, halved
    1 shallot, thinly sliced
    a handful of fresh basil leaves, shredded
    6 tablespoons balsamic and honey dressing (see page 230)
    freshly ground black pepper

1 Arrange the beef tomatoes in a single layer on a large serving plate, then scatter over the tomato wedges and finish with a pile of the baby plum tomatoes. Sprinkle over the shallot and basil, then drizzle the dressing on top. Add a good grinding of pepper and serve at once.

green salad with vinaigrette

The secret of a good salad is to use as little dressing as possible – the leaves should barely glisten. If there's a puddle in the bottom of the salad bowl, you've used too much.

serves 4 • preparation 5 mins • cooking none

Energy 108 kcals • Protein 0.5 g • Carbohydrate 1.3 g • Fat 11.2 g
Saturated fat 1.5 g • Fibre 0.4 g • Salt 0.30 g • Added sugars 0.5 g

    1 whole lettuce, such as butterhead or cos,
        or 1 x 100-g (4-oz) bag mixed green salad leaves
    4–6 tablespoons classic French vinaigrette
        (see page 230, or use ready-made)
    4 spring onions, finely sliced or a small bunch chives,
        snipped

1 Break up the lettuce into individual leaves and gently tear into bite-sized pieces. Wash under cold running water and dry – I normally use a salad spinner, as it never damages the leaves. Tip into a salad bowl, drizzle over 2 tablespoons of the dressing, then toss gently to combine, adding more if necessary (see above). Scatter over the onions or chives and serve at once. This doesn't benefit from hanging around.

VARIATION

MIXED GREEN SALAD

Add 1 diced avocado, a good handful of halved baby plum tomatoes and some thinly sliced red onion instead of the chives.

new potato salad

This is a classic recipe. It's also really good if you stir in one finely chopped pickled dill cucumber and three diced hard-boiled eggs for that posh touch.

serves 4 • preparation 10 mins • cooking 20 mins

Energy 419 kcals • Protein 5.5 g • Carbohydrate 37.6 g • Fat 28.4 g
Saturated fat 5.2 g • Fibre 2.8 g • Salt 0.57 g • Added sugars 0.1 g

    900 g (2 lb) small, waxy new potatoes, scrubbed or
        scraped clean
    2 teaspoons white wine vinegar
    2 tablespoons light olive oil
    3 heaped tablespoons mayonnaise (see page 230, or use
        ready-made)
    1 heaped tablespoon crème fraîche
    1 bunch spring onions, trimmed and thinly sliced
    the leaves from 1/2 x 20-g (3/4-oz) packet dill, chopped
    the leaves from 1/2 x 20-g (3/4-oz) packet flat-leaf parsley,
        chopped
    salt and freshly ground black pepper

1 If necessary, cut the potatoes into 2.5-cm (1-inch) chunks. Place in a pan of cold salted water, bring to the boil and cook for 12–15 minutes, or until tender. Meanwhile, whisk together the vinegar, oil and some seasoning.

2 Drain the potatoes well, transfer to a bowl and gently stir in the dressing. Leave to get completely cold.

3 Mix the mayonnaise and crème fraîche together, then stir into the potatoes, followed by the onions, dill, parsley and some seasoning to taste.

crunchy coleslaw

Stir in the mayonnaise at the last minute, otherwise moisture causes the mayonnaise to lose its texture.

serves 4 • preparation 10 mins • cooking none

Energy 571 kcals • Protein 4.1 g • Carbohydrate 11.9 g • Fat 56.6 g
Saturated fat 7.9 g • Fibre 3.9 g • Salt 0.83 g • Added sugars 0.5 g

- 450 g (1 lb) white cabbage
- 225 g (8 oz) large carrots
- 1 small onion, thinly sliced
- 300 ml (10 fl oz) mayonnaise (see page 230) or use ready-made
- 1 tablespoon Dijon mustard
- salt and freshly ground black pepper

1 Remove the outer leaves from the cabbage, then cut away and discard the hard central core. Cut the rest into very thin slices, separate into strands and place in a large bowl. Peel the carrots, then coarsely grate them by hand or in a food processor. Add to the cabbage with the onion.

2 Mix the mayonnaise with the mustard and season to taste. Stir into the cabbage mixture and serve at once.

warm lentil salad

This salad takes very little time to prepare and is delicious served with a simply cooked fish fillet (see page 172).

serves 2 • preparation 5 mins • cooking 25 mins

Energy 468 kcals • Protein 21.8 g • Carbohydrate 44.4 g • Fat 23.8 g
Saturated fat 3 g • Fibre 8.2 g • Salt 0.12 g • Added sugars none

- 175 g (6 oz) Puy lentils
- ½ teaspoon Dijon mustard
- 1 tablespoon red wine vinegar
- 4 tablespoons extra virgin olive oil
- 1 small garlic clove, finely chopped
- ½ small red onion, finely chopped
- the leaves from 3 sprigs flat-leaf parsley, chopped

1 Drop the lentils into a pan of boiling salted water and simmer for 20 minutes until just tender but still with a little bite left in them. Meanwhile, whisk together the mustard and vinegar, then gradually whisk in the olive oil.

2 Drain the lentils well, return them to the pan and add the mustard dressing, garlic, red onion and parsley. Stir together over a medium heat until warmed through and serve.

broccoli, feta and tomato salad *(ABOVE)*

I just love this salad with its variety of textures and flavours.

serves 4 • preparation 5 mins • cooking 5 mins

Energy 217 kcals • Protein 9.1 g • Carbohydrate 4.9 g • Fat 18.0 g
Saturated fat 4.8 g • Fibre 3.4 g • Salt 1.64 g • Added sugars 0.5 g

- 400 g (14 oz) broccoli, broken into small florets
- 100 g (4 oz) feta cheese, cut into cubes
- 225 g (8 oz) cherry tomatoes, halved
- a handful of good-quality, pitted black olives
- 6 tablespoons mustard vinaigrette (see page 230)

1 Blanch the broccoli for 1–2 minutes in a pan of boiling salted water, then drain and refresh under cold running water. Tip into a bowl and scatter over the feta, tomatoes and olives. Drizzle over the vinaigrette and fold until well combined.

salad dressings

quick mayonnaise *(BELOW)*

This will keep happily in the fridge for up to one week. It takes just minutes to make and is far superior to any shop-bought alternatives. The nutritional information below is per level tablespoonful.

makes 300 ml (½ pint) • preparation 5 mins • cooking none

Energy 103 kcals • Protein 0.4 g • Carbohydrate 0.1 g • Fat 11.2 g Saturated fat 1.6 g • Fibre none • Salt 0.15 g • Added sugars 0.1 g

1 egg, at room temperature
2 teaspoons white wine vinegar
½ teaspoon salt
a pinch of caster sugar
1 teaspoon Dijon mustard
120 ml (4 fl oz) olive oil
120 ml (4 fl oz) sunflower oil

1 Break the egg into the food processor and add the vinegar, salt, sugar, mustard and half the olive oil. Secure the lid and whizz for 10 seconds.

2 Leave to stand for a couple of seconds, then turn on again at medium speed and pour the remaining olive oil and sunflower oil through the feeder tube in a thin, steady stream. This should take 25–30 seconds.

3 Switch off the machine, remove the lid and scrape down the sides of the bowl, then whizz again for 2–3 seconds. Transfer to a bowl or jar, season to taste and cover with cling film. Chill until needed.

classic french vinaigrette

You can adapt this vinaigrette to your own tastes by using red or white wine vinegar, or different oils.

makes enough for 1 large salad (serves 4) • preparation 5 mins • cooking none

Energy 104 kcals • Protein 0.2 g • Carbohydrate 0.9 g • Fat 11.1 g Saturated fat 1.5 g • Fibre none • Salt 0.30 g • Added sugars 0.5 g

1 tablespoon white wine vinegar
a pinch of caster sugar
4 tablespoons extra virgin olive oil
½ teaspoon Dijon mustard
1 small garlic clove, crushed
salt and freshly ground black pepper

1 Place the vinegar in a screw-topped jar, add the sugar and a good pinch of salt, then shake until the salt has dissolved.

2 Add the oil to the jar with the mustard and garlic and shake again until you have formed a thick emulsion. Season to taste and chill until needed.

VARIATIONS

MUSTARD VINAIGRETTE
Increase the Dijon mustard to 1 teaspoon, then add 1 teaspoon wholegrain mustard and a small bundle of fresh chives, snipped.

BALSAMIC AND HONEY DRESSING
Replace the white wine vinegar with balsamic, and the sugar with ½ teaspoon honey. Omit the Dijon mustard.

stocks

vegetable stock

I like to marinate the stock for two days for an intense flavour.

makes about 1.2 litres (2 pints) • preparation 10 mins +
2 days' marinating (optional) • cooking 40 mins

2 leeks, cleaned and finely chopped
2 onions, finely chopped
2 carrots, cut into 1-cm (½-inch) dice
2 celery sticks, finely chopped
1 fennel bulb, cut into 1-cm (½-inch) dice
1 head garlic, sliced in half horizontally
1 thyme sprig
1 bay leaf
1 teaspoon pink peppercorns
1 teaspoon coriander seeds
1 star anise
a pinch of salt

1 Place all the ingredients in a pan and cover with 1.75 litres (3 pints) water. Bring to a simmer, then cook for another 30 minutes until the vegetables are tender. Either set aside to marinate for 2 days in a cool place, or strain through a sieve and taste. If the flavour is not full enough, return the liquid to the pan and heat to reduce until you are happy. Reduce at a simmer with the lid off. Use as required.

chicken stock

I find chicken stock makes a great base for soups and sauces.

makes about 1.2 litres (2 pints) • preparation 10 mins •
cooking 3 hrs 15 mins

1 large chicken carcass, skin and fat removed
2 leeks, cleaned and chopped
2 onions, chopped
2 carrots, chopped
2 celery sticks, chopped
1 thyme sprig
1 bay leaf
a handful of parsley stalks
1 teaspoon white peppercorns

1 Break up the chicken carcass and put into a pan with 1.8 litres (3¼ pints) water. Bring to the boil, then skim off any fat and scum from the surface. Reduce the heat to a simmer and tip in all the remaining ingredients. Simmer gently for another 2–3 hours, skimming occasionally and tasting regularly to check the flavour. When you are happy with it, remove from the heat and pass through a sieve. Leave to cool and remove any fat that settles on the top. Use as required.

beef stock

While this stock does take a long time to make, you can, of course, store it in the freezer for future use.

makes about 1.2 litres (2 pints) • preparation 10 mins •
cooking 7 hrs 15 mins

1.75 kg (4 lb) beef bones
2 large onions, chopped
2 large carrots, chopped
2 celery sticks
4 garlic cloves, peeled
4 plum tomatoes, chopped
2 tablespoons tomato purée
1 thyme sprig
1 bay leaf
1 x 15-g (½-oz) bunch flat-leaf parsley

1 Pre-heat the oven to 200°C/400°F/Gas Mark 6. Place the beef bones in a large roasting tin and roast for 1 hour until well browned. Drain off 2 tablespoons of the fat and place in a large pan. Add the onions, carrots, celery and garlic and sauté for 8–10 minutes until softened and lightly browned. Add the tomatoes and tomato purée and continue to cook for about 5 minutes, stirring occasionally, until reduced to a pulp. Add the thyme, bay leaf and parsley, stirring to combine.

2 Tip the roasted bones into the pan and cover with 2.25 litres (4 pints) water. Bring to the boil, then reduce the heat and simmer very gently for 5½–6 hours, skimming occasionally. Tip into a large colander set over a large bowl or pan and allow to cool. Remove any fat that settles on the top, then use the stock as required, or freeze in 600-ml (1-pint) cartons.

rice recipes

egg-fried rice

Make sure the cooked rice for frying is cold and that all the grains are well separated.

serves 4 • preparation 5 mins • cooking 10 mins

Energy 296 kcals • Protein 8.7 g • Carbohydrate 44.9 g • Fat 10.2 g
Saturated fat 1.8 g • Fibre 1.5 g • Salt 0.80 g • Added sugars 0.1 g

- 2 tablespoons sunflower oil
- 1 small onion, finely chopped
- 2 teaspoons freshly grated root ginger
- 550 g (1¼ lb) cooked long-grain rice
- 100 g (4 oz) frozen peas
- 2 eggs
- 1 tablespoon dark soy sauce
- 1 teaspoon sesame oil
- 2 spring onions, finely chopped

1 Heat the oil in a wok or large frying pan. Add the onion and ginger and stir-fry for 2–3 minutes until tender and just beginning to colour. Add the rice and peas and continue to stir-fry for anther 2–3 minutes, or until sizzling hot.

2 Meanwhile, beat the eggs with the soy sauce and sesame oil, then pour into the rice mixture. Continue to stir-fry for 1–2 minutes until cooked through. Fold in the onions, allowing them just to wilt, then serve at once.

buttery rice pilaf

The combination of buttery rice scented with saffron is unbeatable with most spicy foods.

serves 4 • preparation 5 mins • cooking 20 mins

Energy 355 kcals • Protein 6.7 g • Carbohydrate 77.6 g • Fat 4.1 g
Saturated fat 2.0 g • Fibre 0.3 g • Salt 1.83 g • Added sugars none

- a large pinch of saffron strands
- 15 g (½ oz) butter
- 1 small onion, finely chopped
- 1 garlic clove, crushed
- 1 bay leaf
- 350 g (12 oz) long-grain rice
- 600 ml (1 pint) chicken or vegetable stock (see page 231)
- 1 teaspoon salt

1 Place the saffron in a small bowl, cover with 2 teaspoons hot water and leave to soak for 5 minutes.

2 Melt the butter in a 20-cm (8-inch) heavy-based saucepan, add the onion and garlic and cook gently until soft but not coloured. Stir in the bay leaf and rice and fry gently for 1 minute. Add the stock, the saffron and its water and the salt and quickly bring to the boil. Stir once, cover with a tight-fitting lid and cook over a low heat for 15 minutes. Uncover, remove the bay leaf and fluff up the grains before serving.

pilau rice

This recipe uses basmati rice, the undisputed queen of rice varieties. It actually triples in length as it cooks and fills the house with the most heavenly scent.

serves 4 • preparation 10 mins • cooking 20 mins

Energy 341 kcals • Protein 6.5 g • Carbohydrate 69.8 g • Fat 5.9 g
Saturated fat 0.7 g • Fibre none • Salt 0.62 g • Added sugars none

- 350 g (12 oz) basmati rice
- 2 tablespoons sunflower oil
- 4 cloves
- 4 green cardamom pods, cracked
- 5-cm (2-inch) piece cinnamon stick
- 1 bay leaf
- 600 ml (1 pint) boiling water
- ½ teaspoon salt

1 Wash the rice in numerous changes of cold water until the water runs relatively clear. Cover with more cold water and leave to soak for 7 minutes, then drain well.

2 Heat the oil in a 20-cm (8-inch) heavy-based pan, add the cloves, cardamom pods, cinnamon stick and bay leaf and cook gently over a low heat for 2–3 minutes until they start to smell aromatic.

3 Stir in the rice, add the boiling water and salt and quickly bring to the boil. Stir once, cover with a tight-fitting lid and cook over a low heat for 12 minutes. Uncover, fluff up the grains with a fork and serve.

sauces and dips

béchamel sauce

This classic white sauce is the basis for so many dishes that it really is worth mastering. I have also included a simple variation for cheese sauce.

makes about 450 ml (15 fl oz) (serves 4) • preparation 15 mins • cooking 15 mins

Energy 121 kcals • Protein 4.4 g • Carbohydrate 10.8 g • Fat 7.1 g Saturated fat 4.4 g • Fibre 0.2 • Salt 0.53 g • Added sugars none

- 450 ml (15 fl oz) full-cream milk
- 1 small onion, peeled and cut into quarters
- 1 bay leaf
- ½ teaspoon black peppercorns
- 25 g (1 oz) butter
- 25 g (1 oz) plain flour
- a pinch of freshly grated nutmeg
- salt and freshly grated pepper

1 Place the milk in a pan with the onion, bay leaf and peppercorns. Bring to scalding point (just before the milk comes to the boil and rises up the sides of the pan), then remove from the heat, cover and set aside to infuse for at least 10 minutes, preferably up to 30 minutes. Strain through a sieve into a jug.

2 Wipe out the pan and use to melt the butter. Add the flour and cook for 1 minute, stirring. Remove from the heat and gradually pour in the infused milk, whisking until smooth after each addition. Season to taste and add a pinch of nutmeg.

3 Bring the sauce to the boil, whisking constantly, then reduce the heat and simmer gently for 5 minutes until smooth and thickened, stirring occasionally. Use as required or transfer to a jug, cool, cover with cling film and keep in the fridge for up to 2 days.

VARIATION

CHEESE SAUCE
When the sauce is cooked, remove from the heat and stir in 50 g (2 oz) freshly grated Parmesan cheese or 75 g (3 oz) Cheddar cheese until melted.

beurre blanc *(BELOW)*

This is one sauce for which you really need to make your own stock, as stock cubes are just too salty. Alternatively, try using the cartons of chilled stocks available in most supermarkets.

makes about 300 ml (½ pint) (serves 4) • preparation 5 mins • cooking 15 mins

Energy 421 kcals • Protein 0.9 g • Carbohydrate 0.4 g • Fat 44.2 g Saturated fat 29.2 g • Fibre none • Salt 0.75 g • Added sugars none

- 600 ml (1 pint) chicken or vegetable stock (see page 231, or use ready-made)
- 225 g (8 oz) unsalted butter, diced and chilled
- ½ lemon, pips removed
- salt and freshly ground black pepper

1 Place the stock in a pan and reduce to about 50 ml (2 fl oz). This should take about 10 minutes. Turn the heat right down and whisk in the butter a few cubes at a time (or use a hand-blender) until the butter has melted and the texture is light and frothy. Add a squeeze of lemon juice and season to taste.

béarnaise sauce

This sauce is wonderful served with steak. Omit the vinegar and tarragon and you've got hollandaise sauce, which is great ladled over muffins topped with ham and eggs (see page 24).

makes about 450 ml (15 fl oz) (serves 4) • preparation 5 mins • cooking 5 mins

Energy 476 kcals • Protein 3.9 g • Carbohydrate 0.05 g • Fat 51.1 g Saturated fat 30.6 g • Fibre none • Salt 0.33 g • Added sugars none

**2 teaspoons tarragon or white wine vinegar
the leaves from 2 sprigs tarragon, chopped
2 egg yolks
1 egg
a pinch of salt
225 g (8 oz) unsalted butter**

1 Place the vinegar, tarragon, egg yolks, egg and salt in a food processor or liquidizer and blend until the tarragon is very finely chopped.

2 Gently melt the butter in a heavy-based pan until just beginning to foam. Turn on the food processor or liquidizer and, with the motor running at medium speed, pour the melted butter through the feeder tube in a thin, steady stream. Continue to blitz for another 5 seconds, then pour back into the pan, but do not return to the heat.

3 Allow the heat from the pan to finish thickening the sauce as you stir it gently for another minute before serving. Alternatively, the sauce can be kept warm if put it in a heatproof bowl set over a pan of simmering water, or in a switched-off but warm oven.

creamy peppercorn sauce

This rich sauce should be served with pepper-crusted, chargrilled steaks or slices of rare roast beef. The quantity should be enough to serve 6 people, as a little goes a long way.

makes about 175 ml (6 fl oz) (serves 6) • preparation 5 mins • cooking 15 mins

Energy 105 kcals • Protein 0.7 g • Carbohydrate 1.53 g • Fat 10.8 g Saturated fat 6.7 g • Fibre 0.05 g • Salt 0.52 g • Added sugars 0.06 g

**25 g (1 oz) butter
2 shallots, finely chopped
150 ml (5 fl oz) beef stock (see page 231)
2 teaspoons Worcestershire sauce
6 tablespoons double cream
2 teaspoons Dijon mustard
1 teaspoon coarsely ground black pepper
Maldon sea salt**

1 Heat the butter in a heavy-based frying pan and sauté the shallots for a few minutes until softened. Pour in the stock and add the Worcestershire sauce, then cook rapidly for about 5 minutes, stirring occasionally, until reduced by half.

2 Add the cream, mustard and pepper and simmer for another minute or two, stirring occasionally, until well combined. Season to taste with salt and serve at once.

bread sauce

This sauce can be made up to two days in advance and kept covered with cling film in the fridge until needed.

makes about 450 ml (15 fl oz) (serves 4) • preparation 15 mins • cooking 25 mins

Energy 198 kcals • Protein 6.07 g • Carbohydrate 20.52 g • Fat 10.9 g Saturated fat 6.65 g • Fibre 0.43 g • Salt 0.89 g • Added sugars none

**2 whole cloves
1 small onion, peeled
450 ml (15 fl oz) full-cream milk
1 bay leaf
75 g (3 oz) fresh white breadcrumbs
25 g (1 oz) butter
2 tablespoons double cream
salt and freshly ground white pepper**

1 Stick the cloves into the onion and place in a small, heavy-based pan with the milk and bay leaf. Slowly bring to the boil, then remove from the heat. Cover and set aside to infuse for at least 10 minutes, preferably up to 30 minutes.

2 Remove the onion and bay leaf from the milk, then sprinkle in the breadcrumbs, stirring to combine. Season to taste, then cover and simmer very gently for 10–15 minutes, stirring occasionally. Whisk in the butter and cream, allow just to warm through and serve.

apple sauce

This tart sauce is perfect for counteracting the richness of roast duck or pork. For a really smooth finish, you can purée it in a food processor or liquidizer, but I don't usually bother.

makes about 300 ml (½ pint) (serves 4) • preparation 15 mins • cooking 15 mins

Energy 100 kcals • Protein 0.37 g • Carbohydrate 13.9 g • Fat 5.22 g
Saturated fat 3.25 g • Fibre 1.8 g • Salt 0.12 g • Added sugars 3.75 g

**450 g (1 lb) cooking apples, peeled, cored and chopped
25 g (1 oz) butter
caster sugar, to taste**

1 Place the apples in a pan with 2 tablespoons water and cook gently for about 10 minutes, stirring occasionally, until soft. Beat the apple mixture to a pulp with a wooden spoon, then stir in the butter and enough sugar to taste, depending on how tart the apples are. Leave to cool, then use as required. If covered with cling film, this will keep in the fridge for up to 1 week.

mint sauce

Roast lamb wouldn't be the same without this traditional accompaniment.

makes about 75 ml (3 fl oz) (serves 4) • preparation 5 mins + 30 mins' infusing • cooking none

Energy 13.2 kcals • Protein 0.3 g • Carbohydrate 3.07 g • Fat 0.05 g
Saturated fat none • Fibre none • Salt none • Added sugars 2.5 g

**the leaves from 2 x 20-g (¾-oz) packets mint, chopped
2 teaspoons caster sugar
1 tablespoon boiling water
2 tablespoons white wine vinegar**

1 Place the mint in a serving dish with the sugar. Stir in the boiling water and set aside for 5 minutes, stirring occasionally, until the sugar has dissolved. Stir in the vinegar and set aside for 30 minutes to allow the flavours to infuse. Use as required. If covered with cling film, this will keep in the fridge for up to 2 days.

pouring custard *(BELOW)*

To avoid the possibility of curdling, you can beat 2 teaspoons cornflour in with the egg yolks.

makes about 600 ml (1 pint) (serves 8) • preparation 5 mins • cooking 15 mins

Energy 128 kcals • Protein 5.1 g • Carbohydrate 9.7 g • Fat 8.0 g
Saturated fat 3.2 g • Fibre none • Salt 0.13 g • Added sugars 6.1 g

**600 ml (1 pint) full-cream milk
6 egg yolks
3 tablespoons caster sugar
a few drops of vanilla extract**

1 Bring the milk to scalding point (see page 233) in a non-stick pan. Meanwhile, mix the egg yolks, sugar and vanilla extract in a bowl, then gradually whisk in the hot milk.

2 Wipe out the pan, pour in the egg mixture, then cook, stirring constantly, over a medium heat, until the custard thickens. Do not let it boil or it will curdle. Serve at once.

guacamole

*The ultimate dipping food that never fails to deliver
... and it costs so much less than the shop-bought version.
It tastes far better, too.*

serves 6 • preparation 10 mins • cooking none

Energy 96 kcals • Protein 0.7 g • Carbohydrate 0.8 g • Fat 10.0 g
Saturated fat 1.2 g • Fibre 1.2 g • Salt 0.01 g • Added sugars none

1 large, ripe avocado
1 medium-hot green chilli, seeded and chopped
2 spring onions, trimmed and sliced
½ x 20-g (¾-oz) packet coriander, chopped
juice of 1 lime (about 2 tablespoons)
2 tablespoons sunflower oil

1 Blend all the ingredients together in a food processor
with ½ teaspoon of salt.

chilli tomato salsa

*Bring on the tortilla chips, grilled fish, steaks and bangers
... this salsa goes with everything!*

serves 4 • preparation 10 mins • cooking none

Energy 21 kcals • Protein 0.9 g • Carbohydrate 3.9 g • Fat 0.3 g
Saturated fat none • Fibre 1.1 g • Salt 0.02 g • Added sugars none

4 vine-ripened tomatoes, skinned and chopped
1 teaspoon minced red chilli, from a jar (sambal oelek)
½ red onion, finely chopped
1 x 20-g (¾-oz) packet coriander, chopped
2 teaspoons lime juice

1 Mix all the ingredients together, adding a little
salt to taste.

pastry

basic shortcrust pastry

*Both this and the following recipe are essentials that
you're bound to use again and again.*

makes 350 g (12 oz) • preparation 3–4 mins

Energy 1825 kcals • Protein 21.5 g • Carbohydrate 174.8 g • Fat 120.4 g
Saturated fat 63.9 g • Fibre 7.0 g • Salt 3.76 g • Added sugars none

225 g (8 oz) plain flour
½ teaspoon salt
65 g (2½ oz) chilled butter, cut into small pieces
65 g (2½ oz) chilled lard or white vegetable fat, cut into
small pieces
1½ tablespoons cold water

1 Sift the flour and salt into a food processor, add the chilled
butter and lard and process for a few seconds until the
mixture looks like fine breadcrumbs. Tip into a bowl and stir
in the water with a round-bladed knife until the mixture just
starts to stick together. Gather it into a ball with your hands
and knead briefly on a lightly floured surface until smooth.

sweet shortcrust pastry

makes 350 g (12 oz) • preparation 3–4 mins

Energy 1825 kcals • Protein 21.5 g • Carbohydrate 174.8 g • Fat 120.4 g
Saturated fat 63.9 g • Fibre 7.0 g • Salt 3.76 g • Added sugars 13.1g

225 g (8 oz) plain flour
100 g (4 oz) chilled, unsalted butter, cut into small pieces
100 g (4 oz) icing sugar
1 egg

1 Put the flour, butter and icing sugar into a food processor
and blend together until the mixture looks like breadcrumbs.
Add the egg and whizz briefly until the mixture just starts to
stick together into a ball. Turn out onto a lightly floured work
surface and knead very briefly until smooth. Use as required,
then chill for at least 20 minutes before baking. N.B. in warm
weather you may want to wrap your pastry in cling film and
chill it for 10 minutes or so before rolling it out.

Index

Page references in **bold** denote illustrations

ackee: Jamaican ackee and salt fish in de pan 34, **35**
amaretti baked peaches with mascarpone cream 186, **187**
anchovy butter topping for jacket potatoes 64
apple(s)
  and berry crumble 162, **163**
  deep apple sour-cream pie **116**, 117
  pancakes 26
  sauce 235
aubergine and potato dhansak **126**, 127
avocado and rocket and prawn wrap 51

bacon
  chicken and bacon burgers 200
  smoked bacon, creamed tomato and pea penne 76, **77**
  stuffing and bacon rolls 156, **157**
bagels 46
baguettes 47
baked potatoes 64, **65**
balsamic and honey dressing 230
banana(s)
  baked bananas with Greek yoghurt 94, **95**
  custard 94, **95**
  griddled bananas with toffee sauce 94, **95**
banoffee pie with chocolate drizzle 161, **161**
béarnaise sauce 234
béchamel sauce 233
beef
  beef and rocket with mustard dressing sandwich 43, **43**
  burgers 200, **201**
  Caribbean beef and red bean stew with dumplings 111, **111**
  Italian meatballs in tomato and basil sauce 146, **146**
  kofta kebabs with mango and mint raita 123, **123**
  marinated steak with crispy onion rings on ciabatta 50
  Mexican beef fajitas 134, **135**
  roast beef with horseradish sauce 176, **176**
  roasting chart 159
  seared sirloin steak with blue cheese butter and shoestring chips 177, **177**

spaghetti bolognese 112, **113**
steak and ale pie 150, **151**
stock 231
and vegetables with black bean sauce stir-fry 58
beetroot: roasted balsamic 224
beurre blanc 233
BLT 50
blueberry
  and coconut and lemon muffins 30
  and lemon and crème fraîche cheesecake **210**, 211
bok choi with Thai-style dressing 227, **227**
bread and butter pudding 160, **160**
bread sauce 234
breakfast, full English **28**, 29
broccoli
  chicken and broccoli gratin 88, **88**
  and feta and tomato salad 229, **229**
bruschetta 98, **99**
burgers 200, **201**
butter bean and rosemary hummus **192**, 193
buttermilk pancakes 26, **27**
butterscotch whip in a whirl **92**, 93

cabbage
  braised red 224
  crisp buttered green 223
  Savoy cabbage with bacon 226
cardamom: creamy cardamom chicken 124, **125**
Caribbean brunch menu 36–7
carrots
  glazed carrots with lemon 225, **225**
  honey-roast carrots and parsnips 224
cauliflower au gratin 223, **223**
celeriac and parsnip mash 221
cheese sauce 233
cheesecake: blueberry, lemon and crème fraîche **210**, 211
chicken
  American-style seared chicken salad **60**, 61
  and bacon burgers 200
  and broccoli gratin 88, **88**
  Cajun chicken wrap 51
  chargrilled chicken on avocado salad 194, **195**
  coq au vin **174**, 175
  creamy cardamom 124, **125**
  griddled chicken with tomato and chilli mayonnaise and rocket bagel 46
  lemon and thyme chicken with grainy mustard butter 198, **199**

noodle soup with lettuce 56, **56**
oven-baked chicken with chorizo and artichokes 102, 103
parmigiana with parsley butter tagliatelle 147, **147**
pasta salad with pine nuts 82, **83**
and pepper and Brie puff parcels **174**, 175
pot-roasted chicken with herby garlic butter 89, **89**
roast chicken with crunchy stuffing and bacon balls 156, **157**
roasting chart 159
spiced chicken with apricot sandwich 43
spicy fried tandoori-style 198, **199**
stock 231
and sweetcorn soup 40, **41**
Thai yellow chicken curry 132
tikka masala 124, **125**
chickpeas: spicy chickpea, cumin and coriander soup 40, **41**
chilli cornbread pie 110, **110**
chilli-glazed mango with yoghurt 118, **119**
chips 177, **177**, 218
chocolate
  krispie fridge cake 52, **53**
  mousse **92**, 93
  pear upside-down pud 162, **163**
  rich chocolate, rum and prune pots with crème fraîche 187, **187**
chutney: roasted red pepper 202
ciabatta 11, 50
clotted cream ice-cream 164, **165**
coconut
  -and-cumin-spiced prawns with chapatis **122**, 122
  treacle tart with quick clotted cream ice-cream 164, **165**
coleslaw 229
coq au vin **174**, 175
corned beef hash with poached egg 66, **66**
cornmeal
  cheesy cornmeal and bacon muffins 30
  chilli cornbread pie 110, **110**
  porridge with nutmeg 23, **23**
courgettes
  fettuccine with melting courgettes and Parmesan 78, **78**
  sautéed courgettes with herbs 226
couscous: roasted vegetable couscous with lemon hummus 62, **62**

crab with rocket and lemon aïoli sandwich 42
curries
  aubergine and potato dhansak **126**, 127
  Caribbean lamb and sweet potato curry with clap-hand roti 128, **129**
  chicken tikka masala 124, **125**
  Jamaican curried snapper with coconut and lime 130, **130**
  lamb rogan josh **126**, 127
  Thai 132, **133**
custard 235, **235**
  banana 94, **95**

dauphinoise potatoes 219
desserts
  amaretti baked peaches with mascarpone cream 186, **187**
  apple and berry crumble 162, **163**
  banana 94, **95**
  blueberry, lemon and crème fraîche cheesecake **210**, 211
  bread and butter pudding 160, **160**
  butterscotch whip in a whirl **92**, 93
  caramelised pineapple with rum and raisin 72, **73**
  cheat's banoffee pie with chocolate drizzle 161, **161**
  chilli-glazed mango with yoghurt 118, **119**
  chocolate mousse **92**, 93
  chocolate-pear upside-down pud 162, **163**
  coconut treacle tart with quick clotted cream ice-cream 164, **165**
  deep apple sour-cream pie **116**, 117
  espresso and crumbled biscotti 72, **73**
  iced mixed-fruit platter with passion-fruit cream **92**, 93
  lemon meringue pie 212, **213**
  lemon posset with raspberries and refrigerator biscuits 186, **187**
  mango kulfi 138, **139**
  pavlovas 182, **183**
  pineapple with lime and mint sugar 138, **139**
  rhubarb and strawberry pudding 118
  rich chocolate, rum and prune pots with crème fraîche 187, **187**

strawberry pancakes 72, **73**
watermelon and lime granita 212, **213**
dressings 207, 230
duck
    five-spiced duck breasts with stir-fried vegetable sticks 178, **179**
    roasting chart 159

egg(s) 24–5
    -fried rice 232
espresso and crumbled biscotti 72, **73**

fennel ratatouille 204, **205**
fettuccine with melting courgettes and Parmesan 78, **78**
fish: Thai-style ginger 104, **105**
fishcakes with lemon crème fraîche 142, **143**
Fourth of July barbecue menu 208–9
Fruit iced mixed-fruit platter with passion-fruit cream **92**, 93
    smoothies 20, **21**

garlic
    and mint and lemon dressing 207
    pitta bread 192, 193
gazpacho: roasted red pepper 190, **191**
ginger: Thai-style ginger fish 104, **105**
girls' night in menu 114–15
Greek salad with feta cheese 44, **45**
green beans, sautéed 222, **222**
gremolata 180, 181
guacamole 98, 236

haddock: cheesy haddock and prawn pie 142, **143**
halloumi and vegetable skewers on spicy chick-pea couscous 207, **207**
ham: cheesy baked ham with cabbage 70, **71**
honey-roast carrots and parsnips 224
horseradish sauce 176
hummus
    butter-bean and rosemary **192**, 193
    and roasted red pepper and spinach pitta 51
    roasted vegetable couscous with lemon 62, **62**

iced lemon pumpkin bars 52, **53**
iced tea, Long Island **214**, 215
Indian take-away menu 136–7
Italian bean salad with griddled red onion and tuna 44, **45**
Italian fusilli sausage 'ragu' 76, **77**

Jamaican ackee and salt fish in de pan 34, **35**
Jamaican curried snapper with coconut and lime 130, **130**
jambalaya: southern-style sausage 131, **131**

kedgeree: hot-smoked salmon and egg 34, **35**

lamb
    braised osso bucco-style lamb shanks with gremolata **180**, 181
    Caribbean lamb and sweet potato curry with clap-hand roti 128, **129**
    chargrilled lamb steaks with fennel ratatouille 204, **205**
    chops on minted pea purée with crispy pancetta **152**, 153
    Greek lamb and feta burgers 200
    roast herb-stuffed leg of 108, **109**
    roasting chart 159
    rogan josh **126**, 127
    shepherd's pie with Irish champ mash topping 155, **155**
lasagne 112, **113**
leeks
    braised peas with 225, **225**
    caramelized leek and bacon pilaff 70, 71
lemon
    iced lemon pumpkin bars 52, **53**
    meringue pie 212, **213**
    posset with raspberries and refrigerator biscuits 186, **187**
    risotto 100, **101**
    and thyme chicken with grainy mustard butter 198, **199**
lemonade float 72, **73**
lentils: warm lentil salad 229
Long Island iced tea **214**, 215

mango(s)
    chilli-glazed mango with yoghurt 118, **119**
    kulfi 138, **139**
    and passion fruit and coconut smoothie 20, **21**

marmalade muffins 30, **31**
mayonnaise 230
meatballs: Italian meatballs in tomato and basil sauce 146, **146**
Mexican beef fajitas 134, **135**
mint sauce 235
monkfish on crispy potato cakes 172, **173**
mousse, chocolate **92**, 93
mozzarella and three-tomato salad 194, **195**
muesli 22, **22**
muffins 30, **31**
mushroom(s)
    baked polenta with creamy mushrooms and Parmesan cheese 170, **170**
    and cheese omelette 56, 57
    crunch brunch 32, **32**
    field mushrooms with spinach, blue cheese and pine nuts 206, **206**
    pork parcels with 90, **90**
    risotto 100
    sweet soy mushrooms on ciabatta toast 33, **33**
    nachos: cheesy nachos with avocado and sweetcorn salsa **60**, 61

nutty vegetable stir-fry 58

omelette: mushroom and cheese 56, **57**
osso bucco-style lamb shanks with gremolata 180, 181
oxtail: braised oxtail with butter beans 107, **107**

pan bagnat 47
pancakes
    American sweetcorn 26, **27**
    apple 26
    buttermilk 26, **27**
    savoury 26
    spinach and ricotta 144, **144**
    strawberry 72, **73**
Parma ham
    with basil dressing on bruschetta 98, **99**
    Parmesan baskets with **168**, 169
    Spanish tortilla with Parma ham and caramelized red onions 48, **49**
Parmesan baskets with Parma ham **168**, 169
parsnips
    celeriac and parsnip mash 221
    honey-roast carrots and 224
pasta 84

chicken pasta salad with pine nuts 82, **83**
creamy spaghetti carbonara 63, **63**
fettuccine with melting courgettes and Parmesan 78, **78**
gratin of penne with spinach and tomatoes 79, **79**
Italian fusilli sausage ragu 76, **77**
luxury lasagne 112, **113**
smoked bacon, creamed tomato and pea penne 76, **77**
spaghetti bolognese 112, **113**
pastrami
    and dill pickle and mustard mayonnaise sandwich 42
    and new potato salad 91, **91**
pastry 236
pâté: salmon and goats' cheese **168**, 169
pavlovas 182, **183**
peaches: amaretti baked peaches with mascarpone cream 186, **187**
pear(s)
    and banana, oat and honey smoothie 20, **21**
    chocolate-pear upside-down pud 162, **163**
pea(s)
    braised peas with leeks 225, **225**
    and ham with new potatoes tortilla 48
peppercorn sauce 234
peppers
    peperonata with bubbling goats' cheese on ciabbata 50
    roasted red pepper chutney 202, **202**
    roasted red pepper gazpacho 190, **191**
    roasted red pepper and goats' cheese tortilla 48
pilau rice 232
pineapple(s)
    caramelized pineapple with rum and raisin 72, **73**
    and lime and ginger smoothie 20, **21**
    with lime and mint sugar 138, **139**
pitta bread
    garlic 192, 193
    hummus, roasted red pepper and spinach 51
pizza toasts 47
pizzas 13, 80, **81**
plaice: pan-fried plaice with crispy bacon 67, **67**
plantains, fried 226

polenta: baked polenta with creamy mushrooms and Parmesan cheese 170, **170**
pork
    chops baked on tomato and rosemary potatoes **152**, 153
    fragrant pork and vegetable stir-fry 58, **59**
    parcels with mushrooms 90, **90**
    roast pork, beetroot and horseradish sandwich 43
    roasting chart 159
    stuffed pork fillets with prunes 106, **106**
    Thai pork chops with sweet-and-sour carrot salad 203, **203**
porridge 23, **23**
potatoes
    aubergine and potato dhansak **126**, 127
    baked 64, **65**
    Bombay spiced 220
    Caribbean lamb and sweet potato curry with clap-hand roti 128, **129**
    chips 177, **177**, 218
    crushed new 220
    dauphinoise 219
    mashed 218
    minted new 220
    monkfish on crispy potato cakes 172, **173**
    new potato salad 228
    pastrami and new potato salad 91, **91**
    pork chops baked on tomato and rosemary **152**, 153
    roast 219
    sautéed 218
prawns
    cheesy haddock and prawn pie 142, **143**
    coconut-and-cumin-spiced prawns with chapatis 122, **122**
    piripiri prawn and lemon skewers **196**, 197
    Thai green prawn curry 132
prunes: stuffed pork fillets with 106, **106**
pumpkin
    iced lemon pumpkin bars 52, **53**
    roasted pumpkin and cumin dip **192**, 193
    warm griddled pumpkin and spinach salad **102**, 103

quiches 148, **149**

ratatouille, fennel 204, **205**
rhubarb and strawberry pudding 118, **119**

rice 13
    buttery rice pilaf 232
    caramelized leek and bacon pilaff **70**, 71
    egg-fried 232
    pilau 232
    risotto 100, **101**
risotto 100, **101**
Roquefort, grape, radicchio and walnut sandwich 42

salads
    American-style seared chicken **60**, 61
    broccoli, feta and tomato 229
    chargrilled chicken on avocado 194, **195**
    chicken pasta salad with pine nuts 82, **83**
    chunky Greek salad with feta cheese 44, **45**
    crunchy coleslaw 229
    green salad with vinaigrette 228
    Italian bean salad with griddled red onion and tuna 44, **45**
    mixed green 228
    mozzarella and three-tomato 194, **195**
    new potato 228
    pastrami and new potato 91, **91**
    roasted vegetable and chickpea salad with feta, cumin and lemon 171, **171**
    Thai pork chops with sweet-and-sour carrot 203, **203**
    three-tomato salad with basil 228
    warm griddled pumpkin and spinach **102**, 103
    warm lentil 229
    see also dressings
salmon
    crispy salmon fingers with sun-blushed dipping sauce **86**, 87
    and goats' cheese pâté **168**, 169
    with herby yoghurt dressing 172, **173**
    royal bagel 46, **46**
    tabbouleh with roasted spiced 68, **69**
    see also smoked salmon
salsa
    chilli tomato 236
    spicy tomato 134, **135**
    tomato and caper **196**, 197
salt cod: Jamaican ackee and salt fish in de pan 34, **35**
sandwiches 42–3
sangria, Mexican **214**, 215

sauces 233-6
sausages
    Cumberland sausages with roasted red pepper chutney 202, **202**
    and garlic mash with onion, red wine and rosemary jus 154, **154**
    Italian fusilli sausage ragu 76, **77**
    southern-style sausage jambalaya 131, **131**
    torpedoes with caramelized onions 47
seafood
    Sichuan chilli seafood stir-fry 104, **105**
    summer seafood marinara 82, **83**
shepherd's pie 155, **155**
shortcrust pastry 236
Sichuan chilli seafood stir-fry 104, **105**
smoked salmon
    and egg kedgeree 34, **35**
    and watercress sandwich 42
smoothies, fruit 20, **21**
snapper: Jamaican curried snapper with coconut and lime 130, **130**
soups
    chicken noodle soup with lettuce 56, **56**
    chicken and sweetcorn **40**, 41
    roasted red pepper gazpacho 190, **191**
    spicy chickpea, cumin and coriander 40, 41
spaghetti
    bolognese 112, **113**
    carbonara 63, **63**
Spanish tortilla with parma ham and caramelized red onions 48, **49**
spinach
    with garlic 223
    gratin of penne with spinach and tomatoes 79, **79**
    and ricotta pancakes 144, **144**
steak and ale pie 150, **151**
stir-fries 58, **59**
stocks 231
strawberry(ies)
    mini strawberry pavlovas 182, **183**
    pancakes 72, **73**
    rhubarb and strawberry pudding 118, **119**
stuffing and bacon rolls 156, **157**
Sunday roast menu 158–9
swede: smashed steamed 221
sweet potatoes with marshmallows 221

sweetcorn
    American sweetcorn pancakes 26, **27**
    chicken and sweetcorn soup **40**, 41
    wheels with harissa 226–7

tabbouleh with roasted spiced salmon 68, **69**
Thai curries 132, **133**
Thai pork chops with sweet-and-sour carrot salad 203, **203**
Thai-style ginger fish 104, **105**
tomatoes
    chilli tomato salsa 236
    mozzarella and three-tomato salad 194, **195**
    spicy tomato salsa 134, **135**
    three-tomato salad with basil 228
tortilla weekend brunch 28, **29**
tortilla wraps 51
tortillas 48, **49**
treacle: coconut treacle tart with quick clotted cream ice-cream 164, **165**
tropical ginger Pimm's 214, **215**
tuna
    chargrilled tuna with Thai butter **86**, 87
    Italian bean salad with griddled red onion and 44, **45**
    mayonnaise bagel 46
    steaks with a tomato, caper and mint salsa **196**, 197

Valentine's day supper menu 184–5
vegetable(s)
    boiled green 222
    halloumi and vegetable skewers on spicy chickpea couscous 207, **207**
    roasted vegetable and chickpea salad with feta, cumin and lemon 171, **171**
    roasted vegetable couscous with lemon hummus 62, **62**
    roasted vegetable and goats' cheese quiche 148
    root vegetable and nut crumble 145, **145**
    and stir-fries 58
    stock 231
    Thai red vegetable curry with basil 132, **133**
vinaigrette 230

watermelon and lime granita 212, **213**

Acknowledgements

Working with people who are not only colleagues but friends as well added to the whole enjoyable experience of putting this book together. So, a massive thank you to friends Orla Broderick and Debbie Major for their creative energy. I could not have done it without you guys. To Lorna Brash for all her attention to detail in the studio. To food photographer Juliet Piddington for more delightful sensiferous moments. To all the team at BBC Books, especially Rachel Copus, my editor, who gently persuades me to get the bleedin' thing done ..., my commissioning editor, Nicky Ross, for allowing me to indulge myself sometimes with the occasional oxtail recipe, and Isobel Gillan for her design work.

Thanks also to my agents and friends at JHA,
my caring wife Clare, our great kids Jimmy and Maddie,
and Oscar, it's time for walkies!

First published 2004
Copyright © Ainsley Harriott 2004
The moral right of the author has been asserted

This edition produced for The Book People Ltd, Hall Wood
Avenue, Haydock, St Helens WA11 9UL by BBC Books,
BBC Worldwide Ltd
Woodlands, 80 Wood Lane
London W12 0TT

ISBN: 0 563 52244 5

With thanks to Denby for the loan of items for photography

Photographs by Juliet Piddington © BBC Worldwide Ltd 2004

Recipes developed and written in association with
Orla Broderick and Debbie Major

Commissioning Editor: Nicky Ross
Project Editor: Rachel Copus
Copy Editor: Trish Burgess
Recipe Analysis: Wendy Doyle
Cover Art Director: Pene Parker
Designer: Isobel Gillan
Production Controller: Kenneth McKay
Food Stylist: Lorna Brash
Props Stylist: Victoria Allen

Set in Bliss
Colour origination and printing by Butler and Tanner